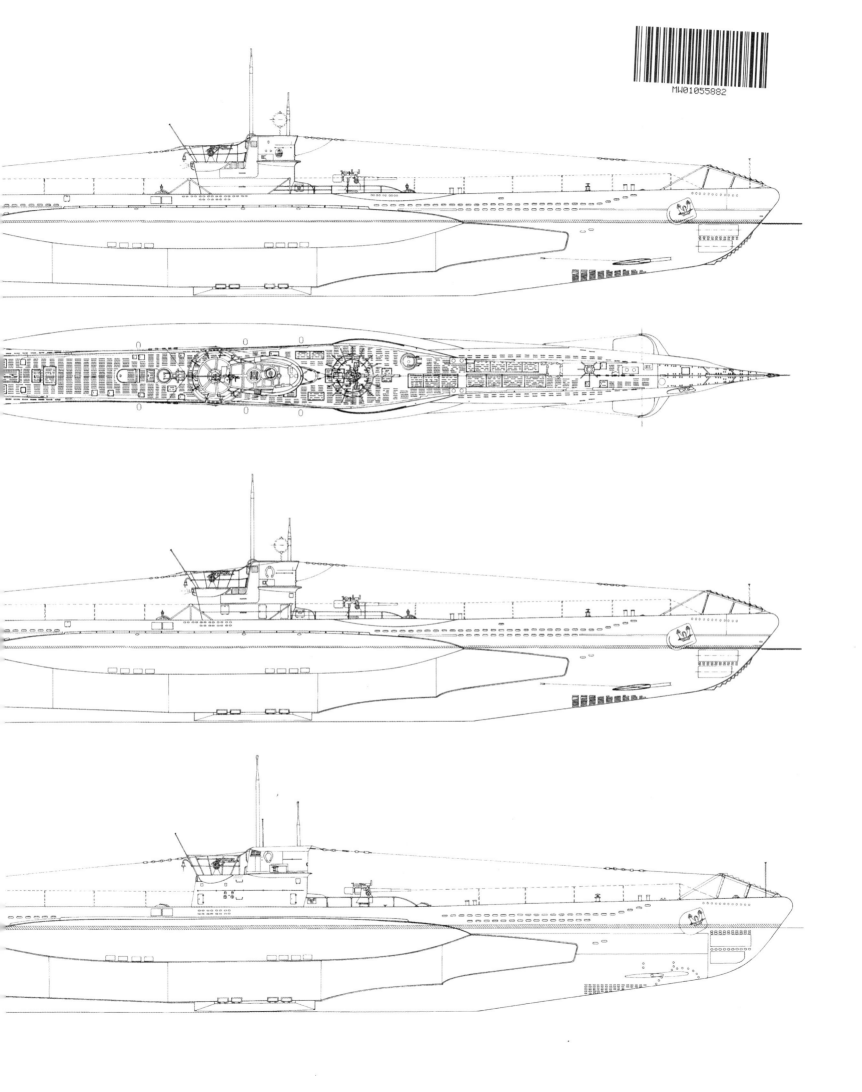

TYPE VII

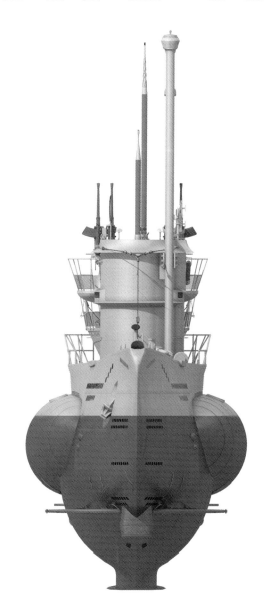

TYPE VII
Germany's Most Successful U-Boats

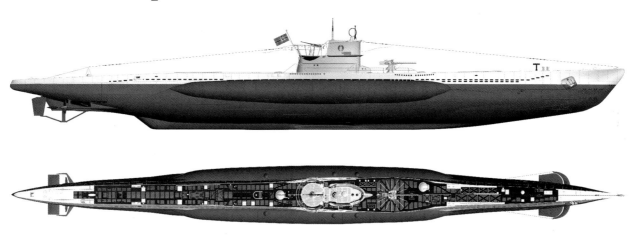

MAREK KRZYSZTAŁOWICZ

NAVAL INSTITUTE PRESS
Annapolis, Maryland

Half title and Frontispiece illustrations: Type VIIC/41 U-boat. (Artwork by Waldemar Góralski)

© AJ-Press 2011

First published in Poland by AJ-Press, Gdansk as *U Boot VII*, Volumes I & II, 2011

This edition first published in Great Britain in 2012
by Seaforth Publishing
An imprint of Pen & Sword Books Ltd
47 Church Street, Barnsley, S Yorkshire S70 2AS

www.seaforthpublishing.com
Email info@seaforthpublishing.com

Published and distributed in the United States of America and Canada
by the Naval Institute Press, 291 Wood Road, Annapolis, Maryland 21402-5043
www.nip.org

LOC number 2012931604

ISBN 978 1 59114 869 2

This edition authorized for sale only in the United States of America,
its territories and possessions, and Canada

Typeset and designed by Mousemat Design Limited
Printed and bound in China by 1010 Printing International Limited

Contents

Introduction

THE IDEA OF ATTACKING the enemy from below the waves is as old as human conflict. An enemy surprised by such an attack would not have much chance to quickly organise an effective defence and, consequently, would be forced to cede the initiative to his opponent, ensuring defeat.

To think of (or even expect) such an attack and to suddenly face it in reality are two different matters. Therefore possessing this filthy weapon, which would allow the execution of such operations, had been forbidden. The submarine had been cursed, considered unethical, perfidious, and – simultaneously – been the subject of great interest. There was another reason for this hostility, however. Thanks to its low price the submarine could easily become a common weapon, an ideal instrument for the world's less powerful navies. Until submarines had appeared the might of a navy had been decided by its number of huge armoured warships, armed with large-calibre guns, powerful enough to crush any enemy who came into range, except of course for ships of the same type. Therefore, the power of a navy had been measured in the number and calibre of guns and the thickness of side armour mounted on large and expensive battleships. Only rich countries could afford to build and operate such warships, which in turn could defend overseas possessions, thus earning a profit for the parent state and dictating the rules to the rest of the world. The small submarine could ruin this *status quo*. It could punch a hole in the soft underbelly of the giant with its torpedoes and sink the enemy in spite of his heavy guns. Thus the new weapon could even the odds in a confrontation between a theoretically weaker navy and a stronger enemy fleet. It could also cut off the supply routes of world powers, threaten their possessions, weaken them, and – provided adequate strategy

▶ *U 1* – the first German submarine. Commissioned on 4 August 1906, this 42m (138ft) vessel displaced only 238 tons. (CAW)

was applied – defeat them – all at a relatively small cost. The story of David and Goliath was becoming true.

Sinking its battleships could lead to the defeat of an entire fleet and that meant destroying the defences of the enemy's coast and also exposing his shipping lanes and – eventually – cutting off his sources of supply and conquering his overseas possessions. Therefore existing strategies were no longer adequate, since defeating a country which owned a powerful navy became a real possibility. All this was caused by a small, slow vessel, only

◀ *U 9* – the boat that first woke the Royal Navy to the seriousness of the underwater threat. On 22 September 1914 its commander Kapitänleutnant Otto Weddigen managed to sink three British armoured cruisers in less than 90 minutes. On 15 October of the same year *U 9* sunk yet another cruiser, HMS *Hawke*. The U-boat, which had been commissioned on 22 February 1910, had a displacement of 493 tons and was 57m (187ft) long. (CAW)

able to submerge for short periods and vulnerable to almost any hit. Surprisingly, both sides of the controversy – traditionalist Admirals who were against using submarines at all, and those who wanted to make use of the new invention – quickly came to the same conclusion: the new weapon is perfidious and unworthy of a skilled tactician, they said, however since it had been already designed it should be used somehow. Such a statement was the origin of the least practical idea for using the submarine in history. The strategists decided, that this unwanted child of war was to fulfil reconnaissance missions . . .

The approach of younger officers was more rational. They had a completely different opinion, since they quickly took note of the possibilities created by this new type of warship. Meanwhile the high command was greatly disturbed by the phantom of invisible U-boats lurking under the waves, which could suddenly strike – and strike hard. Therefore at the outbreak of the First World War 'U-boat fever' broke out – a psychosis that made even a clump of seaweed, a wave or just a reflection on the water be considered the periscope of a U-boat setting an ambush. On two occasions the British Grand Fleet fled its main base in Scapa Flow in total disorder due to – as it turned out later – a frolicking seal. All this resulted in the hasty designing of a special anti-submarine weapon. It consisted of . . . 'special' sacks and hammers. How were they used? Very simply – one needed only to cover a submarine's periscope with the sack and smash its lens with the hammer . . . This is not a joke – such equipment and instructions were issued to His Majesty's seamen, patrolling Scapa Flow base in small boats.

The first German submarine patrol was launched only forty-eight hours after war had been declared, thus starting submarine warfare. On 6 August 1914, the U-boat force commanded by Korvettenkapitän Herman Bauer began its campaign – but achieved nothing, since the patrol had to be aborted due to numerous equipment failures. Soon, however, the submarines showed their claws which resulted in the aforementioned panic. On 22 September 1914 a gloomy record, which so far remains unmatched, was set. On this very day Kapitänleutnant Otto Weddigen encountered in stormy seas an British patrol consisting of three armoured cruisers – HMS *Aboukir*, *Hogue* and *Cressy* – abandoned by their screen of destroyers, which had been forced to return to base due to rough seas. *U 9* needed only a few manoeuvres, well calculated by her skilled commander, and a mere ninety minutes to sink them all. Warships of the proud Royal Navy were going down while warning each other of non-existent mines and stopping their engines to rescue survivors. It was a terrifying demonstration of the effectiveness of submarines. After restrictions on submarine warfare had been relaxed – though not completely abandoned – in 1915, the tonnage sunk by U-boats increased so greatly that Allied commanders genuinely feared that Great Britain might lose the war in less than half a year. Even worse losses threatened the United Kingdom two years later. The U-boat campaign of 1917 was a great shock for both the British and the entire world. Submarines on both sides had already shown what they were capable of.

However, several things were needed to carry out such brilliant operations – skilled and aggressive commanders leading well-trained crews, good conceptions of submarine warfare with all its consequences, effective reconnaissance and good equipment. The last was being developed quickly, but the Treaty of Versailles, enforced on Germany by the

◀ Kapitänleutnant Otto Weddigen, *U 9*'s commanding officer, the first of many German submariners whose exploits were to achieve near-legendary status. On 22 September 1914 he used only six torpedoes (one of which missed) to sink three British armoured cruisers. (CAW)

▼ One of *U 9*'s three victims, the armoured cruiser HMS *Cressy*, built in 1902. She had a displacement of 12,000 tons, over twenty times the size of her nemesis. With the other two ships sunk, *Aboukir* and *Hogue*, Weddigen had accounted for half of the ships of this class built for the Royal Navy. (IWM)

► Oberleutnant zur See Karl Dönitz – creator of the future U-Bootwaffe. The photo was taken aboard *U 39* in 1917, when he was serving as a watch officer. (CAW)

victorious Allies, forbade the German fleet from possessing such vessels. The lessons of 1915 and 1917 had been learned. The British had drawn the proper conclusions from the previous war. But while the British and the French had the Treaty, the Germans had Karl Dönitz. The man who was to be the most brilliant commander of submarine forces on either side had been taken prisoner while commanding *U 60* and attempting to attack – together with other U-boats – a British naval task force. This new tactic ended in disaster then, but would strike a near-lethal blow to the British in the future. The 'wolfpack' tactic – as it became known – needed one more important factor though – large numbers of submarines, which the Weimar Republic was not allowed to have. The prohibition could

be evaded though, and the Germans soon started to do so. Clandestine design bureaus were established in Holland, contracts were awarded to foreign shipyards and submarines were built – for Finland, Spain and Turkey. Sea trials naturally followed. During these, every boat was evaluated in all its aspects by both German officers, who would form the backbone of the future U-bootwaffe, and seamen who learned how to operate those 'Dutch' vessels.

So the personnel were being assembled, there were commanders and tactics – everything and everyone of superb skill and quality. Germany lacked only a good submarine design, but this problem was resolved quickly as well. It was decided to update and mass-produce a model which had already proved its excellent qualities in combat. A wide variety of U-boat types had been designed and operated during the First World War, ranging from small coastal boats to huge underwater freighters. Among them was the progenitor of arguably the most famous Unterseeboot, which would be produced in the largest quantity of any warship in history. The so-called 'Seven', that is the Type VII U-boat and its variants VIIB, VIIC, VIID, VIIE and VIIF, were to play a crucial part in the Second World War. Before this happened, however, there were many clashing conceptions within the Navy Headquarters staff, some of them the result of a total misunderstanding of the nature of modern naval warfare.

Even the construction and capabilities of a submarine raised serious doubts about the proper tactical use of this weapon. It was a perfect, stealthy torpedo boat, though weak as a gunnery platform since its unstable deck placed low above the sea did not allow for precise aiming and the observation point, placed only few metres higher, made

► *UB 64*, one of the UB III class, which were the progenitors of the Type VII. Those submarines had a submerged displacement of 510 tons and were 56m (184ft) long. (IWM)

spotting the fall of shot difficult. A submarine was also a superb minelayer, able to operate unseen close to enemy bases, but it was too slow to cooperate closely with the surface fleet and had too low a bridge to serve as an effective reconnaissance vessel. It was simply in a class by itself. The submarine never needed superiority to its enemy in terms of speed, armour or gunnery firepower as was the case with, for instance, a battleship. That is why submarine designers, guided by the criteria formulated by naval commanders, were free to shape their vessels and select adequate propulsion and armament. Some admirals' megalomania, however, caused those boats to grow and resulted in the absurd sizes of some Japanese, French and American designs. In addition, it is important to remember that in this class of warships combat power is in no way proportional to displacement. In fact, it is the opposite: larger size results in longer diving times and poorer trimming accuracy. A larger submarine was more vulnerable to depth charges, was less manoeuvrable both submerged as well as surfaced, and was generally more difficult to operate, especially at periscope depth. Its larger silhouette was also easier for the enemy to spot. Of course, a large displacement also had some advantages. A submarine of larger size could hold more fuel in its tanks, which allowed longer range. Its larger hull also improved the living conditions of its crew. The latter factor, however, was of secondary importance since – as had been proved by experience – even in the best conditions crews were unable to endure a patrol that was longer than two months. The headquarters of the reborn, though still greatly constrained, German navy had to combine all these often conflicting factors and find an acceptable compromise. The design which would be chosen and put into service had to be technically reliable, but also be able to dive quickly and have good manoeuvrability and long range. It was accepted that commissioning a greater number of smaller (and thus cheaper and easier to produce) boats increased the

ability to deploy them across a large area in order to effectively locate and intercept enemy convoys.

Nevertheless the conditions set by headquarters did not strictly define the priorities for the new submarines, which allowed the designers to shape the new boats with relative freedom. The re-established German navy, which was preparing for a possible war at sea, had to quickly find an ideal solution which would strike a happy balance between all the contradictory requirements.

The father of the U-bootwaffe, Fregattenkapitän (at that time) Dönitz had his own ideas. Contemplating future submarine tactics, he observed that having a larger number of smaller and cheaper submarines was better suited to the idea of 'wolfpacks', since it improved the probability of locating enemy vessels at sea and facilitated executing multidirectional attacks against more valuable targets. One needs to remember that a larger submarine was not able to carry out reconnaissance missions over a larger area. There was yet another factor – more prosaic, though equally important – the Kriegsmarine's budget, which was very restricted before the war and did not allow for full-scale fleet development. The state's leadership was more convinced by hordes of tanks charging across training fields and protected by swarms of roaring planes, which they had seen on numerous exercises, than by cramped warships which made visitors feel sick.

Therefore, considering all the criteria mentioned above, the requirements for a future U-boat were eventually defined. The medium submarine was to displace some 600–700 tons and have a range of about 3000–6000 nautical miles, with an armament consisting of at least four torpedo tubes with a reasonable number of torpedoes. The vessel also had to be easy to manufacture in order to allow for mass production, but at the same time should be sturdy, reliable and able to dive quickly.

Such guidelines forced the engineers designing the boat to seek intensively for an optimal solution. Despite the

◀ A UB III class submarine. It is very similar to the later 'VII', apart from the masts. This is *UB 70*, which entered service on 17 August 1917. The boat was sunk in the Mediterranean on 8 May 1918 after a depth-charge attack by an American destroyer. (IWM)

▲ Another photograph of a UB III class boat, this time with its masts folded down. The similarity to the future Type VII is very close. This is *UB 119*, which entered service on 13 December 1917. (NHC)

time that had passed since the end of the First World War, in spite of endless brainstorming, numerous deliberations and discussions as well as the huge emotions fed by reminiscences of submarine exploits, submarine technology had not substantially changed. All the solutions which had been used in the past were still valid. Such a conclusion was in fact favourable for the Kriegsmarine's command. To avoid any possible faults it was decided to stick to old ideas and only improve the manufacturing technology, which permitted predicting good boat performance. This technical stagnation also facilitated the choice of a type which would satisfy all of the U-bootwaffe's requirements. In fact, such a submarine had been already designed and its combat performance, operational characteristics and the possibility of mass production already proved. Although it had been used in the previous war this idea was supported by the future Admiral Dönitz, one of the most distinguished military commanders and an excellent submariner, and also by his subordinate engineers Schürer (a shipbuilding expert) and Bröking (a talented maritime propulsion specialist). Therefore the twin-hull UB III type submarine, mass-produced from 1915 to 1918, was accepted as a future star of submarine warfare. It had been built in a long series during the last war by every important German shipyard along with other cooperating industrial plants.

A total of fifty-three submarines of this type had been commissioned, entering service from 1917. Even more such boats had been built, though they had not entered service before the end of the war. Therefore the shipbuilding industry had numerous well-trained and experienced staff, and the techniques of mass production had been fully developed and tested. Undoubtedly such shipyards as Blöhm und Voss and Vulcan in Hamburg, Weser in Bremen or Germania in Kiel, along with their engineers, foremen and workers, were looking forward to the resumption of production of the boat, even with changed characteristics and a slightly modified design – updated, though still similar to the one produced earlier.

During the First World War, Type UB III U-boats had sunk a total of 500 ships of 1,125,715 GRT altogether. Some of their commanders' achievements are listed below:

- *UB 48* – 34 ships – 106,927 GRT.
- *UB 49* – 41 ships – 79,683 GRT.
- *UB 50* – 38 ships – 93,773 GRT.
- *UB 51* – 18 vessels – 48,634 GRT.
- *UB 57* – 47 ships – 130,679 GRT.
- *UB 80* – 20 ships – 35,679 GRT.
- *UB 105* – 24 ships – 64,587 GRT.

As well as all the above, UB IIIs also managed to sink the following enemy warships:

- *UB 50* (Oblt.z.S H Kukat) – battleship HMS *Britannia* (displacement 17,500 t).
- *UB 65* (Kptlt. M Schelle) – sloop HMS *Arbutus* (1290 t).
- *UB 67* (Oblt.z.S H von Doemming) – minesweeper HMS *Ascot* (860 t).
- *UB 73* (Kptlt. K Neureuther) – British submarine *D-6* (620 t).
- *UB 91* (Kptlt. W H Hertwig) – patrol vessel USS *Tampa* (1181 t).
- *UB 105* (Kptlt. W Marschall) – sloop HMS *Cowslip* (1290 t).

UB IIIs had carried out a total of 267 combat patrols. The Type UB III was the only high seas U-boat designed to operate in the open ocean, featuring a twin-hull layout and with good performance. It could reach a top speed of over 13 knots while surfaced and 7 knots while submerged, and was also very durable, manoeuvrable and seaworthy, dived quickly and had a very good range for its time. The Type UB III was also quite well armed. Undoubtedly, the UB III was a significant achievement of German engineering and industry.

Almost all significant industrial plants in Germany of that time had been involved in manufacturing equipment for this U-boat type. They were well-known to the future Befehlshaber der Unterseebote, Admiral Dönitz, who had gained his experience while commanding – among others – one such boat, namely *UB 68*. The tactical guidelines which had been framed earlier, as well as the criteria of choice of the new primary submarine earmarked for operations against British shipping, fitted well with the concept of further development and improvement of the Type UB III boat. Therefore the new submarine that was being developed was based on a well-tried ancestor. All calculations and research were being done in secret German design offices which had been established abroad; the projects were also realised there. The final product, in the form of the submarine *Veteninen* built for Finland, underwent thorough sea trials in which a series of German officers and crews – the future U-bootwaffe's personnel – actively participated.

Thus the Germans were killing two birds with one

◄ *UB 88*, another UB III, surrenders to the Americans. The emblem of the Iron Cross, which was awarded for heroism, is painted on the boat's conning-tower – this custom had been introduced by Otto Weddigen, who put such a cross on his *U 9*. Later, in the 1930s, another U-boat designated *U 9* also wore such a cross. (NHC)

stone. They were designing a boat and also training a group of experts, who helped to improve the new U-boat. Extensive trials were continued with their 'own' *U 27* and subsequent boats, starting in 1936. This stage of testing was prolonged and included new tactical situation schemes, and was willingly carried out in extreme weather conditions. The resulting experimental data was becoming more and more precise and valuable, which quickly paid off in two ways: with many improvements in the vessels already built and also many corrections to the design itself. The trials' results proved also beyond all doubt that Dönitz's assumptions were correct, and influenced the decisions to abandoning the larger Type I U-boat design and discontinue work on the smaller coastal Type II. Thenceforward German designers concentrated on only two types: IX and VII. The latter is the subject of this publication – the famous 'Seven', workhorse of the U-bootwaffe and a warship produced in the greatest numbers ever, which caused much trouble to the Allies and almost won the Battle of Atlantic – a battle the significance of which cannot be overestimated.

Hence the specific mix of imagination (Dönitz),

necessity (something was needed to win the war and to realise Dönitz's plans) and logic (using an old but tested model) resulted in what was arguably the most perfect and effective of all instruments of war used in the Second World War – the Type VII U-boat with all its variants. Beside the above-mentioned factors, German precision and reliability were needed to create such a lethal machine. It soon turned out that the choice of the model and the design work aimed at its modernisation were the proverbial bull's-eye. They resulted in a relatively well-armed, manoeuvrable submarine, with exceptional diving time and excellent seaworthiness both surfaced and submerged. Even the 'Seven's' range turned out longer than had been expected, which particularly pleased Dönitz and his staff since from the very beginning it had been planned that hunting for Allied shipping would have to be carried out on both sides of the ocean.

▼ Grossadmiral Karl Dönitz awarding decorations to U-boat men. (CAW)

▼ The U-boats' primary weapon – the torpedo. The picture shows torpedoes being loaded aboard U-boats in port. (CAW)

1. Versions of the Type VII

Type VII (VIIA)

THE TYPE VII U-BOAT, as has been mentioned, can be traced straight back to the exceptionally successful UB III model. The 'A' letter in the variant's designation was not used when the first boats entered service, they were just known as 'Type VII'. The additional letter was added later to distinguish the 'original' design from the variants which followed, which were designated 'B', 'C', etc.

The Type VII U-boat had a double hull, the pressure hull being covered by a streamlined outer casing to which the main ballast saddle tanks were fitted, though the extra ballast tank for rapid diving was inside the pressure hull. The displacement was 626 tons surfaced and 745 tons submerged, and total displacement (taking into account the theoretical displacement of the outer hull shape) was 915 tons. The length of the pressure hull was 45.50m (149.28ft) and the outer casing was 64.51m (211.65ft) long. The widths (diameters) of both hulls were 4.70m (15.42ft) – pressure – and 5.85m (19.19ft) – outer. The height of the submarine from the keel to the top of the tower was 9.50m (31.17ft) and the draught was 4.37m (14.34ft). The boat could dive exceptionally quickly – it could reach a depth of 100m (approximately 330ft) in 30 seconds and 200m (660ft) in 50 seconds, which gave it a great advantage compared to other contemporary submarines.

U-boats of this type, just like any other submarine of their time, carried two kinds of armament: primary – torpedoes, and auxiliary – guns. They were fitted with four 535mm bow torpedo tubes (two on each side, one above the other) and one more in the stern, placed above the waterline in the outer hull, which could be reloaded only while the boat was surfaced. A total of eleven torpedoes were stored in the tubes, in the forward compartment under the deck and under the seamen's berths,

and in the motor room, also under the deck. The 'Seven' could also carry mines: thirty-three of the TMB type or twenty-two of the TMA type, which were laid through the torpedo tubes. The gun armament of the submarine consisted of a single 88mm SK C/35 deck gun on the Ubts.L. mount and a single 20mm C/30 cannon. Ammunition carried was 250 88mm shells and 4380 20mm rounds.

The Type VII submarine, like all other contemporary boats, was propelled by two diesel engines while surfaced and two electric motors while submerged. Later, when the so-called snorkel ('Schnorchel' in German) had been invented, the diesels could be also used to propel the boat while submerged. The diesel set consisted of two naturally-aspirated four-stroke, six-cylinder MAN diesel working at speeds of 470–485 rpm. The maximum output of a single engine was 1160hp. The electric motor room was fitted with two BBC GG UB 720/8 motors of 375hp each; their maximum speed was 322rpm. Power for them was provided by two storage batteries with sixty-two type AFA 27 Mak 800 cells and a total capacity of 7500 Ah. The fuel tanks' capacity was 67 or 58.6 tons of diesel oil, which allowed for a range of 6200nm at 10 knots and 2900nm at 16 knots surfaced, and the batteries gave a submerged range of 73–90nm at 4 knots. The 'Seven's' top speed was 16–17 knots while surfaced and 8 knots submerged. The crew consisted of four officers (the commander, two watch officers and a chief engineer) and forty to fifty-six petty officers and seamen.

Since the first of the Type I and Type VII U-boats entered service almost simultaneously they became natural competitors. However, the official comparison proved the 'Seven' superior. Her only disadvantages were an excessive turning radius, too few reload torpedoes, insufficient surfaced speed and range.

▼ One of the first Type VII (VIIA) U-boats built. (CAW)

The following Type VIIA U-boats entered service:

Boat No.	Commissioned	First commander	Manufacturer
U 27	12 Aug 1936	KKpt. Ibbeken	Deschimag AG Weser, Bremen
U 28	12 Sep 1936	Kptlt. Ambrosius	Deschimag AG Weser, Bremen
U 29	16 Nov 1936	Kptlt. Fischer	Deschimag AG Weser, Bremen
U 30	8 Oct 1936	Kptlt. Cohausz	Deschimag AG Weser, Bremen
U 31	28 Dec 1936	Kptlt. Dau	Deschimag AG Weser, Bremen
U 32	5 Apr 1937	Kptlt. W Lott	Deschimag AG Weser, Bremen
U 33	25 Jul 1936	Kptlt. Junker	Krupp Germaniawerft, Kiel
U 34	12 Sep 1936	Kptlt. Sobe	Krupp Germaniawerft, Kiel
U 35	3 Nov 1936	Kptlt. Ewerth	Krupp Germaniawerft, Kiel
U 36	16 Dec 1936	Kptlt. Michahelles	Krupp Germaniawerft, Kiel

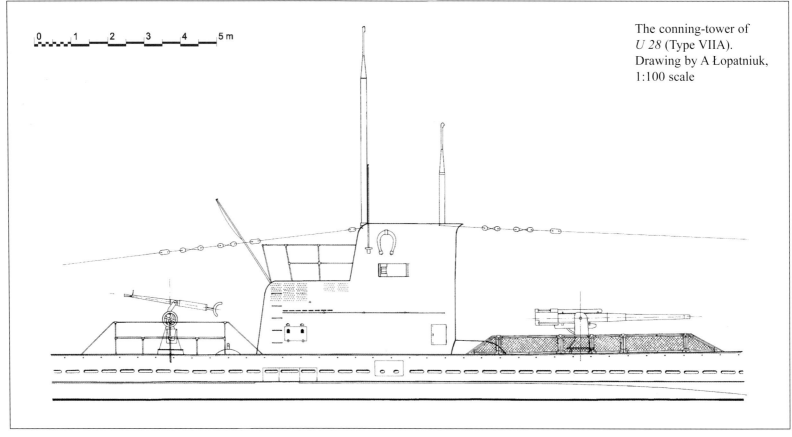

The conning-tower of
U 28 (Type VIIA).
Drawing by A Łopatniuk,
1:100 scale

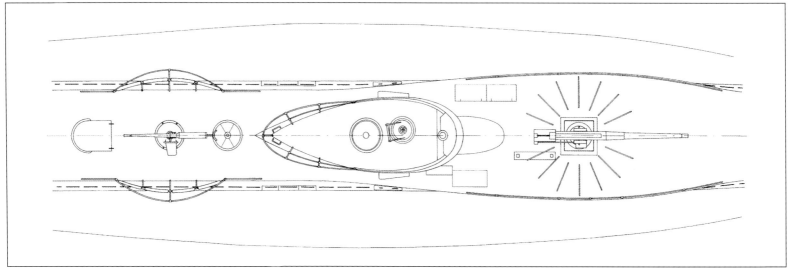

▶ The conning-tower of a Type VIIA U-boat with a different arrangement of drainage slots. The 20mm cannon has been removed from its deck mount. (CAW)

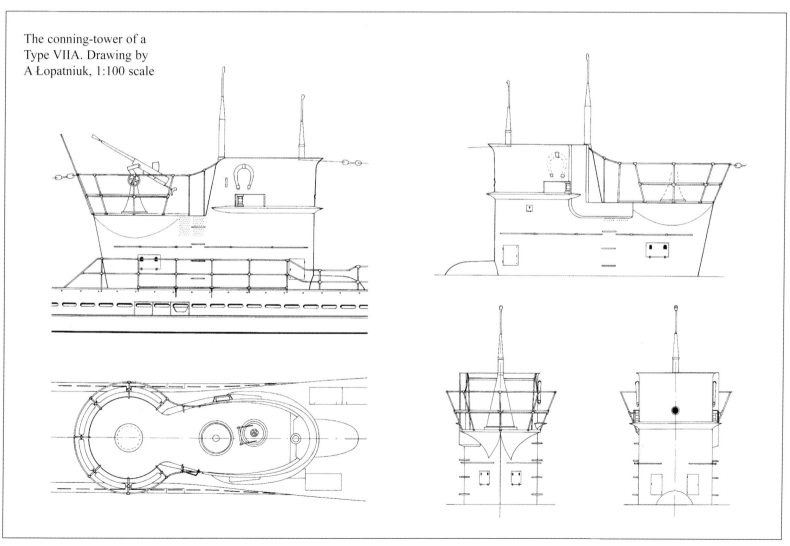

The conning-tower of a Type VIIA. Drawing by A Łopatniuk, 1:100 scale

◄ The differently-shaped conning-tower of a Type VIIA U-boat fitted with the platform for a 20mm cannon. (CAW)

◄ A Type VIIA U-boat fitted with an earlier type of conning-tower (without an anti-aircraft gun platform) slips into its base. (CAW)

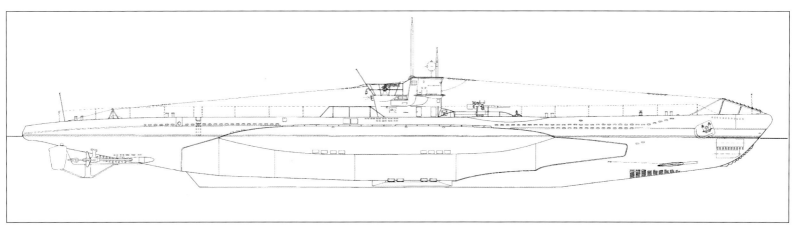

▲ *U 52*, a Type VIIB
U-boat of the first series.
Drawn and traced by
Mirosław Skwiot

▼ Amidships aboard a Type
VIIB. Ventilation ducts are
visible on the tower just
behind Prien's charging bull
emblem. (CAW)

Type VIIB

Constant exercises, ordered and run by Dönitz, simulated combat conditions as closely as possible. They were intended not only to train excellent skippers and crews but also to test the equipment and help to evaluate the boat's construction. The results of such trials, together with analyses of commanders', engineers' and staff officers' suggestions, led eventually to the designing of a new version of the Type VII U-boat – namely the VIIB. Despite the fact that Dönitz attributed the credit for designing the VIIB to Fregkpt. (Ing) Otto Thedsen, Chief Engineer of the Flotilla, the design was the result of many men's work. The excessive underwater turning radius was improved by fitting a second rudder, doubling the rudders' area, and placing both of them directly behind the propellers. This modification also allowed an increased number of torpedoes to be carried, solving another problem with the Type VIIA. The aft torpedo tube was repositioned inside the pressure hull (where the steering engine had been in the 'A' model), which allowed it to be reloaded while submerged and also permitted another reload torpedo to be stowed under the deck of the same compartment. The

vacant space between the pressure and outer hulls now served as a stowage space for two more torpedoes.

The boat's top speed had been increased by adding a supercharger for the diesel engines. To increase its range the whole vessel had been lengthened by 2m (6.6ft), to accommodate larger fuel tanks. Since these by themselves did not permit the desired increase in range, other fuel tanks had been added inside the enlarged saddle tanks. To improve the vessel's stability, which would be affected by the new tanks, two compensation tanks had also been fitted inside the saddle tanks – one on each side – which resulted in reduced rolling while the submarine was on the surface. The fuel tanks inside the saddle tanks were self-regulating, which meant that they had open bottoms and the fuel used was automatically replaced by heavier seawater freely flowing in. All the changes described had caused an enlargement of the saddle tanks' dimensions, which – along with the increased length of the hulls – increased the U-boat's displacement by almost 120 tons.

The first of the new variant U-boats, *U 45*, built by the Krupp Germaniawerft in Kiel, was commissioned on 25 June 1938. Subsequent boats were built by the same shipyard as well as two others: Vulkan in Bremen and Flender-Werke in Lübeck.

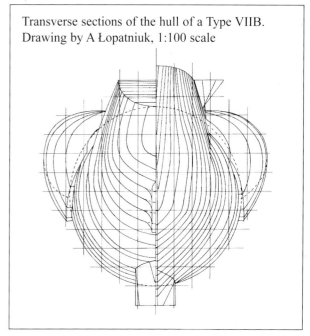

Transverse sections of the hull of a Type VIIB.
Drawing by A Łopatniuk, 1:100 scale

The VIIB also had a double hull, with its pressure hull divided into three compartments. The boat was fitted with saddle tanks of similar construction to its predecessor, but of a rounder shape and stretching down almost to the keel. The 'B' variant also differed – as has been already mentioned – with the placement of its fifth torpedo tube, which was now fitted in the lower part of the hull below the waterline, eliminating the characteristic muzzle over the stern. The new variant was also larger, which determined her superiority. As has been mentioned, the VIIB's displacement was almost 120 tons greater than the original Type VII (VIIA). The new submarine was also 2m (6.6ft) longer (both the pressure and outer hulls had been lengthened). It had more powerful diesel engines, which allowed greater surface speeds. The enlargement of the ballast tanks resulted in increased diving times: the VIIA could reach 200m (660ft) in some 50 seconds, while the new 'B' variant could dive to that depth in only 30 seconds. There was also a significant difference in the amount of fuel carried. The VIIA had 67 tons of diesel fuel, while her successor could carry 108.3 tons, which increased her range by 1500nm (surfaced at 10 knots).

Such progress was very significant for an ocean-going submarine. However, the badly-designed ventilation system had not been improved and remained the same as on the 'A' variant. The air ducts used in the system were inefficient, which forced designers to find a provisional solution. This

▲ Another Type VIIB, *U 83*, operating in the Mediterranean, wearing the 'spotted' camouflage often used in that theatre. This particular boat does not have the expanded ventilation ducts on the tower, only a vertical pipe with two holes protruding from the rear, under the gun platform. However, the twin rudders and the position of the stern tube marked it out as a Type VIIB. (CAW)

▼ The conning-tower of *U 33*. Despite the additional external ventilation ducts visible on the sides, the boat was in fact a Type VIIA. (CAW)

was eventually eliminated by mounting additional ducts, which supplied the air for fans and then to the boat's interior, on the side of the conning-tower (in most cases on the left). Those rectangular (not round) pipes were bent in several places and were a visual differentiation of variants 'A' and 'B' from their successor, the VIIC, as the 'C' version was the first one with an improved internal ventilation system. This was achieved by fitting it with internal ventilation ducts, which could be seen from outside only as rectangular drain-covered slots placed in the aft part of the bridge coaming.

The Type VIIB U-boat's technical and tactical data were as follows: displacement: surfaced 753 t, submerged 857 t, full 1040 t. External hull length 66.50m (218.18ft), diameter 6.20m (20.34ft). The pressure hull was 48.80m (160.10ft) long and 4.70m (15.42ft) in diameter. The boat could dive to 200m (660ft) in 30 seconds. The 'B' variant's armament was very similar to that of the 'A' model – it consisted of four bow torpedo tubes and another one in the stern with the increased number of fourteen torpedoes carried in total. The boat could alternatively carry up to thirty-nine mines. In terms of gun armament however, the number of light-calibre weapons changed over time, according to changes in tactics and theory throughout the war. The basic gun armament was still an 88mm SK C/35 deck gun and one

20mm C/30 cannon. In the later period either two 20mm cannons or a single 37mm cannon were mounted. The boat carried 250 shells for the deck gun and 1195 37mm rounds or 4380 20mm rounds. The submarine was propelled by two F46 four-stroke, six-cylinder supercharged diesel engines designed by Germaniawerft. They had a maximum output of 1400hp each, though a temporary emergency power of 1600hp could be achieved; and maximum speed was 470–490rpm. These engines were installed aboard *U 45–50*, *U 83*, *U 84*, *U 87*, *U 99*, *U 100* and *U 102*, while *U 51–55*, *U 73–76*, *U 85*, *U 88* and *U 101* were propelled by MAN M6V40/46 engines, which were also four-stroke, six-cylinder supercharged diesels. Their maximum output was 1160hp at a maximum speed of 470–485rpm. The motor rooms of *U 45*, *U 46*, *U 49*, *U 51*, *U 52*, *U 54*, *U 73–76*, *U 85*, *U 86*, *U 99* and *U 100* was fitted with two BBC GGUB 720/8 electric motors with a maximum output of 375hp and a speed of 295rpm, while *U 47*, *U 48*, *U 50*, *U 53*, *U 55*, *U 83*, *U 84*, *U 87*, *U 101* and *U 102* had AEG GU 460/8–276 motors of the same power and speed. In terms of range there were differences between boats of this type: for those powered with MAN engines it was 9400nm at 10 knots, while for vessels with F46 engines it was 9700nm at the same speed. The fuel tanks' capacity also differed – the former group could carry 99.7 tons, the latter 108.3 tons of diesel oil. The Type VIIBs could reach a top speed of 17.2–17.8 knots on the surface and 8 knots submerged. At a speed of 17.2 knots the range dropped to 3850nm. While submerged they could travel for 90nm at a speed of 4 knots. Power for the electric motors was stored in two batteries consisting of sixty-two MAK 800 W AFA 270 cells with a total capacity of 7500 Ah, mounted in rubber containers (*U 45–47*, *U 51*), or AFA 33 MAL 800 W cells of 9160 Ah mounted without containers in the other boats. The crew consisted of four officers and forty petty officers and seamen.

The following Type VIIB submarines were commissioned: *U 45*, *U 46*, *U 47*, *U 48*, *U 49*, *U 50*, *U 51*, *U 52*, *U 53*, *U 54* and *U 55* built by Bremer Vulkan; *U 83*, *U 84*, *U 85*, *U 86* and *U 87* built by Flender-Werke in Lübeck; and *U 99*, *U 100*, *U 101* and *U 102* built by Krupp Germaniawerft in Kiel.

▲ *U 46* on its way back from patrol with its conning-tower damaged. This boat lacked the external ventilation ducts, but it was a Type VIIB, since it had twin rudders and its stern torpedo tube inside the pressure hull. (CAW)

Type VIIC

On 2 November 1940, with the commissioning of *U 69*, the most numerous series of submarines in history entered service. These were the Type VIIC U-boats. For the first time the changes introduced in a new version were aimed not at eliminating any observed shortcomings in the boat but to create space for mounting new electronic equipment. The Kriegsmarine's high command was completely satisfied with the Type VIIB design, and only the need to introduce new, modern hydrophones (which demanded more space) forced the designers to develop a new variant. In the Type VIIB's hull there was simply no room for the new S-Gerät (Such Gerät – seeking device) active sonar, which allowed detection of both targets and mines. This required adding a new hull section and an additional frame in the middle part of the control room, which increased the overall length of the boat by 60cm (24in). Other results of this were: enlargement of the cramped conning-tower placed directly above the control room by 30cm (11.8in) in length and 6cm (2.4in) in width, and lengthening the fuel tank situated below the control room, which allowed an additional 5.4m³ (264 US gallons) of fuel to be carried. The saddle tanks were also lengthened in the process, allowing the designers to fit two quick-dive tanks inside them, one on each side. In additional the submarine received a modernised filtering system, which reduced consumption of lubricating oil, and a new Junkers air compressor driven by the diesel engine, which allowed electrical power to be conserved (up to now the compressor had been powered by an electric motor). The Type VIIC U-boat was of larger dimensions and displacement and was superior to her predecessors in terms of diving speed. However, since the change of dimensions was not accompanied by increasing the engines' output, both top speed and range fell. Nevertheless this model became the standard submarine of the German navy and a main actor in the Battle of the Atlantic.

The Type VIIC's displacements were 769 t (surfaced), 871 t (submerged) and 1070 t (total). The pressure hull was 50.50m/49.40m (165.68ft/162.07ft) long and 4.70m (15.42ft) wide, while the dimensions of the outer hull were 66.50m/62.10m (218.18ft/203.74ft) and 6.20m (20.34ft) respectively. The submarine's height (measured from the keel to the top of the conning-tower) was 9.60m (31.50ft), and the draught was 4.74m (15.55ft). The boat had an exceptional diving speed – it could dive to 150–165m (some 500ft) in a mere 30 seconds. Although the maximum operational depth was set at 280m (920ft), in fact it could dive even deeper without being crushed by the water pressure.

As with the other Type VII variants, the gun armament varied over time as tactical requirements changed. The main deck gun remained an 88mm SK 35 gun with 250 shells, but the lighter armament could consist of 20mm or 37mm cannons in several combinations. In the first case – when only 20mm guns were used – it could be either one or two guns. When the 37mm was fitted it was usually a single gun. Apart from the 88mm shells, 1195 37mm rounds and 4380 20mm rounds could be carried. The torpedo armament was also the same as on the Type VIIB: four bow and one stern 535mm torpedo tubes with fourteen torpedoes or thirty-six TMA or thirty-nine TMB mines.

The subs were propelled by two types of diesel engine: MAN or Germaniawerft F 46 (both of similar performance) and electric motors designed by AEG, BBC and SSW. Six-cylinder, four-stroke supercharged MAN MV 40/46 diesels were fitted into *U 79–82, U 90* and *U 132–136*. A single MAN engine had an output of 1160hp at

▼ The bow of a Type VIIC submarine on the slipway. (CAW)

▶ Another photograph of a Type VIIC on the slipway, this time from the stern. The rudders and planes, as well as the door of the stern torpedo tube, are clearly visible. The presence of officers in full dress uniforms suggests that the submarine is being prepared for launching. (CAW)

▼ A Type VIIC U-boat on the slipway in a shipyard. Note the open torpedo tube doors. (ADM)

470–485rpm. The remaining Type VIIC U-boats were propelled by Germaniawerft engines. These type F46 diesels, also four-stroke and six-cylinder with superchargers, had a maximum output of 1400hp at 470–490rpm and were able to achieve temporary emergency power of 1600hp. The ranges of all those boats, although similar, differed slightly and depended on the type of engine installed. Two MANs gave 8850nm at 10 knots and 3450nm at 17 knots, while two F46 diesels gave 8500nm at 10 knots and 3250nm at 17 knots. While submerged (without snorkel) the boats were propelled by two AEG GU 460/8–276 375hp motors at 295rpm, BBC GG UB 720/8 motors (375hp at 295 rpm), SSW GO 343/38–8 (375hp at 295rpm) or GL RP 137/c. The AEG motors were installed aboard *U 69–72*, *U 89*, *U 93–98*, *U 201–212*, *U 221–232*, *U 235–291*, *U 331–348*, *U 351–374*, *U 431–450*, *U 731–750*, *U 1051–1058* and *U 1191–1210*. *U 77–82*, *U 88*, *U 90–92*, *U 132–136*, *U 401*, *U 451*, *U 452*, *U 551–650*, *U 751*, *U 821*, *U 822*, *U 825*, *U 826* and *U 951–994* had two BBC motors, while *U 301–316*, *U 375–400*, *U 701–722*, *U 752–782*, *U 1131* and *U 1132* had GL RP 137/c motors manufactured by the Gable Lahmeyer und Co. factories. Siemens Shuckert Werke provided GO 343/38–8 motors for *U 349*, *U 350*, *U 402–430*, *U 453–458*, *U 465–486*, *U 651–686*, *U 901–908*, *U 921–928*, *U 1101*, *U 1102*, *U 1161* and *U 1162*.

The power for the motors was stored in two batteries consisting of sixty-two AFA 33 MAL 800 E cells with a total capacity of 9160 Ah, weighing 61,996kg (136,678lbs) with an approximate discharge time of twenty hours. Each cell's dimensions were: length 478mm (18.81in), width 381mm (15.00in), height 1123mm (44.21in). The electric drive allowed a top speed of 7.6 knots while submerged; diesel engines propelled the boat at a maximum of 17–17.7

Transverse sections of a Type VIIC U-boat. Drawing by A Łopatniuk 1:100 scale

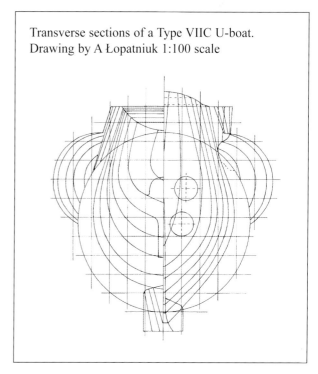

▲ A Type VIIC U-boat is being scuttled by charges laid by the crew of the Polish destroyer escort ORP Ślazak during Operation 'Deadlight'. (MMW)

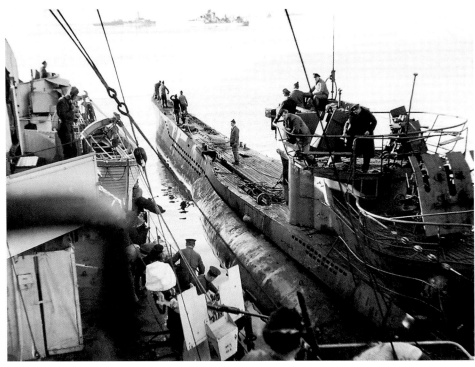

▲ An almost de-stored Type VIIC rides very high in the water in one of the shelters on the French coast. The drainage slots in the outer hull are clearly visible. (CAW)

▼ U 471, a Type VIIC, one of the numerous boats described as 'Kampfboote' because of their strengthened anti-aircraft armament. (CAW)

▲ Another 'Kampfboot' – a Type VIIC U-boat stripped of all armament waits to be sunk as part of Operation 'Deadlight' after the end of the War. (MMW)

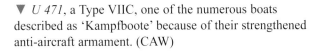

► This photograph shows *U 673*, a Type VIIC. Note the altered tower with strengthened anti-aircraft armament, the so-called Flak U-boot-Turm IV. There is a twin 20mm 38MII cannon installed on the additional platform forward of the bridge. The large 'box' on the top contained the FuMO 30 radar antenna. (CAW)

► The antennae of the FuMO 29 radar, made by the GEMA company, wrapped around the conning-tower of *U 231*, a Type VIIC U-boat. (CAW)

knots. Ranges on electric propulsion were as follows: 80nm at 4 knots and 130nm at 2 knots. Total fuel capacity was 105.3–113.5 tons of diesel oil. The crew consisted of the commander, two watch officers, a chief engineer and forty petty officers and seamen.

The Type VIIC U-boats were built in the following shipyards:

- Vulkan Bremen, Vegesack: *U 77–82, U 132–136, U 251–300, U 1271–1279, U 1280–1300.*
- Flender Werft, Lübeck: *U 88–92, U 301–330, U 903–904, U 1331–1400.*
- Nordsee-Werke, Emden: *U 331–350, U 1101–1130.*
- Flensburger Schiffbau Ges: *U 351–370, U 1301–1330.*
- Howaldtswerke, Kiel: *U 371–400, U 1131–1160.*
- Danziger Werft, Danzig: *U 401–430, U 1161–1190, U 1801–1900.*
- Schichau Werft, Danzig: *U 431–450, U 731–750, U 825–840, U 1191–1220, U 2301–2320.*
- Deutsche Werke, Kiel: *U 451–458, U 465–486.*
- Blohm und Voss, Hamburg: *U 551–650, U 951–1050, U 1401–1404, U 1417–1500.*
- Howaldtswerke, Hamburg: *U 651–700, U 2001–2100.*
- Stülcken, Hamburg: *U 701–730, U 905–920.*
- Kriegsmarine-Werft, Wilhelmshaven: *U 751–790, U 1901–2000.*
- Oder Werke, Stettin: *U 821–824.*
- Vulkan Werke, Stettin: *U 901* and *U 902.*
- Neptun Werft, Rostock: *U 921–950.*

◄ Type VIIC/41 U-boats
with their 88mm deck guns
removed. Towards the end of
the war the U-boats had few
opportunities to use their
guns and instead attacked
with their primary weapon,
torpedoes, staying concealed
themselves. From the right,
U 1109, *U 1058*, *U 278* and
U 901. (CAW)

Type VIIC/41

The changing demands of war led to the designing of another three variants of the Type VIIC submarine, known as types VIIC/41, VIIC/42 and VIIC/43. Only the first was produced in limited numbers, the others were not built at all.

The United States' entry into the war created new hunting-grounds for the U-boats off the American coast. The weak defences in those waters, along with the negligence of the American command, allowed the Germans to strike a painful blow at Allied shipping. This period is known in the U-bootwaffe's history as the 'Happy Time' (in fact the second period to be so called). However, despite successes in the Western Atlantic, the German command could not ignore the fact that Allied countermeasures in the primary theatre of war, the Atlantic, were becoming more and more effective. Thorough analysis of the tactical situation indicated that U-boats needed greater surfaced speed (some 22 knots) and a deeper operational depth, reaching 300m (985ft), to effectively carry out their operations. As a result of that research the new version – the Type VIIC/41 – was designed. The basic plan was to introduce modifications which would fit into the Type VIIC's layout, thus not disturbing the mass-production process which had already been established. This objective was achieved by replacing some old equipment with new

models which were much smaller, thus allowing the entire boat's weight to be reduced. It had been decided to use the 11.5 tons saved in this way to introduce new, thicker steel in the hull's construction – 21mm (0.83in) instead of the previous 18mm (0.71in). This increased the hull's strength, allowing a greater operating depth (increased from 150m [490ft] to 180m [590ft]). The crush depth also increased to 300m (985ft) as opposed to 250m (820ft) for a production Type VIIC. To reduce drag the bow was also redesigned – lengthening it by 13cm (5.1in) to create the so-called 'Atlantic bow'. Introducing this sub-variant into the production lines was not to be a revolution. The shipyards which had been already producing the Type VII boats were simply ordered to modify them to the new standard and employ the new materials. Technical data, except for the boat's overall length, which increased by 10cm (0.33ft), remained exactly the same as they were on the Type VIIC. Nevertheless, the first such boats only entered service in 1943.

The results achieved by these modifications encouraged the Kriegsmarine to introduce further modifications. This time, to achieve a greater speed and improve the U-boat's diving characteristics, it was decided to change its parameters. First of all, a new two-stage supercharger was to be used. This device, combined with an increase in the engines' rpm, would result in increasing a single engine's output to 2200hp, which would increase

◄ Late Type VIIC and VIIC/41 U-boats were fitted with the GHG passive sonar array. It was fitted under the bow, below the torpedo tubes, as show here on *U 1105*.

maximum speed by 1.6kts. However, to do that the designers would be forced to lengthen the whole engine room by 80cm (31in). The submarine's range was to be increased by larger fuel tanks – external, fitted into saddle tanks widened by 35cm (1.15ft), and internal, inside the pressure hull whose diameter increased by 30cm (11.8in). With all these modifications, together with using special armoured 'Wotan' steel which increased hull thickness up to 28mm (1.10in), the submarine's overall weight was increased by some 68 tons. The U-boat's theoretical diving depths were now excellent: operational depth was 300m (985ft) and crush depth 500m (1640ft). The technical data

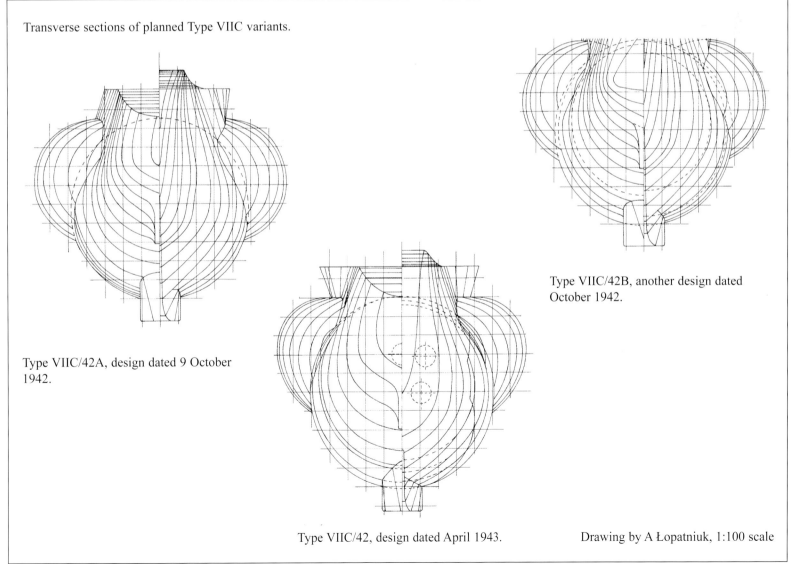

Transverse sections of planned Type VIIC variants.

Type VIIC/42A, design dated 9 October 1942.

Type VIIC/42, design dated April 1943.

Type VIIC/42B, another design dated October 1942.

Drawing by A Łopatniuk, 1:100 scale

of the boat, designated Type VIIC/42, was as follows:

- Displacement:
  - surfaced   999 t
  - submerged   1050 t
  - total   1369 t
- Length:
  - outer hull   67.3m (220.8ft)
  - pressure hull   53.0m (173.9ft)
- Height   9.0m (29.5ft)
- Draught   5.0m (16.4ft)
- Engine output:
  - diesel   2700hp
  - electric   750hp
- Top speed:
  - surfaced   16.7kts (18.6kts also possible)
  - submerged   7.6kts
- Range:
  - surfaced, at 12kts   10,000nm
  - submerged, at 4kts   80nm
- Emergency dive: 280m in 30 seconds
- Depths:
  - maximum operational   400m (1310ft)
  - crush   500m (1640ft)
- Fuel tanks' capacity: 180 t
- Armament:
  - torpedo tubes (bow/stern):   4/1
  - number of torpedoes carried: 14
  - deck gun: 1 × 88mm (250 rounds)
  - AA guns: 1 × 37mm (1195 rounds)
                            4 × 20mm (12,000 rounds)

◀ The Turm IV of *U 995*, a Type VIIC/41. Note the 'Wintergarten' with 20mm cannon abaft the bridge. (W Trojca collection)

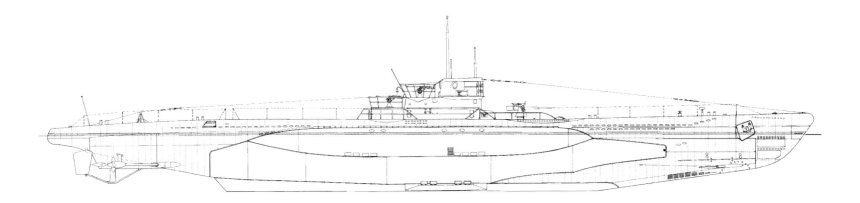

▲ *U 237*, a Type VIIC U-boat with additional gun platform aft of the tower. Drawn and traced by Mirosław Skwiot

The boat was to be powered by two four-stroke, six-cylinder MAN MGV 40/46 supercharged diesel engines of 2200hp each (max. speed 530rpm). While submerged it would be propelled by two electric motors of 375hp each, powered by a battery of sixty-two AFA 33 MAL 800 W cells with a total capacity of 9160 Ah, weighing 61,996kg (136,678lbs). Like all other 'Sevens', it would be fitted with two cast-iron propellers 1620mm (63.78in) in diameter. Unfortunately this project was never realised and all contracts were eventually cancelled.

Yet another version was designed – the Type VIIC/43. It differed from the Type VIIC/42 only in its number of torpedo tubes. In order to increase the submarine's combat effectiveness in the Battle of Atlantic (which had been becoming harder and harder for German submariners), six bow tubes (in two columns of three) and another four (two columns of two) in the stern were planned. All the changes introduced into the boats' blueprints were directly linked with the torpedo armament and thus affected only the bow and stern sections.

This project was also abandoned, since to continue the war the U-bootwaffe needed an all-new submarine designed from scratch. Therefore all the efforts of the designers and shipyards were diverted to the new Type XXI U-boat.

Type VIID

The next version of the 'Seven', the Type VIID, was introduced in 1941–2. It was to meet the requirement for a new submersible minelayer, earmarked for acting in nearby operational areas, while more distant missions of that type would be carried out by the Type X U-boats. The Type VIID was almost identical to the Type VIIC, although it was lengthened by 9.8m (32.2ft). This space was used to mount five vertical, 'wet' mine shafts. The added section was placed directly behind the conning-tower and could hold three mines in each shaft. The greater length of the hull also improved the boat's range, though significantly reducing top speed. The more spacious interior also contained two additional berths, for seamen who would help in mine operations, and also two freezers for food. Additional ballast tanks, which were to compensate the change of the boat's weight after releasing mines, were also fitted under the mine containers.

► A Type VIID in a base shelter. The raised deck aft of the conning-tower, a distinctive feature of this variant of the 'VII', is clearly visible. (CAW)

The data for this new variant were as follows: displacement 965 tons (surfaced), 1080 tons (submerged), 1285 tons (total). Dimensions of hulls: external 76.60 × 6.38m (251.31 × 20.93ft) and pressure 59.80 × 4.70m (196.19 × 15.42ft). The boat's height from keel to the top of the tower was 9.70m (31.82ft) and the draught was 5.01m (16.44ft). This type of U-boat was able to dive to 100–160m (330–520ft) in 30 seconds; the maximum operational depth was 200m (660ft). The submarine's armament still consisted of four bow and one aft torpedo tubes and twelve torpedoes could be carried. Alternatively –instead of torpedoes – she could carry, like all previous versions, thirty-nine TMB or twenty-six TMA mines (as well as the fifteen mines in the containers).

This U-boat was powered by two four-stroke, six-cylinder supercharged Germaniawerft F 46 diesel engines of 1400hp at 470–490rpm. It was possible to achieve an output of 1600hp temporarily. Electric drive consisted of two AEG GU 460/8–276 motors (375hp, 295rpm each) powered from two 62-cell AFA 33 MAL 800 E batteries (capacity 9160 Ah, weight 61,996kg [136,678lbs]). The Type VIID could reach a top speed of 16.0–16.7 knots surfaced and 7.3 knots submerged. Range of the vessel was impressive – 11,200nm at 10 knots, 13,000nm at 10 knots on combined diesel-electric drive, and 5050nm at 16 knots. The electric motors provided a submerged range of 69 nautical miles at 4 knots and 127 miles at only 2 knots. The U-boat carried 155.2–169.0 tons of diesel oil in its normal tanks and an additional 115.3 tons in special tanks.

The gun armament of the Type VIID consisted of a single 88mm deck gun (250 rounds), a single 37mm cannon (1195 rounds) and two twin 20mm cannon (4380 rounds). The U-boat was manned by a crew of four officers (commander, first and second watch officers, chief engineer) and forty petty officers and seamen.

As the war situation changed, the mine warfare requirement was dropped and the Type VIIDs were considered functional combat units only thanks to their standard torpedo armament. They also proved useful as tankers.

The whole series of six such U-boats, designated U 213–218, was built by the Krupp Germaniawerft in Kiel.

Type VIIE

At roughly the same time development of a new engine – the Deutz V-12 – began. It was meant for a new series of U-boat. This engine would be a super-light two-stroke diesel in a V configuration. Since predictions of the new motor's performance were enthusiastic, it was decided to build a new U-boat, designated Type VIIE, 'around' this new propulsion unit. The weight saved thanks to the lighter engine could be used to further strengthen the pressure hull and increase the allowed diving depths. Apart from the new propulsion gear it would not differ from the standard Type VIIC. Development of Type VIIE U-boat began promptly, but was abandoned soon after since it turned out that the new engine was extremely unreliable and its performance was below expectations. Abandoning the Type VIIE programme left a specific 'gap' in the 'Seven's alphabet' – the Type VIID was followed by the Type VIIF.

Type VIIF

More distant theatres of operations created the need to deliver additional torpedoes to U-boats far from their bases, since the lack of those forced shorter patrols. It was thus decided to build a new variant of the Type VII able to carry out such missions, since basing it on an existing model guaranteed a shorter development process and allowed quicker commissioning of the new supply boats. The new vessel would be similar to the Type VIID. The means of gaining the space required to carry additional torpedoes had also already been tested: an additional 10.5m (34.4ft) section was inserted into the Type VIIC hull. The internal space of this section was used to store an extra 25–27 torpedoes (in the aft part of the new compartment, 7.8m [25.6ft] long) and two additional berths for seamen (forward of the torpedo storage). The bottom part of this section housed additional compensation tanks and larger fuel tanks. This time – contrary to the Type VIID's enlarged hull – the hull's diameter was also increased – by 1.1m (3.6ft) as compared to the Type VIIC type – which gave the new design similar performance to the 'C' variant.

Technical and tactical data of the Type VIIF U-boat

▼ *U 218*, a Type VIID, sets out on an operation. (CAW)

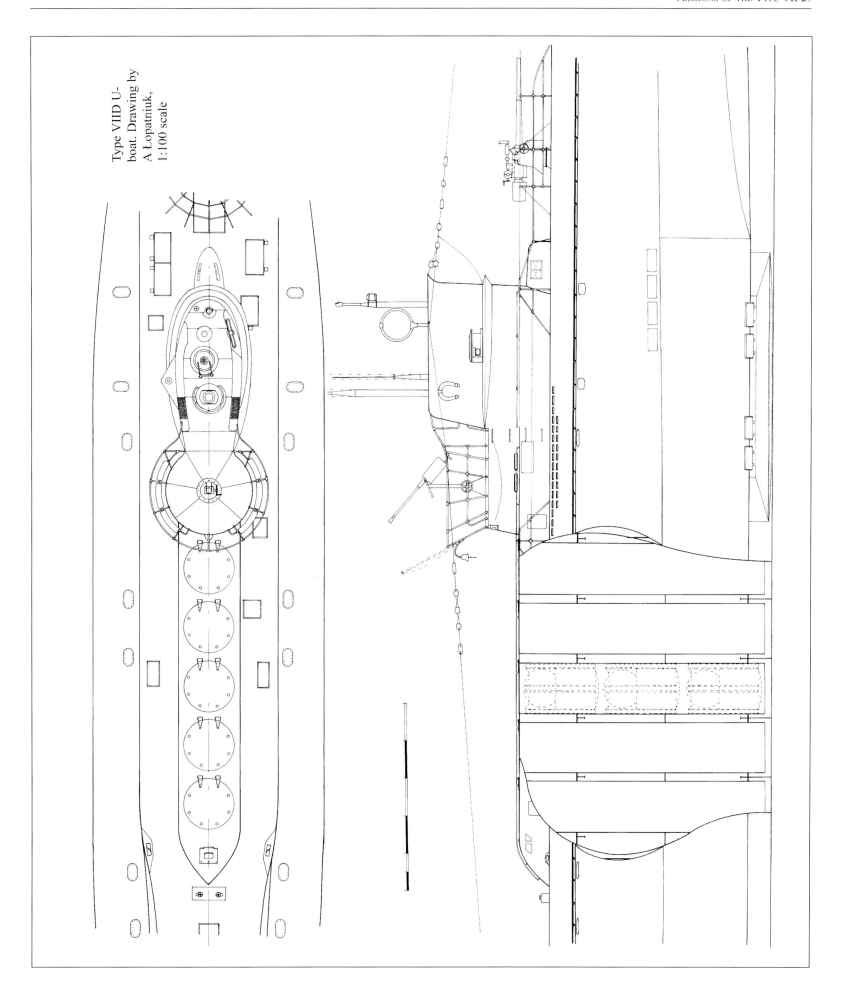

Type VIID U-
boat. Drawing by
A Lopatniuk,
1:100 scale

were as follows:
- Displacement:
  - surfaced 1084 t
  - submerged 1181 t
  - total 1345 t
- Length:
  - outer hull 77.63m (254.69ft)
  - pressure hull 60.40m (198.16ft)
- Height 7.30m (23.95ft)
- Draught 4.70m (15.5ft)
- Top speed:
  - surfaced 16.7kts (18.6kts also possible)
  - submerged 7.6kts
- Pressure hull thickness 20.5mm (0.81in)
- Diving speed 35 sec to 100m (330ft)
- Emergency dive 280m (920ft) in 30 sec
- Maximum depth 200m (660ft)
- Top speed:
  - surfaced 16.9–17.6kts
  - submerged 7.9kts
- Range:
  - surfaced, at 10kts 14,700nm
  - surfaced, at 12kts 9500nm
  - surfaced, at 16.9kts 5350nm
  - submerged, at 4kts 74nm
  - submerged, at 2kts 130nm
- Armament:
  - torpedo tubes (bow/ stern): 4/1
  - number of torpedoes for own use: 14 (including 9 spare)

▲ The crew of a Type VIID minelayer gathered on the raised deck aft of the tower. Note the perforated hatches of the 'wet' mine shafts here. (CAW)

▼ The conning-tower of *U 1060*, a Type VIIF. The 'Wintergarten', the platform for anti-aircraft armament, is clearly shown. Note the niche housing the antenna of the FuMO 30 radar on the port side. (A Szewczyk collection)

The boat's 'freight' was 24 torpedoes carried in the new section in four layers of six and five, or six torpedoes in containers on deck. The Type VIIF was powered by two six-cylinder, four-stroke supercharged Germaniawerft F 46 diesel engines, working at a maximum speed of 470–490rpm and – while submerged – two AEG GU 460/8–276 (295rpm) electric motors. Total output of the diesel engines was 2880hp (temporarily 3200hp), while the electric drive had altogether 750hp. Since all Type VII U-boats had two propellers, their largest variants – namely Types VIID and VIIF – also had two cast-iron propellers of 1600mm (5.25ft) diameter. Power for the electric motors was stored in two batteries (62-cell AFA 33 MAL 800 E, discharging time 20 hours, capacity 9160

Ah, weight 61,966kg [136,678lbs]). Fuel tank capacity was 198.8 tons of diesel oil. The U-boat had a single 88mm deck gun (250 rounds), a single 37mm cannon (1195 rounds) and two twin 20mm (4380 rounds). The crew consisted of four officers and forty-two petty officers and seamen.

All submarines of this type were launched from the Krupp Germaniawerft shipyard in Kiel, though their construction seemed unending. When *U 1059*, *U 1060*, *U 1061* and *U 1062* were eventually commissioned in mid-1943 (all but the first one equipped with a snorkel), plans to supply submarines at sea with torpedoes had been already abandoned due to the improved effectiveness of Allied defences. They were used instead as normal attack submarines, thanks to their standard armament, and also as freighters shipping torpedoes to the northern Norwegian bases and bringing scarce resources back to the homeland.

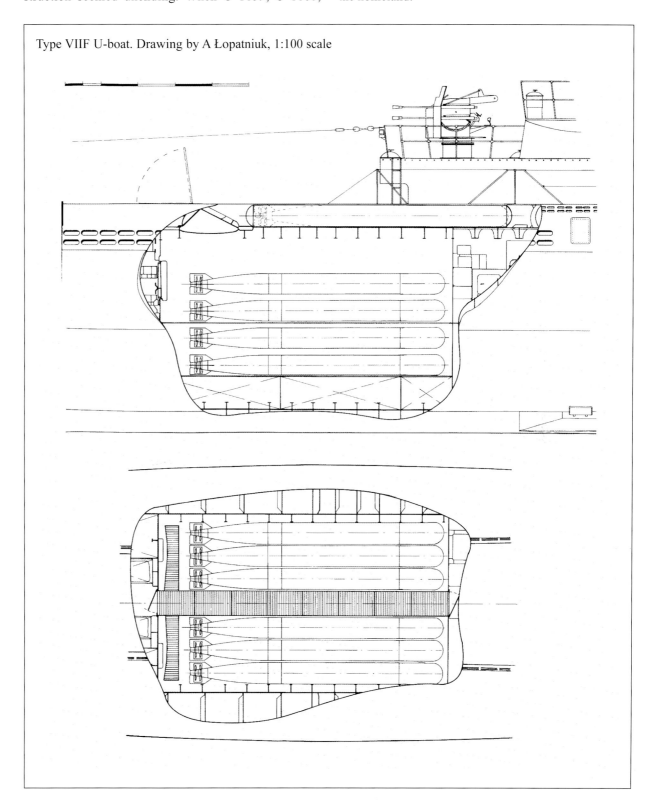

Type VIIF U-boat. Drawing by A Łopatniuk, 1:100 scale

2. Production

Manufacturers

THE TYPE VII PROVED to be a relatively cheap boat, costing the Kriegsmarine only four million Reichsmarks each, permitting full-scale mass-production of the type. The programme involved all the major German shipyards and other industrial concerns, as well as a large number of larger and smaller subcontractors. The boats themselves were built in the following shipyards: Krupp Germaniawerft and Deutsche Werke (both in Kiel), Deschimag A G Wesser in Bremen, Blohm und Voss in Hamburg, Vulkan in Bremen-Vegesack, Schichau-Werft in Danzig (now Gdańsk in Poland), Flender-Werft in Lübeck, Nordsee-Werke in Emden, Flensburger Schiffbau Gesellschaft in Flensburg, KM-Werft in Wilhelmshaven,

Danziger Werft, also in Danzig, Neptun Werft in Rostock, Stülcken Sohn and Howaldtswerke in Hamburg, Howaldtswerke in Kiel and Oder Werke and Vulkan in Stettin (now Szczecin in Poland). Most of them, particularly those which were the first to start production, had had previous experience of building submarines. The subcontractors, which manufactured most of the boats' equipment (both primary and secondary) were:

• diesel engines:
- Maschinenfabrik Augsburg-Nürnberg, the famous MAN
- MAN – Blohm und Voss
- MAN – Weser
- MAN – BBC
- MAN – Vulkan

▼ A plan of the Germania shipyard in Kiel, one of the main builders of U-boats. (W Danielewicz collection)

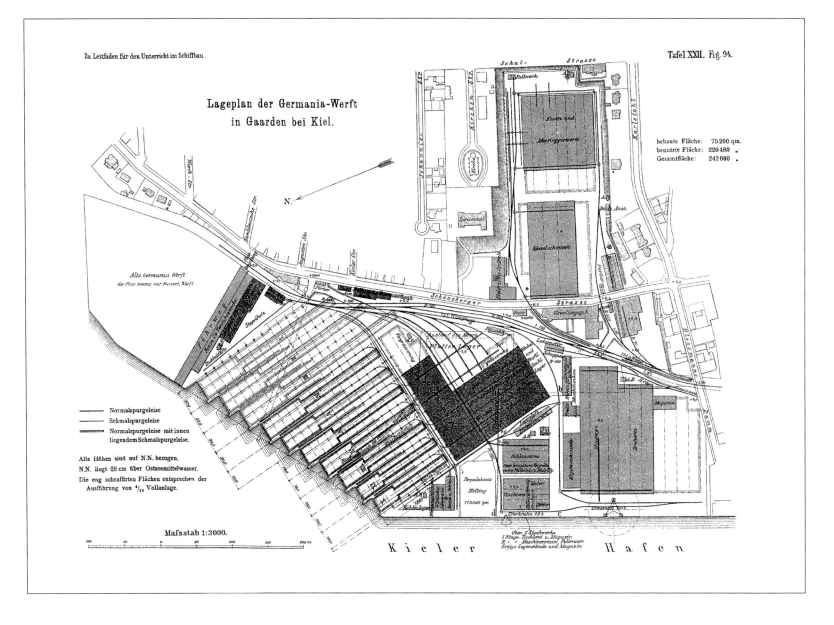

▶ An aerial photo of another large U-boat manufacturer, the Blohm und Voss shipyard, taken during the War. (IWM)

▼ The frames of a pressure hull spaced out on the slipway. Welding is underway on the brackets which held the frames in place. (CAW)

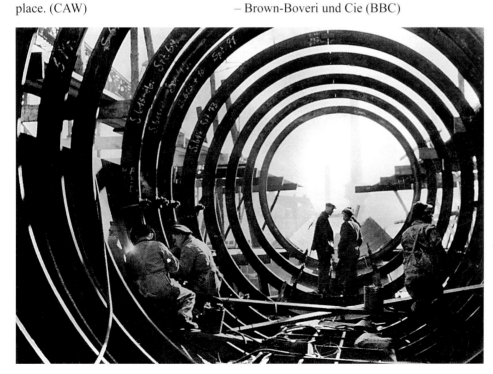

– Krupp Germania
– Geber. Karting
– Daimler Benz
– Linked-Hoffman-Junkers
• electric motors:
    – Elektricitäts-Gesellschaft (AEG)
    – Deutsche Elektromotoren Werke
    – Lahmeyer und Co.
    – Brown-Boveri und Cie (BBC)

– Schiffsunion
– Siemens-Schuckert-Werke (SSW)
– Pichler und Co.
– Maffei-Schwartzkopf
• radio equipment: Lorenz
• hydroacoustic equipment: Askania
• batteries:
    – Watt Akkumulatoren-Werke
    – Akkumulatorenfabrik AG (Afag)
    – AG für Akkumulatoren (AFA)
• magnetic compasses and gyrocompasses:
    – the famous Anschütz
    – C P Goerz
    – and the greatest of the great – G Zeiss
• hulls:
    – W Fitzner
    – Lanrahütte O/S (geschweißte Innenkörper für Uboote)

There was also an even greater number of smaller companies manufacturing cables, pipes, panelling, chains, anchors, furniture, and also suppliers who delivered for instance tableware, mattresses and all the other equipment necessary for the successful operation of the boat.

Construction

The 'Sevens' were mass-produced, a process usually associated with completely identical products leaving a production line. But the Type VII U-boats, undoubtedly a record-holder for the sheer number of examples built, were not identical in the way that modern cars leaving a production line are. Shipbuilding has its own rules. Differences between individual submarines, often unnoticeable by an unskilled observer, were obvious to an expert. Series-built submarines were by no means clones of each other. This was because, although they were all based on one set of blueprints, they were constructed in different shipyards, each of varying capabilities and experience, which immediately adapted those plans to their capabilities. That is why Dönitz established the 'Baubelehrung' programme, in which an entire crew was assigned to a U-boat at the start of its construction in order to become fully acquainted with their boat as it was built. Every officer, petty officer and seaman therefore participated in the construction of the vessel and saw every system being installed. This was an excellent way for the men to 'learn' their boat, preparing them to operate the submarine and handle it in emergency situations, but it also increased the differences between individual boats. The introduction of new equipment in the course of the War, which due to the problems suffered by German industry often arrived irregularly and in small numbers, further increased the differences between the U-boats. The introduction of new devices and equipment as a result of changes and progress in warfare and navigation theories also did not help.

Further modifications were made when the boats were overhauled. Damage due to enemy action or just from the conditions encountered on patrol meant that they were frequently docked for repairs, when the opportunity was taken to make further modifications. Therefore the introduction of new equipment and changing tactics produced differences in the appearance of these supposedly mass-produced vessels. For example, some Type VIIs had distinctive crescent-shaped wave deflectors added to the front of the bridge, while others had a similar breakwater forward of the 88mm gun, and many had their 'Wintergarten' enlarged to accommodate more 20mm guns and their ammunition. These modifications automatically changed the whole appearance of the boat, since they also caused changes to the entire conning-tower, thickening its walls or mounting additional supports or railings. There were also other minor alterations, for example mounting steps for the lookouts at the sides of the bridge, and adding various handgrips, containers and weapons mounts. The new equipment previously mentioned, such as improved radios, radar, snorkels and a range of other retractable antennae and masts, required channels to be fitted in the walls of the tower, thickening them and thus creating another difference between individual 'Sevens'. At one time, distinctive 'hammers' appeared on the foredecks of some U-boats – these were the vibrators of hydrophones which also changed the hull's streamlined silhouette. Of course, these changes are just those which altered the appearance of boats of the same variant of the Type VII: the different variants, i.e. Type VIIA, B, C, etc, were built to

▶ Finished hull sections wait to be transported to the slipway.

◀ Prefabrication of a Type VII hull section. Full-scale production has not been geared up at this point in time, as can be judged by the lack of mechanisation. (CAW)

▼ Prefabrication of hull plates. The change in the process as compared to the previous photograph can be clearly seen – now it is real mass-production. (CAW)

different plans and were already distinguished from one another by their different dimensions, and the different arrangement of drainage slots and air intakes.

From when they first entered service, the 'Sevens' were popular with their crews for their excellent manoeuvrability, seaworthiness and durability. The strength of their construction was particularly valued, as it permitted deep dives significantly exceeding their theoretical limits. So, how was a Type VII actually built? Although they were mass-produced, nevertheless every boat was built individually, just as with larger warships. In the shipyard's workshops every component of the boat's structure, her hull, tanks or section, was numbered or designated according to the particular shipbuilder's specification for that vessel alone. Then all the elements were assembled on

▼ This photograph shows the pressure hull being covered with its shell plating. Note that hulls are not yet assembled from prefabricated sections – U-boats were built this way before the War and shortly after its outbreak. (CAW)

▲ The bow section of a Type VII's pressure hull with four distinctive holes for the torpedo tubes. (CAW)

the slipway. This method had basically remained unchanged since the First World War, the only significant difference being the large-scale use of electric welding. Riveting was still used, but only in a few parts of the hull, and then more because of the shortage of skilled welders than for any technical reason. Electric welding required good conditions, protected from rain and humidity, so the sections of the pressure hull, the most important part of the submarine, were built in sections in roofed-over halls and then the sections were joined together on the slipway outside.

Each section comprised four to six steel plates welded along their shorter sides, bent to fit round the frames. Construction of a whole section began with laying two metal plates on the semi-circular keel blocks and welding them together from the inside, by welders standing inside what was to be the hull, creating something like a gigantic former. After joining those plates the frames were carefully put onto them in predetermined spots and welded in. Then a third plate was mounted at the right place with bolts and the whole section was turned over in such a way that the 'fresh' plate's connection with the previous plate was at the

◄ Fitting-out work on a 'Seven's' hull. Note the already-completed side ballast tanks. (CAW)

bottom, and it was welded just like the previous two – from the inside. This operation was repeated until the section became an enclosed steel cylinder. The last plate was cut in place to fit the gap left between the previously-welded parts. After a while that last plate was no longer necessary since, in the course of numerous assemblies, templates for every section had been created. They were simply put in the right place and welded together without any further metalwork being necessary. External seams and their edges were also welded from the inside.

The placement of the watertight bulkheads determined how every section was finished. If the bulkhead was placed inside the cylinder, it was mounted along with its respective frame as the section was assembled. If the bulkhead was at the end of the cylinder it was welded in just before the final hull plate closed the section. Finally, if there were bulkheads at both ends, the shipyard workers fitted all the equipment inside that section before it was finally closed. Thus all the tanks, boards, bulkheads and decks were installed and then temporarily secured with screws and bolts until the boat was completed on the slipway.

Thanks to the large-scale use of electric welding it was not necessary to for the keel to be used to stiffen the whole construction and it could be replaced with a lighter ballast keel. This was made up of box-like sections reinforced with internal transverse braces, which were laid parallel to the completed hull sections. They were then laid on keel blocks on the slipway and then – without any concern about the forces inside them which would be of key importance in the case of a traditional stiffening bilge – sections of the

◄ Another Type VII hull during fitting-out. (CAW)

► Assembly work on a Type VII's hull. The frames of the ballast tanks, which have not yet been covered with plating, can be seen on both sides of the hull. The base of the mount for the deck gun is visible in the background. (CAW)

► ► Electric welding of an early Type VII's hull. The frames of the ballast tanks are clearly visible. In the background the cylindrical conning-tower can be seen; it would later be enclosed in the streamlined outer casing, which reduced drag. (CAW)

► The outer hull casing being fabricated. (CAW)

pressure hull were precisely set on top of them. This stage of construction began with the hull section containing the control room, in the middle of the U-boat. Then the next two sections were added: one forward of the control room, the other aft of it. Further sections were also laid in this manner – one forward and one aft of those already assembled. When this stage was completed the conning tower was mounted above the control room, thus finishing the pressure hull, though without installing the trim compensation tanks, which would be fitted externally. When all the above had been done an air-tightness test was performed, by increasing the pressure inside the hull up to three atmospheres. Only after this did work begin on the installation of equipment and the construction of the outer hull.

Just as with the pressure hull, this was done by working from amidships towards the bow and stern. First of all the heavy high-pressure ballast and compensation tanks, along with their internal bulkheads, were fitted to the pressure hull. Then the frames and stringers which would support the shell of outer hull were welded to the pressure hull. The entire construction was closed by the bow and stern sections, which were in fact completed elements, already plated. Assembly was finished by mounting the external hull shell, welded plate by plate to the frames and stringers.

The upper deck, composed of wooden planks 8cm (3.1in) wide, was laid by hand with every plank being fixed 2cm (0.78in) apart in small sections; the whole process was closely coordinated with the installation of the engines, electrical wiring etc, since all the pipes, ventilation ducts and exhaust manifolds had to be placed in the empty space between the pressure hull and the deck and thus had to be installed before the latter could be completed. The hatches fitted into the deck were finished earlier in the assembly hall and mounted in their proper places with great accuracy, so that they exactly fitted the holes left for them. That stage of the work was carried out by designated shipyard workers when the boat was already launched, on the water and moored to the fitting-out pier. The outer shell of the U-boat's tower, which had been previously completed in the hall, was mounted on the deck covering the prepared apertures and the conning tower like a hood.

The boat was then fitted-out. All the internal components were built by the subcontractors in such a way that they could fit through the boat's narrow hatches or through special holes left in the hull during construction for that purpose. The largest of these was for the diesel engines, electric motors, main switchboard and other equally bulky equipment. One can imagine the congestion around this largest hatch and how well all the work at this stage had to be coordinated. Since all those parts had to be brought into the hull through this one 'hatchway' of sufficient size, it was then necessary to move them inside the boat to their own compartments. For example, when the electric motors had been got into the hull through the aperture in the side of the diesel engine room, they had to be moved into their own adjacent compartment. The bulkhead between the two was therefore cut and bent back like a door, parallel to the boat's axis, and then re-welded into place once the motors and their

▲ Mass production of Type VIIC U-boat hulls. (A Szewczyk collection)

associated equipment had been installed in their proper compartment. Then it was time to install the propeller shafts, thrust bearings, clutches and – obviously – the diesels themselves along with their transmissions. The other compartments were also being equipped simultaneously. Therefore it is hard to overestimate the significance of careful and precise planning and accurate scheduling, in this phase of a boat's construction. Furthermore, the yard would have been working on several boats simultaneously. The design offices provided accurate blueprints, although these did lack some exact dimensions which the shipyard's engineers and technicians had to complete; this reduced the designers' workload, though it added to that of the ship-builders. The last major phase of construction was mounting the bow and stern torpedo tubes and the batteries. The tubes were pulled inside the boat through the outer doors and fixed in the places prepared for them

Once the batteries were installed the construction of the U-boat was essentially complete. Once the boat was launched and finally fitted-out, it was commissioned and entered service. Where possible the completed U-boats underwent pressure trials inside a special pressurised dock built at the Flenderwerke shipyard in 1937–8. It consisted of a cylinder 12m (39.3ft) in diameter, which was placed in the floating dock. The U-boat was brought into the partially flooded cylinder, which was then raised along with all the dock. The boat was braced and then the dock submerged, while the cylinder containing U-boat was flooded under pressure for two hours. Hull integrity was checked by rep-resentatives of the shipyard in the presence of the boat's

► The finished conning-tower of *U 393*, a Type VIIC U-boat, fitted with a 'Wintergarten', is being transported to the slipway of the Kriegsmarinewerft in Kiel where it will be mounted on the assembled hull. (CAW)

future skipper, his chief engineer and members of the Acceptance Committee, who observed the operation and looked for any flaws or shortcomings from inside the boat.

Due to many skilled workers being drafted into the armed forces, the shipyards were forced to pass some work on to the steelworks and other factories working with them. Both the assembly of pressure-hull sections and the manufacture of plating for the outer hull was put out to these subcontractors. The completed elements were then transported to the shipyard by barge on rivers and canals, the sections having been redesigned to facilitate easy transportation and reassembly on arrival on the slips. In 1942/43 as many as twenty-four other manufacturers were producing components for the sixteen shipyards involved in the production of Type VII U-boats. This system produced a significant reduction in building times. The construction of the first eight Type VIIs in the Flensburg shipyard, when it was still burdened with a number of subsidiary operations, took 400,000 man-hours per boat. By the twenty-second boat this had dropped to 240,000 man-hours. Larger shipyards, such as Blohm und Voss, were able to do it in only 180,000 man-hours. This was due both to the sub-contracting of the manufacture of whole sections of the boats and to the fact that the workforce became more skilled as their experience of serial production of Type VIIs grew as they were required to produce one U-boat per week.

Below is an example of the cost calculation for building a single Type VII U-boat launched in late 1943 in the Blohm und Voss shipyard.

- 180,000 man-hours: 180,000 Reichsmarks
- 160 per cent government grant: 288,000 Reichsmarks
- Materials and sections already assembled: 1,420,000 Reichsmarks
- 5 per cent shipyard's revenue: 95,000 Reichsmarks
- Overall cost: 1,983,000 Reichsmarks

Obviously, this involves a huge shipbuilder, which could manage to cut down both production time and cost so effectively.

The following table shows the recorded achievements of the same shipyard on 1 April 1943.

Type	Building time (man-hours)	Engine building time (man-hours)	Overall time building time (man-hours)
VIIC	147,000	107,000	254,000
VIIC/41	150,000	105,000	255,000
VIIC/42	175,000	115,000	290,000
VIID	271,000	130,000	401,000
VIIF	235,000	125,000	360,000

Summary

Some problems were discovered with the Type VIIs in the early years of their service. Firstly, the beds of the diesel engines were found to be too weak, which limited their ability to operate for long periods at sea and was also a drawback in combat where the boat might have to endure sustained depth-charge attacks. The beds had to be replaced, meaning that the boats had to be withdrawn from operations for prolonged periods in dockyard hands. Secondly, the valves that sealed the diesel exhaust when the boat dived were found to be faulty, causing potentially disastrous leaks during deep dives. It was suspected that a number of U-boats lost in the early stages of the War had sunk for this reason, including even the famous *U 47*, commanded by the ace Korvkpt. Günther Prien, though of course he and his crew took the truth of their fate to their graves.

Despite these problems, the Type VII was in all an outstanding design, meeting and in many cases exceeding the requirements of the U-boat command, thanks to careful planning, well-specified requirement, the basing of the design on a tried and tested predecessor from the previous war, and not least the skills of its designers Schürer and Bröking. Being able to build a prototype for Finland and conduct extensive sea trials with naval officers aboard was also very helpful, allowing problems to be identified and improvements made before series production began. It was also relatively cheap at four million Reichsmarks, allowing for mass production, although this was not without other problems.

In conclusion it can be said that the Type VII was a specific compromise between tactical requirements, financial constraints and the terms of the 1935 London Naval Treaty. However, the rate of production of these boats – at least initially – was too slow, and by the time it reached an acceptable level the time of the Type VII had definitely passed, and the future belonged to the new generation of Type XXI and Type XXII U-boats. They may have been obsolete towards the end of the War, but they were still dangerous, and the losses they had inflicted during the Battle of the Atlantic were truly terrifying.

◀ The full-scale mass-production of Type VIIC U-boats. The boat in the centre of the photograph is ready to be launched – the scaffolding has already been dismantled. (CAW)

► Mass-production
of U-boat in one of
the German
shipyards during the
later years of the
war. (CAW)

So it was a boat with good performance, relatively cheap and durable; a boat superior in terms of both speed and range to its most modern British counterparts, though with lesser firepower in one torpedo salvo. A Type VII could fire five torpedoes to the 'T' class' ten (six from bow tubes, two from deck tubes and two from waist tubes). The German boat was also smaller than, for instance, American and Japanese subs. The Kriegsmarine crews inhabited more cramped and less luxurious accommodation than their Yankee colleagues, though this did not bother them as the living conditions of U-boat men were entirely up to German fleet standards. The Type VII was, however, undoubtedly superior to all other submarines of its time in terms of diving speed, manoeuvrability and resistance to depth charges. Their solid construction allowed them to dive much deeper than their 'competitors' could. Superbly commanded, reliable and effective, manned by elite crews, they became a highly dangerous instrument of war, something that – in Churchill's own words – terrified him the most.

The 'Sevens' were excellent war machines, designed as a perfect weapon. German U-boats also had – as is agreed among the subject's researchers – the worlds' finest optical equipment. The Zeiss-made 7 × 50 binoculars used by the U-bootwaffe were the best in the world. They were watertight, durable instruments of high lens clarity, and provided the lookouts with excellent observation. The very light German attack periscopes were also outstanding when compared to those used by other navies. The prisms and lenses used in their construction, also manufactured by Zeiss, were of exceptional clarity, were not prone to flattening, and stayed tuned allowing for very accurate observation and aiming. Zeiss periscopes had a single eyepiece and a folding saddle used during the attack by the skipper, who could freely rotate and elevate the scope in all planes using control pedals and levers. The other achievement of German optics was the Überwesserzieloptik (UZO) – a combined optical sight, binoculars and rangefinder combined in one device, set on a special mounting on the bridge. The data acquired by the UZO were automatically passed to the Vorhaltrechner torpedo fire-control computer. The UZO was undoubtedly the finest such instrument used aboard any country's submarines during the War.

◄ A U-boat launching ceremony. The speech is under way. (CAW)

◄ Assembly completed. The U-boat slips into the water in the Germaniawerft in Kiel, 8 August 1940. The boat is *U 93*, one of the early Type VIICs. (CAW)

3. Technical Description

ASUBMARINE IS A VERY special vessel. It has to be designed to easily withstand high pressures in its operational environment, and also to dive quickly when its ballast tanks are flooded. For these reasons it has a very special hull shape and equally unusual stability properties. However, the design must also permit it to operate on the surface, so the shape and profile of the hull, as well as its stability, has to meet that that requirement as well.

The Forward Compartment

The Type VII U-boat was a very typical submarine design and like all others was similar to a steel pipe – the pressure hull – with another pipe (or a partial one) built around it (the outer casing). The front of the pressure hull was closed with a convex bulkhead. Four torpedo tubes passed through it. In other words the whole boat began with the torpedo tubes – its main weapon. The tubes themselves, together with their complicated controls and equipment, made up the forward bulkhead of the forward compartment. This also accommodated twelve bunks for seamen along both sides, in three rows and on two levels. This section was inhabited by the 'Lords', as the deck department seamen were nicknamed in the Kriegsmarine. Each seaman put his own bedclothes on the leatherette-covered bunks, because three men were assigned to each pair of bunks. Except during alerts, when every man was at his battle station, only one-third of the 'bow' crew – such as torpedomen, sonar operators or radio operators – at a time was on watch, the others being more or less forced to lie on their bunks owing to the lack of space aboard. Not all off-duty time could be spent lying down, however. At mealtimes, for instance, the foldaway tables had to be lowered from the deckhead above and opened out, and the upper bunks folded away so the men could sit on the lower ones to eat. Another interruption was when the four reload torpedoes stored under the deck of the forward compartment, and another two actually kept under the lower tier of bunks, needed their periodic maintenance.

Officers' Accommodation, Hydrophone and Radio Compartments

The next compartment was for the petty officers – the backbone of the Kriegsmarine – the boatswain, the chief helmsman and two machinists. Each had his own bunk, on

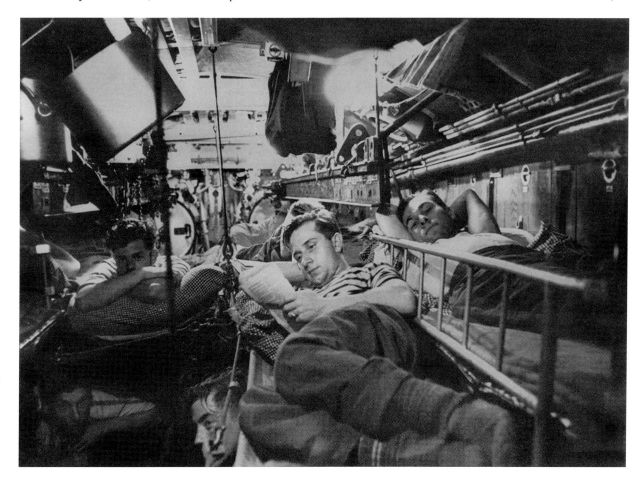

► The forward compartment of a Type VII U-boat. Note the cramped conditions. The hatches of the forward torpedo tubes can be seen in the background. (CAW)

◄ Off-duty, the crew of a 'Seven' spent most of their time resting on their bunks. (CAW)

two levels on both sides of the hull. The compartment was also a little more comfortable than the crew quarters forward. The compartment was lined with imitation-wood panelling and the bunks had folding sides to keep the occupant from falling out if the boat rolled, as well as curtains and reading lights, although they still had to eat on folding tables set up in the central passageway, which ran the length of the boat. The forward section of this compartment housed the forward toilet.

A rectangular hatch in the after bulkhead of this compartment lead to the officers' mess, which had the same panelling and the more comfortable bunks with curtains and reading lights. The single bunk on the port side was the First Officer and the two – one above the other – on the port side were for the Chief Engineer and Second Officer. Officers had lockers tall enough for uniforms to be hung up normally, while the other ranks only had small lockers above and below their bunks.

The next compartment aft consisted of three 'rooms' and the main battery switching room, in the after corner on the port side, which partially enclosed the captain's 'cabin', which was in fact little more than a niche with a comfortable bunk, a table with a lamp above it, three lockers and a mirror. The panelled 'cabin' could be screened off from the main passageway with a curtain. Opposite the CO's 'nest', on the starboard side, were two small cabins with doors. The forward one was the hydrophone room and the after one was the radio room. The after wall of this compartment formed a pressure

bulkhead between the whole bow section of the boat and the control room.

Hydrophones and sonar

The sonar systems used by German submarines, including the Type VIIs, were divided into three groups. The first were passive devices, commonly known as hydrophones,

▼ And this was how meals were eaten aboard. (CAW)

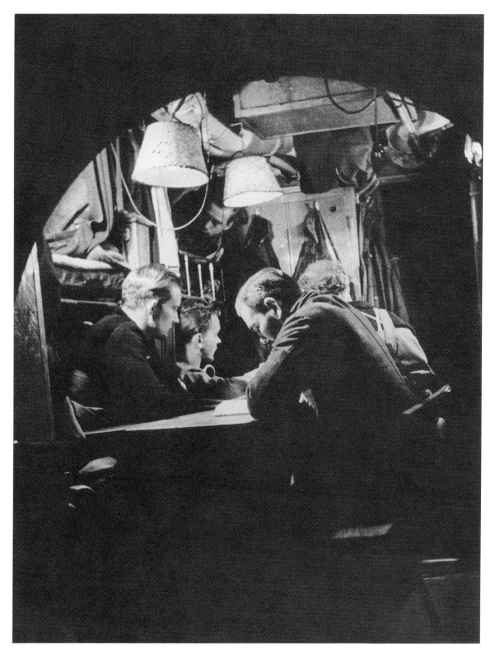

▲ The officers' mess was a little less cramped and they could eat in slightly more tolerable conditions. (CAW)

which allowed the bearing to be determined by identifying the sensor which had picked up the signal. In order to increase accuracy the designers constantly experimented with increased numbers of microphones and eventually came up with the GHG Balkon system with forty-eight sensors installed in two rows. The GHG was able to detect a single ship at 20km (11nm), and a convoy at approximately 100km (55nm) – not a bad performance for the time. The microphones of the system were made of very high quality Seignette-Salz-Kristall crystals, which actually came as a surprise to the Allies – the Americans kept using these until the 1950s. The performance figures given above of course apply to good hydroacoustic conditions and could significantly deteriorate in stormy seas or varying water densities. In order to get a more accurate bearing on a target, another instrument, called KDB (Kristallbasisgerät), was used. This anvil-shaped sensor was installed in the bows of a boat, on the deck. It was 500mm (19.68in) long, could rotate freely all, and incorporated six microphones. It provided a bearing-to-target with an accuracy of ± 1°. Two Type VII boats – *U 1008* and *U 393* – were also equipped with SP-Gerät sonar outfits as part of the 'Ursel' project, which were very accurate. Another development was the NGH-L system used for detecting torpedoes.

The second group were the active sonars. The first of these installed aboard U-boats was the Mob-S-Anlage type manufactured by GEMA. Originally these were dual band (SZ-Anlage) and had a power of 5kW. The pulse frequency was 15kHz, wavelength 20m and the range 10,000m (5.4nm). The Type VIIC/42s were equipped with SU-Gerät Nibelung sonars, able to provide bearing and distance to the target after emitting only a few pulses, which made them hard for the enemy to detect. The bearing of the reflected signal provided the bearing to the target, while the time the echo took to return provided the range. However, active sonar could betray the U-boat's presence as its pulses could be picked up and tracked back to their source.

Sonar countermeasures were also developed for U-boats, such as canisters containing calcium hydroxide, which produced clouds of bubbles when opened to the sea, interfering with enemy sonar. A special anechoic rubber coating for U-boat hulls, codenamed 'Alberich', was also experimented with.

which were similar to those used in all other navies at that time. They emitted no signals, only picking up external sounds, for example from the propellers of other vessels. From the very beginning the Type VIIs carried GHG (Gruppenhorchgerät) hydrophones, used to detect targets and provide an approximate bearing and estimation of range. Of course, range estimation was largely guesswork, based on the skill and experience of the operator in judging the distance to the target from the volume of sound picked up. To help with this, the Kriegsmarine built up a library of recorded underwater sounds, recorded at different ranges and bearings, which included natural noises, providing a basic 'textbook' for hydrophone operators. Target bearing could be determined with reasonable accuracy, although not sufficiently to provide a torpedo firing solution. The GHG consisted of electronic amplifiers and twenty-two microphones installed in the bows (eleven on either side of the hull). Each of them had its axis at a precise angled,

Communications equipment

The wireless compartment was equipped with a 150W long-wave 2113 S transmitter operating at a frequency of 300–600 kHz with a 200 W, short-wave S 406 52/563 transmitter operating at 750–15,000 kHz, both manufactured by Telefunken. They were coupled to an EBG control panel, allowing both to be used. Installed receivers were Telefunken T9K39 or Köln T8K44 Großschift, or a shortwave receiver E 437 S operating on the 1500–25,000 kHz band from Telefunken or long-wave T3 PLLa 38 operating on15–33 kHz and 75–100 kHz. Communications were encrypted with a five-rotor Enigma machine. Towards the end of the war also UHF Lo 10 UK Lorenz wireless sets were installed for direct communications.

The Control Room

Aft of the concave bulkhead was the control room. This filled the entire central watertight compartment and contained all the equipment necessary to sail and fight the boat. The helmsman's station was the foremost position on the starboard side, with the rudder control equipment: two electric buttons and an emergency wheel, the rudder position indicator, the gyrocompass repeater and engine room telegraphs. Carbon dioxide absorbers were mounted beside it, while compressed air bottles were hidden under the deck. The helmsman sat on a small L-shaped bench without a backrest, at the end of the L's shorter arm. On the longer arm sat two planesmen – one for the bow and one for the stern hydroplanes. Like the rudder, these were controlled with electric buttons and also had emergency wheels. In front of the planesmen, at their eye level, was a large depth gauge – the famous Papenberg, for rough measurements, tube depth indicators for periscope-depth cruising, and a boat trim indicator. According to the readings from these instruments, the planesmen kept the boat at the depth ordered by the officer of the watch, who could correct both heading and trim. The officer of the watch stood right behind the planesmen, by the search periscope in its well in the centre of the control room. He had a special harness to keep him in place if the boat rolled suddenly. Above the round hatches at either end of the compartment, and also near the periscope, there were pairs of blue handwheels controlling the vent flaps on all six ballast tanks. Opening these let the air in the tanks out, which let water in and dived the boat. Further aft on the starboard side was the control panel for the compressed-air valves, with red levers for high pressure, black for medium pressure and light blue for low pressure commonly nicknamed the 'Christmas tree'. This panel controlled the filling of the compressed air reservoirs and blew the ballast tanks to surface the boat. At the after end of the control room was one of the two main air compressors, surrounded by an array of valves (for fresh water tanks, bilges, trim tanks, fuel tanks, compensation tanks, ballast tanks, day tanks, sea inlet valves etc.). In the middle of the compartment, behind the watch officer and his periscope, there was the trunk of the attack periscope, which could only be operated from the commander's station, located above the control room in the conning tower. Forward of the periscope there was a control panel for the ballast tanks. On the starboard side, near the compressor, there was the torpedo control panel, with the switches for selecting the tubes to be fired. On the port side there was the machinery for raising and lowering the periscopes, the navigation table, under which there were selectors for control location and engine room telegraphs, another table with a map container and sextant boxes, with an echo depth finder and log gauges mounted above it. In the left-hand corner of the control room was the other main air compressor. Aft of the trunk of the search periscope there was the main gyrocompass made by Anschütz – a popular device, world-renowned for its accuracy and easy error compensation. It was linked to eight repeaters installed at vital points in the submarine, i.e. the helmsman's station, the periscope station, the sonar room, the bow torpedo room, the UZO (U-boot-zieloptik, surface targeting device) station, the navigation plotting table, and the radio direction-finder. U-boats were commonly equipped with echo depth finders and logs supplied by Atlas-Krupp. The navigation equipment was supplemented by a magnetic compass installed in a distinctive 'hump' at the base of the conning tower, just forward of it.

The entire control room was a maze of pipes and cables, totally confusing to the untrained eye, and the lack

◀ Planesmen at their stations. (CAW)

▲ The commanding officer surveys a target through the attack periscope. The men standing behind the scope are ready to read off the target's bearings when the captain gives the order. (CAW)

binoculars attached to it. In a surfaced torpedo attack, it provided the exact bearing and range to the target which was automatically passed to the fire-control computer which produced the firing solution, i.e. the torpedo gyro angle. During a submerged attack, this information was provided by the periscopes.

A Type VII had two periscopes, the larger search periscope operated from the control room and the smaller attack periscope, used by the commanding officer at his attack station in the conning tower. During an attack the commander received target information from the sonar, the fire-control computer and his periscope. The ASR (Angriffssehor) attack periscope was quite slender and therefore difficult for the enemy to spot. Hydraulically elevated, its diameter at the base was 180mm (7.09in). Its optical length was 7500mm (295.18in), focal length 2000mm (78.74in) and free-standing length 5300mm (208.66in). The head was 31mm (1.22in) in diameter and the external diameter of the lenses was 4mm (0.16in). The angle of observation was from −15° to +20°. It had two zoom modes, 1.5 × and 6 ×, switched with the handle. Target range and bearing could be read from the periscope (which was coupled to the gyrocompass) and distance to the target, and it could also control gunnery thanks to the mils scale on the reticule. The colours of the digits, markings, aiming cross and scale could be changed. The mirrors and lenses were heated, which prevented them steaming-up, and the eyepiece was designed to allow a camera to be fitted to it.

of space might induce claustrophobia, but despite this all the systems were perfectly clear to the crew – as indeed they had to be.

The UZO and the periscopes

The UZO and the attack periscope had no equals anywhere in the world. The precision and lens speed of the equipment produced by Zeiss was unmatched.

The UZO was mounted on the bridge and had

▼ The bridge of a Type VII, photographed from the AA gun platform. The housing of the attack periscope is in the foreground and in the background, behind the seaman's head, is the mounting for the UZO (the binoculars have been unshipped). (CAW)

▼ Similar view of the bridge from a different angle. On the right is the housing for the radio direction-finder (RDF) antenna. (CAW)

◀ The bridge of a Type VIIC/41, looking forward. On the left is the radar antenna and the UZO with binoculars mounted. The raised attack periscope is in the foreground. (Drawing by Waldemar Góralski)

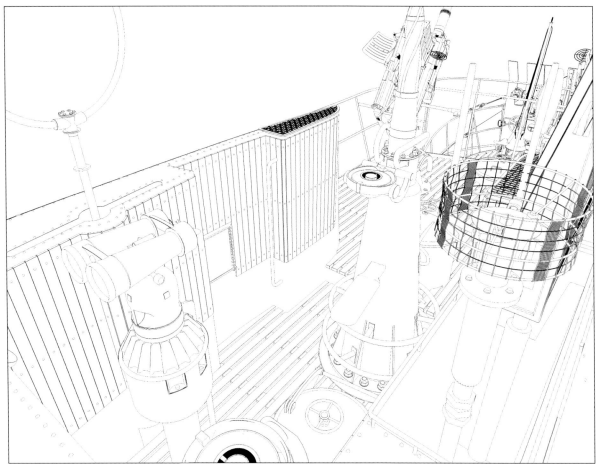

◀ Looking aft. On the left is the RDF antenna, and on the right is the FuMB 29 Bali I aerial. (Drawing by Waldemar Góralski)

► The UZO with binoculars mounted. To the left is the raised FuMB 28 Naxos radar antenna. (Drawing by Waldemar Góralski)

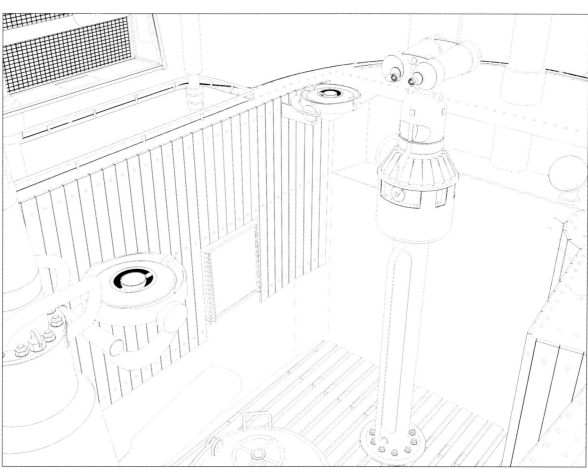

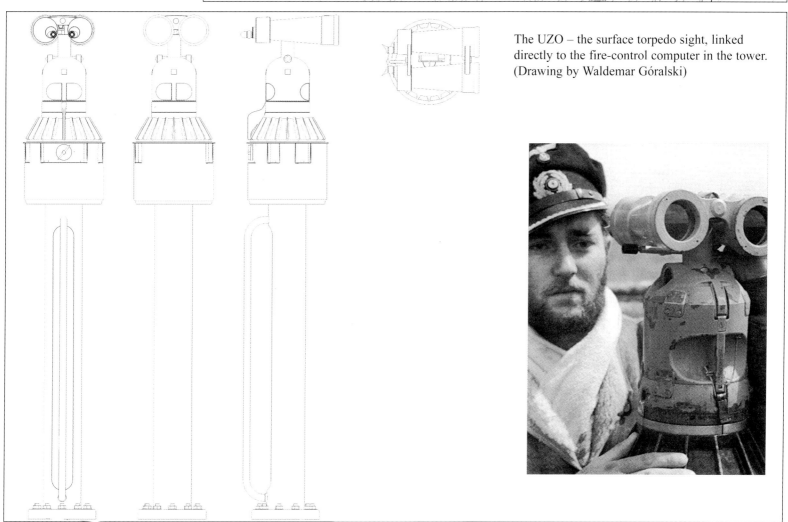

The UZO – the surface torpedo sight, linked directly to the fire-control computer in the tower. (Drawing by Waldemar Góralski)

▲ The bridge of a Type VIIC, most likely *U 340*. In the centre is the FuMB Ant 2 ('Biscaya-Kreuz') antenna, for the FuMB–1 Metox radar detector, and on the right is the circular RDF antenna. (CAW)

▼ Close-up of the 'Biscaya-Kreuz'. (CAW)

▲ *U 333* (Type VIIC) entering La Pallice harbour. The cylinders in the FuMO antenna housing contain hydrogen for the FuMT Aphrodite radar decoy balloons the boat was carrying out tests with. The commanding officer, Kptlt. Peter-Erich Cremer, nicknamed 'Ali', is in the white cap. On the right are the two twin 20mm guns that less than two months later, on 12 June 1944, would be used to shoot down a Short Sunderland flying boat of 228 Squadron RAF. (CAW)

Radar

In 1857 Rudolf Hertz succeeded in generating electro-magnetic waves from sparks, which in 1898 allowed Marconi to transmit the first wireless message to a distance of 14.5km (9 miles) – radio communications had been invented. But the concept of radar was of equal age. Hertz had already pointed out that radio waves were reflected by objects they encountered. This phenomenon was the subject of extensive research in military and governmental laboratories. Further inventions, such as the directional YAGI antenna and the electron tube, appeared, and when Dr Rudolf Kühnold combined these two devices to obtain an echo on the screen of an oscilloscope, the era of radar had begun.

In 1938 the Germans already had an effective radar system, codenamed Freya, which could detect a Junkers Ju 52 aircraft at 92km (50nm). In July 1939 the German anti-aircraft artillery received Telefunken's Würzburg A radar, a very advanced device with a power of 8 kW operating at a wavelength of 50cm. An additional rotating dipole increased its bearing accuracy to half a degree, and it gave a range accurate to within 100m (110yds). Later however, the British (in cooperation with the Americans) took the lead in this technological race and introduced radars superior to those of the Germans.

Originally U-boats were not equipped with radar. During the Battle of Atlantic, the convoy escorts, which had priority for radar equipment, were able to detect their opponents on the surface at night or in fog, whilst the U-boats were effectively blind. U-boat commanders initially punished their lookouts who 'failed to spot' attacking aircraft, but the men were not guilty as the aircraft could 'see' their targets through cloud cover with their on-board radars – initially the ASV Mk II type, later superseded by the Mk III and finally by the Mk XII, which initially could not be detected by the German Metox radar warning devices. It was a technological race – the Allies kept developing improved radars, while the Germans constantly worked on improved countermeasures. The Germans were lucky in this area, though it took some time until they realised this. Before the war a French inventor, Metox Grandin, developed a device for monitoring radio signals with wavelengths between 1.3m and 2.6m, known after him as the Metox, which proved capable of detecting radar

▲ The antenna of the FuMO–61 Hohentwiel; Type VIIs began to receive this in March 1944. (National Archives)

signals with the same wavelengths. The device was simple and had a wooden cross-shaped support for the antenna. This antenna, combined with the bad reputation of the Bay of Biscay – the U-boats' graveyard – earned it the nickname 'Biscaya-Kreuz' ('Biscay Cross'). It was a simple passive radar of the FuMB NVK R600 A type, produced by the French companies Grandin and Metox, fitted with the FuMB Ant 2 antenna. However, extensive tests showed that it could actually betray the position of a U-boat fitted with it, as it itself emitted some radiation. An aircraft flying at an altitude of 500m (1650ft) could detect a Metox at 22km (12nm), at 1000m (3300ft) at 33.4km (18nm) and at 2000m (6550ft) as far away as 46.3km (25nm).

The Metox was liked by the U-boat crews as it helped them to survive – some commanding officers would even abort their patrols if the Metox malfunctioned – but it was disliked because it was terribly cumbersome to use. After the boat surfaced the antenna – connected by a long cable to the receiver – had to be set on the bridge, and then regularly rotated by 90° to eliminate 'blind' sectors. It also had to be dismantled before the boat dived, as the cable would prevent the hatch from closing. The Metox could detect radar signals in the 62 to 264 HZ band at a range of up to 80km (45nm). Changes in signal amplitude gave the source's bearing – it increased if the aircraft was closing and decreased if it was moving away.

Metox sets began to be installed aboard U-boats in August 1942, but they were rendered useless when the Allies began to use centimetric-band radar, which they could not detect. It was proved that the Allies were using these short-wave radars when a petty officer aboard *U 124* installed an oscilloscope aboard his boat that could detect these wavelengths when the Metox could not. New radar-warning receivers were therefore introduced. From autumn 1942 U-boats were equipped with the FuMB4 Samos with a wavelength of 157–333cm in the 87–470 MHz band. In April 1943 this was replaced by Bali with a FuMB Ant–3 dipole antenna. August 1943 brought the new detectors FuMB8 Zypern (W. Anzg. 1), FuMB9 Zypern 2 (wavelength 118–192cm, frequency 156–254 MHz, with the Fu MB Ant 3 Bali and Timor antennae) and FuMB 10 Borkum (wavelength 75–300cm, frequency 100–400 MHz with the Bali and FuMB Sumatra antennas and the FuMZ 6 amplifier). Initially German scientists claimed that it was impossible to construct a radar operating on a 10cm wavelength, but analysis of U-boat logbooks by Konterad-miral Ludwig Stummel, head of the naval radar department, lead him to deduce that such a device had to be being used by the enemy. A British radar retrieved from an aircraft shot down over Rotterdam – and therefore nicknamed by the Germans the 'Rotterdam Gerät' – confirmed his deduction. Therefore a new detector, the Naxos FuMB7 was introduced. Its range was 5000m (27mm) and it was equipped with the manually-rotated FuMG Ant 1X antenna. The equipment was supplied by NVK Telefunken and installed on U-boats from October 1943. In March 1944 the Naxos was combined with the FuMB antenna into a device codenamed Cuba 1 or Fliege. Its range was 20km (11nm) and it could detect radars operating on 8–12cm wavelengths. A German response to Allied 3cm radars was the Mücke antenna providing a detection range of up to 50km (27mm). In 1944 the newly developed FuMB 35 Athos antenna was added to the Bali device resulting in a new radar warning device called FuMB 37 Leros.

These radar-warning devices certainly reduced the ef-fectiveness of enemy ASW forces, but they did nothing to help the U-boats in their own attacks. Although they kept improving existing equipment, the Germans neglected development of radar and fell well behind the British, who became the leaders in this field. Both jammers and decoys were developed in the sonar field, but only radar detectors. The German navy was particularly poorly equipped. It was not until Dönitz and his chief of signals met with represen-tatives of industry and scientists that he realised that they had no idea about requirements of the navy in general and the U-bootwaffe in particular, and he took this opportunity to make them aware of what the Kriegsmarine was actually doing and what it needed. As we have seen, it was not until January 1944 that the Germans realised that the Allies were operating on 'impossible' centimetric wavelengths, and this produced the Naxos detector, but there were still no search radars available for the U-boats. There had in fact been some development of naval radar and several types of search radar had been designed, but these were all fitted aboard large ships, U-boats not coming into the programme until much later. As we know, no earlier than in January 1944 did the Germans realise that the enemy radars were operating on 'impossible' centimetre wavelengths. The detector response was Naxos, but search radars remained unavailable for U-boat commanders. That said, it cannot be stated that there was no development at all in this area. Indeed, there were radar-related experiments in the Kriegsmarine, and several search radar models were actually designed, but all those were tested aboard large warships. U-boats were only included in the programme quite late. The first to carry Dete Gerät radars supplied by the Gema company were the larger Type IXA boats. This set was quite bulky and heavy, provided only a 30° sector of observation, had a range of 7000m (3.7nm) and was rather inaccurate (bearing error ± 2°). After tests with the Dete Gerät aboard *U 39* and *U 41* (both Type IXAs) in the autumn of 1941 similar set were installed aboard on other Type IX submarines. In 1942 some Type VIIs finally got them as well. The model used in this case was Dete Gerät 500, now redesignated FuMO29, operating on a 82cm wavelength. The first boats to carry this radar were *U 623* and *U 231*.

Technical parameters

Type	Wavelength	Frequency	Power	Range	Error – bearing	Error – distance
FuMO27	81.5cm	368 MHz	8 kW	24km (13nm)	5°	70m
FuMO26	81.5cm	368 MHz	8 kW	26km (14nm)	2°	50m
FuMO29	81.5cm	368 MHz	8 kW	26km (14nm)	2°	50m

The FuMO29 used an array composed of two rows of dipoles, six in each, installed in the forward part of the conning-tower. Therefore in order to scan the entire horizon the boat had to carry out a full 360° turn. In 1942 a new 1000 × 1400mm (39 × 55in) antenna with two rows of four dipoles each was introduced – this version was called FuMO30.

In 1943 new parabolic antennas installed in the after part of the tower were introduced. In 1942, despite opposition from the Kriegsmarine designers, the FuG 200 Hohentwiel aircraft radar also started to be installed aboard U-boats. This set was developed by Dr Christ and Dr Müller from the FMG 40 Kurmark model. It operated at a frequency of 550 MHz, wavelength 56cm, and had a power of 30 kW. The naval version of this device was called FuMO61 Hohentwiel U. Its range was 10km (5.4nm) and distance accuracy was 300m (1000yds). It was tested aboard *U 763* (Type VIIC).

The process of equipping Type VIIs with radar proceeded very slowly due to the difficulty German industry had with manufacturing radar equipment due to damage done by air-raids. By September 1944 only sixty-four U-boats had been equipped with the FuMO64 set. New variants of this radar set were successively introduced, e.g. FuMO65 Hohentwiel U 1 (frequency 110–160 MHz or 25–575 MHz) which provided sectoral or panoramic displays. In late 1944–early 1945 testing of the FuMO84 Berlin U 1 began – the new design operated at 9cm wavelength and a frequency of 3300 MHz. It had power of 20 kW and its antenna was installed on a watertight mast which could be raised from the conning-tower.

The After Compartment

Abaft the after watertight hatch of the control room was the third and last watertight compartment. The foremost part of this was another petty officers' mess with eight bunks, four on each side on two levels, with lockers for personal items. As with its forward counterpart, it was panelled and relatively comfortable. Abaft this cabin, on the port side, was the galley, where meals for 40–50 men were cooked on small electric stoves. Hot meals were usually only prepared at night, while the boat was on the surface charging its batteries. During the day the crew only ate cold dishes and snacks. Opposite this, to starboard, was the second toilet, but it was usually used as a food store (!), so for most of a patrol the crew only had the one toilet forward.

Next aft was the diesel engine room, with a narrow gangway between the two engines and the engines' control panels next to the hatch, and then the quieter electric motor room. As the motors were much smaller and mostly

◄ 'Dive! Dive!' The watch-keepers in the engine room have switched off the diesels and are closing the muffler valves to prevent seawater rushing into the boat. (CAW)

▶ Diesel engines being serviced before being installed aboard a U-boat. (ADM)

hidden under the deck the motor room seemed quite spacious and uncluttered – by the standards of a U-boat! The control panels for the motors were on either side, and the motor room also housing the steering engine and – at the far end – the after torpedo tube, with the after hydroplane engines either side of it. In an emergency both the rudder and the hydroplanes could be controlled from here. In the engine room, just next to the entrance, there was a valve cutting off the flow of exhaust gases to the manifolds, which passed through the room and rear part of the fin to the exhaust.

Propulsion

The submarines' diesel-electric drive consisted of four engines – two internal combustion engines for surfaced propulsion and two electric motors, which propelled the boat underwater. The 'fuel' of the latter was direct current, fed from storage batteries. The electric motors also charged the batteries when the submarine was on the surface. To do this the diesels were started and coupled to the electric motors, which then functioned as DC generators, with an output of 465 kW (300 V, 1550 A at 450 rpm). The capacity of the batteries, after twenty hours of charging, reached 9160 Ah. The propulsion system of a U-boat consisted of two propellers, shafts, transmission gears, electric motors, clutches and diesel engines. It was also possible to use the engines and motors in different combinations. For example, one diesel and one motor could be used to propel the boat on the surface while the other diesel, coupled to the other electric motor, simultaneously charged the batteries.

▶ A six-cylinder engine being installed in a Type VIIC on the slipway. (CAW)

The snorkel

The air aboard a U-boat was consumed both by the diesel engines and the crew themselves. Carbon dioxide could be removed by special absorbers and some of the compressed air could be released inside the boat, but this was only done in dire emergencies and the amount of air released was relatively small. The boat could only be properly ventilated on the surface, until the development of the snorkel allowed the boat to 'breathe' while submerged.

The snorkel was invented in 1933 by a Dutch Lieutenant, Jan Jacob Wichers, who later collaborated with Lieutenant J C van Pappelendam. It was first installed for trials aboard the Dutch submarine *O-21* in February 1940. When the Germans conquered the Netherlands later that year, the *O-21* fell into their hands, although the snorkel did not enter service aboard U-boats for several years. Development of the German snorkel (in German: 'Schnorchel') was inspired by Professor Walter with Dönitz's support and carried out by the engineers Ulrich Gabler and Hepp. The original design consisted of two concentric pipes which could be raised and lowered like periscopes. The intake pipe was equipped with a valve with a ball-shaped float to prevent accidental flooding. The

other was used to vent the exhaust gases, and had no such safety device. By June 1943 the blueprints were ready and the first boats were selected for testing – *U 57*, *U 58* and *U 236*. Trials revealed that the cut-off valves did not operate properly, so *U 235* and *U 237* – the next boats earmarked for the snorkel development programme – were equipped with an improved model. The new device had a diameter of 220mm (8.66in) and a total length of 8300mm (326.77in). The exhaust was located 1300mm (51.18in) lower than the air intake, to prevent the gases just being sucked back into the boat.

By July 1944 only 120 snorkels had been installed aboard Type VII and Type IX U-boats. The commanders of the upgraded submarines invented a quite interesting, non-combat application for their equipment. Running on diesels, they would order the air intake valve to be partially

▲ Whilst submerged the engine-room crew did not have much to do. (CAW)

◄ The motor room. The control panels are in the foreground.

▶ A Type VIIC/41 after the surrender of Germany. The boat has a 37mm AA gun on the lower platform, with two twin 20mm above it. The snorkel, lowered into its housing in deck, can be seen in the background. *National Archives)*

▶ Another Type VIIC/41 with its snorkel and periscopes (the attack periscope is the taller one). There is no 88mm deck gun – by the end of the war Type VIIs only carried AA guns. (National Archives)

closed, so the engines quickly sucked the air from the boat. Then the valve was fully opened again and the fresh air rapidly filled the entire interior of the submarine, thus ventilating the boat much more quickly.

The snorkel turned U-boats from submersibles into true submarines. They no longer had to surface to run the diesels and charged their batteries or to ventilate the boat. But the fitting of snorkels did not begin until 1943 and was painfully slow thereafter, as the equipment was not available in sufficient quantities. Even if it had been, fitting it required a major reconstruction of the boat, meaning it would have to be withdrawn from service for a considerable time and also increasing the workload in the already overburdened shipyards, which were barely able to keep up with ordinary maintenance requirements

The Type VII U-boats were equipped with a snorkel composed of two concentric pipes with a hinged base, allowing it to be lowered and laid flat in a special cradle, forward of the conning tower. Its use was restricted by the height of the waves and the rolling of the boat when cruising at periscope depth. Rough seas could close the intake valve, causing the diesels to start to suck the air out of the interior of the boat, the drop in pressure causing discomfort to the lungs and ears of the crew. The speed of the boat was also restricted. Theoretically the snorkel should have allowed the boat to achieve the same speed as it would have done on the surface, but in practice it could make only 6 knots, just what it would have done on the electric motors. But it did provide the undisputed advantage that the boat could now remain at periscope depth for prolonged periods, without being forced to surface.

The Lower Deck

The lower deck, below the panels of the main deck, housed numerous tanks, the batteries and the magazine. The surfacing and submerging of a Type VII was controlled by a ballast system consisting of three main ballast tanks, two trimming tanks, a crash-dive tank, and two compensation tanks. Two of the main ballast tanks were installed in the bow and stern, outside the pressure hull. The third one was located directly under the control room and its volume was equal to the other two combined, as the designers had assumed that the external tanks might be damaged in action and this one would have to take on the whole job. When the boat was surfaced, all three tanks were filled with air, providing positive buoyancy. The bottoms of the tanks were always open, though the air pressure prevented water from getting in. Opening the vent flaps in the top of the tanks let the air be pushed out by the influx of water, which dived the boat. All the valves could be operated remotely from the control room, or manually from control positions next to the tanks. Maintaining neutral buoyancy, achieved by trimming the boat, due to some hydrological anomalies and the constant shifting of weight, was virtually impossible, so the boat could not 'hang' neutrally in the depths, so the boat always had to have way on and control its depth with the hydroplanes.

To surface the boat, the water had to be forced out of the tanks. Initially this was done by pumping compressed air into them. Once the conning tower had broken the surface, the exhaust valves were opened and the diesels coupled to the shafts and quickly started, the remaining water in the tanks then being forced out by the exhaust gases. This helped both to reduce the consumption of compressed air and to preserve the

insides of the tanks themselves by coating them with an oily film. The crash-dive tank (capacity 5 tonnes), was also located under the control room, and was always filled after the boat surfaced and emptied after it dived. Its task was to add weight during the initial moments of a dive, helping to defeat surface tension of water and any initial inertia, especially when the boat was rolling heavily – in such conditions it took longer to flood the regular ballast tanks.

The compensation tanks, also located near the control room, were supposed to trim the boat, assuring its desirable fixed buoyancy, which had to be constantly updated. Trimming in a fresh-water environment would have been quite simple, but in seawater it was much more complicated. Changing water salinity, as well as currents, insulation, water temperature, the presence of plankton etc., altered the conditions. On the other hand the boat's weight also changed over time, as food and fuel were consumed. Therefore the First Officer and Chief Engineer had to adjust the weight of the boat as conditions changed by pumping water in or out of the compensation tanks. Trimming tanks locating on both 'tips' of a U-boat compensated for all changes in longitudinal distribution of weight along the boat, by transferring water between them. Loss of weight caused by launching torpedoes was compensated with tanks installed beneath the torpedo tubes themselves. The ballast and fuel systems of a Type VII were very simple, reliable and easy to operate – proving that this design was the correct one for mass-production.

The layout of the lower deck followed the that of the hull frames. Frames are always numbered from the stern – in the case of U-boats, from the after end of the pressure hull.

▲ Three Type VIIC/41s moored in Wilhelmshaven after the surrender in May 1945. All are equipped with snorkels. Note the containers for liferafts in the forward deck: the boat on the left has three, while the others have four. (National Archives)

▶ A 'Seven' in dry dock. The external saddle tanks, for fuel oil, can be clearly seen. (CAW)

Tank	Frames
Ballast tank No 1	–11 – +6.5
Trimming tank	1 – 6
Compensation tank No 1, starboard	6 – 10
Compensation tank No 1, port	6 – 10
Bilge	10 – 29
Battery No 1	29 – 36, centrally
Used oil tank	19 – 15, along sides
Engine oil tank	21 – 25, centrally
Port and starboard fuel tanks	18 – 26
Fresh (drinking) water tank	19 – 31 (port)
Fuel tank No 1, starboard	19 – 40
Fuel tank, port	32 – 40
Waste water tanks	31 – 32
Ballast tank no 3	40 – 49
Deep fuel tank	49 – 63 (along sides)
Ammunition magazine	51 – 53 (centrally)
Waste water tank	53 – 54 (port)
Washing fresh water tank	53 – 54 (starboard)
Compensation/fuel tanks No 1	35 – 38 port/starboard (external saddle tanks)
Fuel tanks	18 – 35
Compensation/fuel tanks No 2	35 – 44 (port/starboard)
Untertriebszelle	44 – 46 (port/starboard)
Fuel tanks	46 – 66 (port/starboard)
Battery no 2	54 – 63 (centrally)
Compensation tanks no 2 and no 3	63 – 69.5 (port/starboard, centrally)
Bow trimming tank	64.5 – 74
External ballast tank no 2	76 – 90

▼ 'All hands, man your battle stations!' The crew runs to prepare the 88mm deck gun to fire. Note the plug in the muzzle. (CAW)

Armament

Guns

The gun armament of Type VII U-boats changed several times in response to changing tactical requirements. These changes mostly affected the anti-aircraft guns, involving different combinations of 20mm and 37mm cannon, beginning with a single 20mm gun, then two 20mm and a single 37mm and then one or two quadruple 20mm. But throughout this the main deck gun remained the same – a single 88mm. Although it was the same calibre as the excellent army and Luftwaffe 8.8cm FlaK, it was a completely different weapon designed and used only by the Kriegsmarine – they could not even fire the same ammunition. The Schiffskanone 8.8cm C/35 in Unterseebootslafette C/77 had a range of 14,834m (15,556 yards) and an anti-aircraft ceiling of 10,476m (34,370ft) and was the basic artillery armament on all variants of the Type VII. It was a pretty good gun, although with a slow rate of fire, well made and highly reliable. Its crew consisted of six men: the training gunlayer, the elevation gunlayer, the loader and his two assistants, and the commander (the second watch officer). In rough weather – one has to remember that the gun crew had to work on a narrow, low and lively deck – the gunners were strapped to the mount with special harnesses. Of course the ammunition carriers had to be able to move freely so they only had their lifejackets. The gun was manually loaded with shells handed from inside the boat through a special hatch in the conning-tower. Shells were delivered by the shortest route possible, that is always to the side of the gun closest to the tower. Therefore if the gun was, for example, firing to port, it was turned with its left side to the conning tower and so the ammunition was delivered from the left. To avoid the crew colliding with one another, the gun was fitted with identical aiming controls (both for elevation and training) on both sides of the barrel. In the situation described above, both gunlayers would use the controls on the right-hand side of the gun. A single optical sight of the finest quality was used, which could be dismounted and attached to either side of the gun. Both gunlayers used it to aim the gun at a target, standing on the same side, always the outer one, while the loaders were delivering shells from the other side of the mount. The U-boats' anti-aircraft outfit changed like the picture in a kaleidoscope. Initially the Type VIIAs were all fitted with a single 20mm cannon on the deck behind the conning-tower. Later the gun was moved to the rebuilt conning-tower behind the bridge, on a small platform called the 'Wintergarten' ('winter garden', i.e. 'bandstand') fenced in with a characteristic overhanging railing.

Later, beginning with the Type VIIBs, two single cannons of the same calibre were used. Type VIIC U-boats usually had two single 20mm and a single 37mm cannon or two twin 20mm cannons or even three twin 'twenties' and a 37mm. When *U 333* scored a rare success in shooting down an attacking Wellington bomber, the U-bootwaffe command was inspired to order all U-boat commanders to stay on the surface and shoot it out with attacking aircraft. An exceptionally dangerous area, extensively patrolled by the RAF, was the Bay of Biscay which had to be crossed by every U-boat stationed in France when leaving on patrol or returning from one. The proper solution to this problem, of course, was for the U-boats to have their own fighter escort. Dönitz was well aware of this, just as he knew that he would never get them from Oberkommando der Luftwaffe, so he decided that boats transiting the Bay of Biscay would do so in groups escorted by specially adapted, heavily-armed U-boats, the so-called 'U-bootflaks'. *U 441*, a Type VII, had been

▲ A U-boat gun crew in action. The target has already been hit and is on fire. In the foreground stands the loader with another round. (CAW)

◄ Loading a U-boat's 88mm deck gun. (ADM)

Cannon	Calibre (mm)	Barrel length (mm/calibres)	Muzzle velocity (m/s)	Barrel life (shots)	Range/ceiling (m)	Length of round (mm)	Rate of fire (theoret./pract.]	Weight (kg /lbs)
2cm Flak C/30	20	1300/65	835	22,000	4900/3700	203	280 (20-rd mag)	420/926
2cm Flak C/38 double	20	1300/65	835	22,000	4900/3700	203	480/220	416/917
2cm Flak Vierling C/38a/43 quadruple	20	1300/65	835	22,000	4900/3700	203	1800/880	2150/4740
3.7cm SK30	37	2960/83	1000	7500	6800/8500		160/80	3670/8091
3.7cm M42	37	2568/69	1000	7500	4800/6400		160/80	3670/8091

► Empty 88mm shell cases piled next to the tower of a Type VIIC. Their number suggests that the gun crew has been busy recently. (CAW)

chosen for this role and was armed with two quadruple 20mm and a single 30mm cannon. However, the idea was soon abandoned. Production of quadruple 20mm mounts for the U-boats was badly delayed by the effects of the war on German industry, although some did finally reach the submarines later on. See the table below for details of the anti-aircraft cannon carried by the Type VIIs.

▲ The 20mm (2-cm Flak C/30) cannon mounted on the rear platform of a Type VIIC U-boat's conning-tower. (CAW)

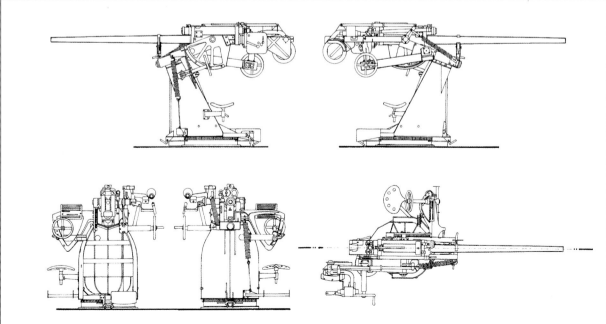

► 3.7cm SK C/30 U gun in Ubts. LC/39 mount. (Drawn and traced by Mirosław Skwiot)

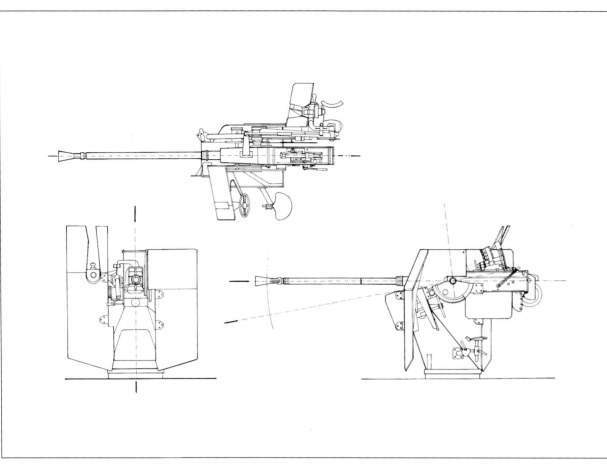

◀ 3.7-cm LM 43U gun. (Drawn and traced by Mirosław Skwiot)

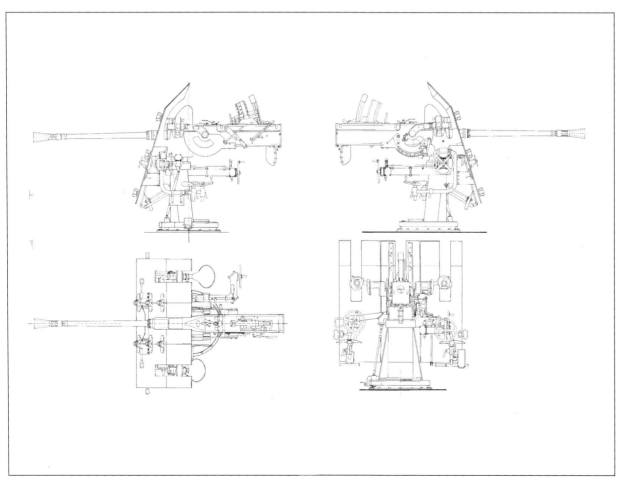

◀ 3.7cm Flak 42 gun in LM 42 mount. (Drawn and traced by Mirosław Skwiot)

▶ 3.7cm Flak LM 42 gun in a twin DLM 42 mount. (Drawn and traced by Mirosław Skwiot)

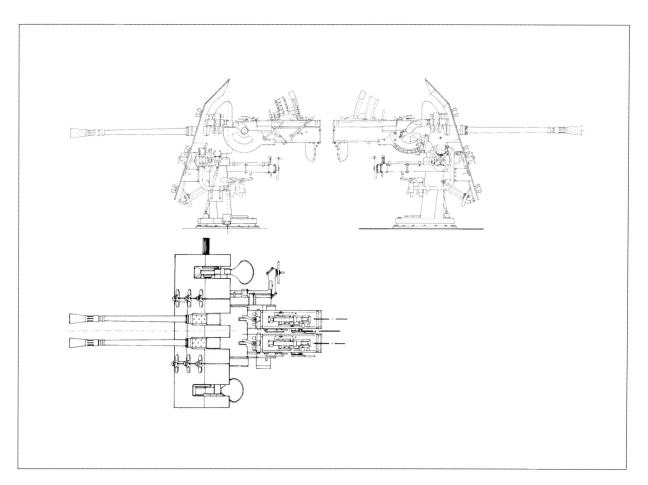

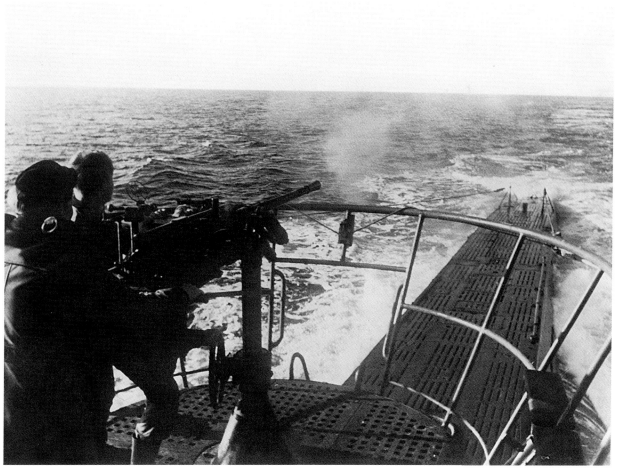

▶ A 20mm Flak C/30 AA gun aboard a Type VIIC. (CAW)

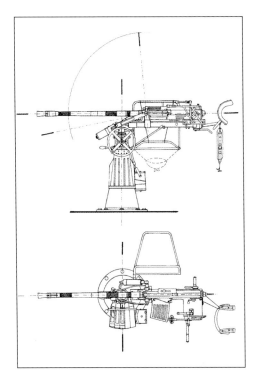

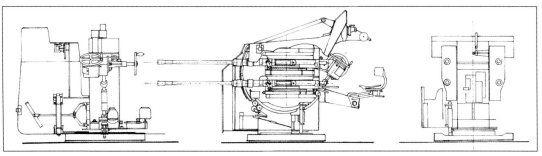

▲ 2cm Flakvierling C/38 in Vierlingslafette 38/43U mount. (Drawn and traced by Mirosław Skwiot)

◄ Mauser 2cm Flak 30 in C/30 pedestal mount. (Drawn and traced by Mirosław Skwiot)

Torpedoes

The primary armament of the U-boat (just like every other submarine in the world) was always torpedoes. During the Second World War two types of torpedo were in use: with compressed air and electric propulsion respectively. The former, propelled by a combustion engine, had a higher speed and greater range, although they betrayed the position of the attacking U-boat by the trail of exhaust gas bubbles they left on the surface. The latter was a more discreet weapon, since it generated no exhaust gases, although it was slower and shorter-ranged. In this period the Germans were the world leaders in torpedo design, which they were constantly modernising though they encountered problems in the process. The Norwegian campaign was a clear example of this. A special inquiry had to be set up to discover the reasons for the large number of

	Ships sunk	Ships damaged
With 1 hit:	210 ships (40.3%)	83 ships (15.9%)
With 2 hits:	149 ships (29.9%)	29 ships (5.7%)
With 3 hits:	39 ships (7.4%)	4 ships (0.6%)
With 4 hits:	6 ships (1%)	1 ship (0.2%)
Total:	404 ships (77.6%)	117 ships (22.4%)

dud shots and premature explosions that had occurred. It turned out that the torpedoes had not kept to their set running depth due to water leaking into their steering mechanisms, and also that the iron-rich rocks in Norway had distorted the Earth's magnetic field, affecting the torpedoes' magnetic fuses. Two types of fuse were then in use: contact and non-contact. The explosion of a torpedo with a contact fuse was initiated by a special inertial

◄ ▼ A torpedo store in one of the pens at a U-boat base. (W Trojca collection)

▼ Torpedoes being serviced aboard a repair ship. (CAW)

▲ A training torpedo being loaded aboard a Type I U-boat – *U 26*. Note the special folding ramp designed for this purpose. (A Jarski collection)

which gives two torpedoes per sunken ship. The magnetic fuse brought this ratio down to one torpedo per ship.

German torpedoes had the advantage that they could be fired with an angle on the bow of up to 90°, meaning that the whole boat did not have to be aimed towards the target. Indeed, later this angle was increased to 180°, allowing the U-boat to fire at targets directly behind them as they moved away from a convoy, greatly increasing their chances of survival. Later still, the designers gave the torpedoes the ability to manoeuvre: having covered a set distance, the torpedo would then start to zigzag or circle, increasing the possibility of a hit.

Every U-boat began its patrol with all tubes loaded and reload torpedoes stowed under the deck in the forward compartment. The tubes were reloaded using sling slides in the compartment's deckhead, the so-called 'Flaschen-zuge', chain hoists with a system of blocks, and of course the hard work of the crew! Regulations stated that each torpedo had to be serviced every five days, so one torpedo had to be withdraw from its tube every day.

The torpedoes were fired by compressed air. Before firing the outer doors of the tube had to be opened, the tube flooded and the torpedo calculator connected. The torpedoes could be fired both submerged and on the surface from several locations aboard the boat: directly from the forward torpedo compartment itself, from the control room, from the commander's station above the control room inside the conning-tower, and from the bridge on top of the tower. The main switch, which activated the selected tubes, was mounted in the rear corner of the control room, with a bank of coloured lights showing which tubes had been armed. Before firing, as well as deciding which tubes to use and which control position they were to be fired from, the torpedoes and tubes themselves had to be checked, and the firing solution calculated. The device used by the Germans for this was among the best in the world and was considerably superior to that used by other navies. It was essentially what would be called today a simple analogue computer, characterised by advanced technology and a high degree of miniaturisation for its time. When one of these devices was captured, the Allies were unpleasantly surprised by both its degree of sophistication and its capabilities. Aiming the UZO (Überwesserzieloptik – Above Water Optical Aiming Device, a combined optical sight, binoculars and rangefinder, set on a special mounting on the bridge) or pointing the periscope (which was linked to the gyrocompass) at the target which automatically sent the target's bearing to this Vorhaltrechner, which was also fed with other necessary information such as the boat's own course and speed. With these and any changes in the bearing and range of the target acquired from the periscope or UZO, the machine calculated the target's movement, resolved the shooting equation and automatically sent the results of the firing solution directly to the torpedoes as the firing angle. As we have seen, the torpedoes could be fired at an angle on the bow of up to 90°, and later this was increased still further. The Vorhaltrechner could constantly update this data for up to five targets at once, more than its

mechanism and occurred as the result of a direct hit, while the non-contact fuse was initiated when the torpedo entered the target's magnetic or acoustic field. The difference between the two was considerable. Firing the former required a direct hit, and even that was often not enough to sink a target. A vessel with a hole in its side often remained seaworthy and could limp into harbour, while a non-contact torpedo's explosion occurred beneath the target and could break her keel like a twig, thus dealing a mortal blow. The performance of contact-fuse torpedoes is shown in the table opposite:

In total 404 ships were been sunk by 806 torpedoes,

best counterpart aboard Allied or Japanese submarines could do. Each individual torpedo could have its own firing solution sent to it and then all five could be fired at 1.5-second intervals, each one at a different target. The torpedo officer's job was to keep the target in the UZO, or in the periscope's crosshairs when the U-boat was executing a submerged attack. The submarine could even turn while shooting without affecting accuracy. To increase the system's reliability a petty officer – the chief of the torpedo section – was in the bow torpedo room, stretched like a spider with his hands and feet on emergency firing levers, ready to fire the torpedoes manually should the remote control systems fail in the control room or on the bridge. Torpedoes were launched by compressed air; the interval of 1.5 seconds between shots was kept automatically in order to prevent possible interference between them. Immediately after the shot the regulating tanks were filled with sea water of the same weight as the torpedoes fired, in order to maintain the submarine's trim and its ability to change depth quickly.

The output of the German engineers developing torpedo weapons was truly impressive. In total they designed six models of thermal-engine powered torpedoes (four-cylinder engines fed with a steam-gas mixture), nineteen electric designs and twelve propelled by the Walter turbine (an oxygen-free engine). There were also experimental designs with a closed-cycle motor, and even jet-powered ones. All torpedoes used on U-boats had a calibre of 534.6mm and were 7.165m (23.507ft) long.

▲ A torpedo with a combat warhead is being loaded onto *U 331* (Type VIIC) commanded by Ritterkreuzträger (Knight of the Knight's Cross of the Iron Cross) Hans Dietrich von Tiesenhausen, who sank the British battleship HMS *Barham* in the Mediterranean.

▲ The tricky operation of lowering a torpedo down a Type VIIC's loading hatch. The 88mm deck gun is visible in the foreground. (ADM)

◀ A torpedo being transported from a depot to a pier. Note the special carriage. (CAW)

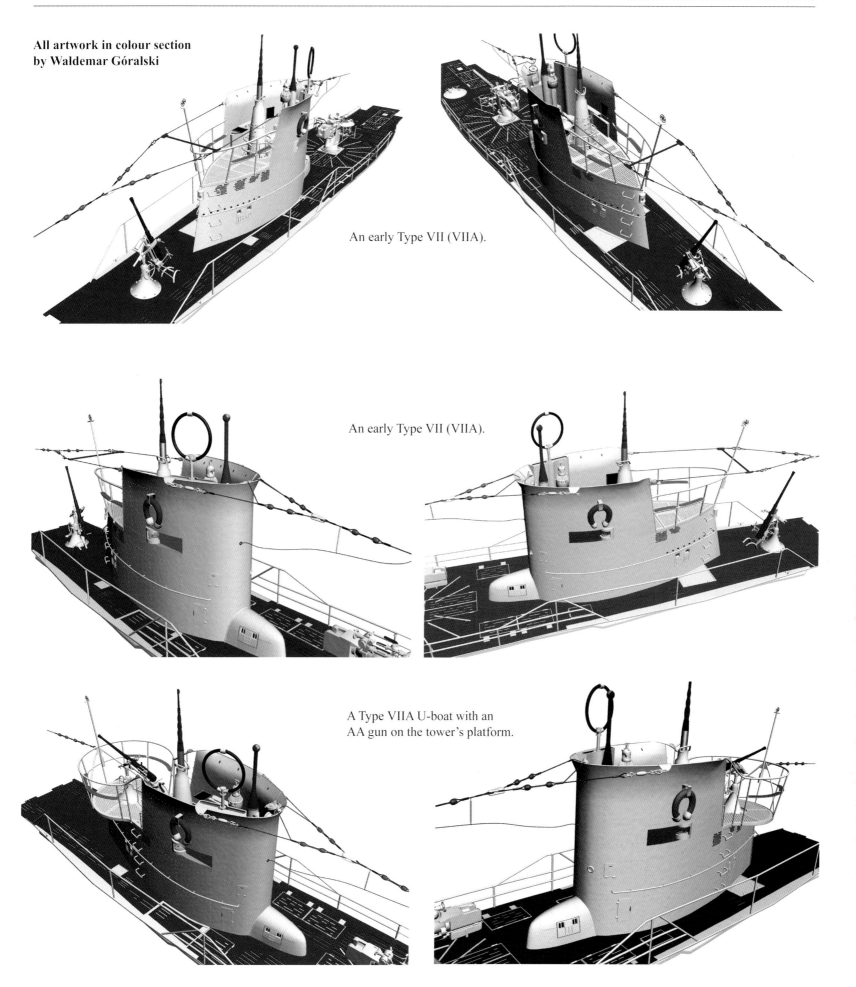

**All artwork in colour section
by Waldemar Góralski**

An early Type VII (VIIA).

An early Type VII (VIIA).

A Type VIIA U-boat with an
AA gun on the tower's platform.

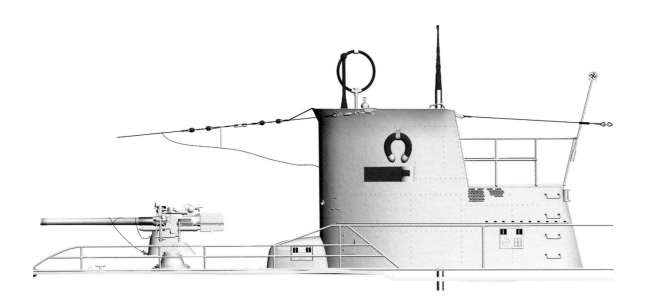

An early Type VII (VIIA).

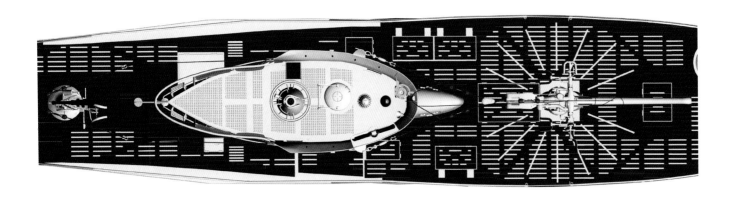

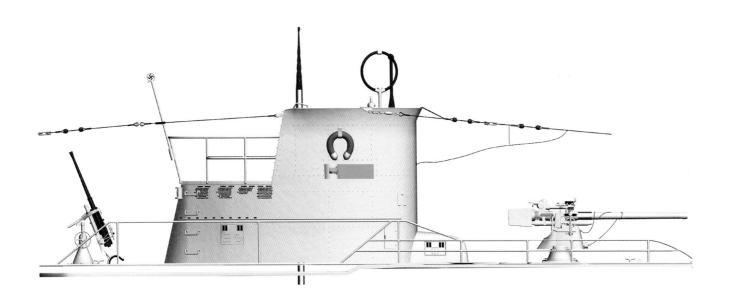

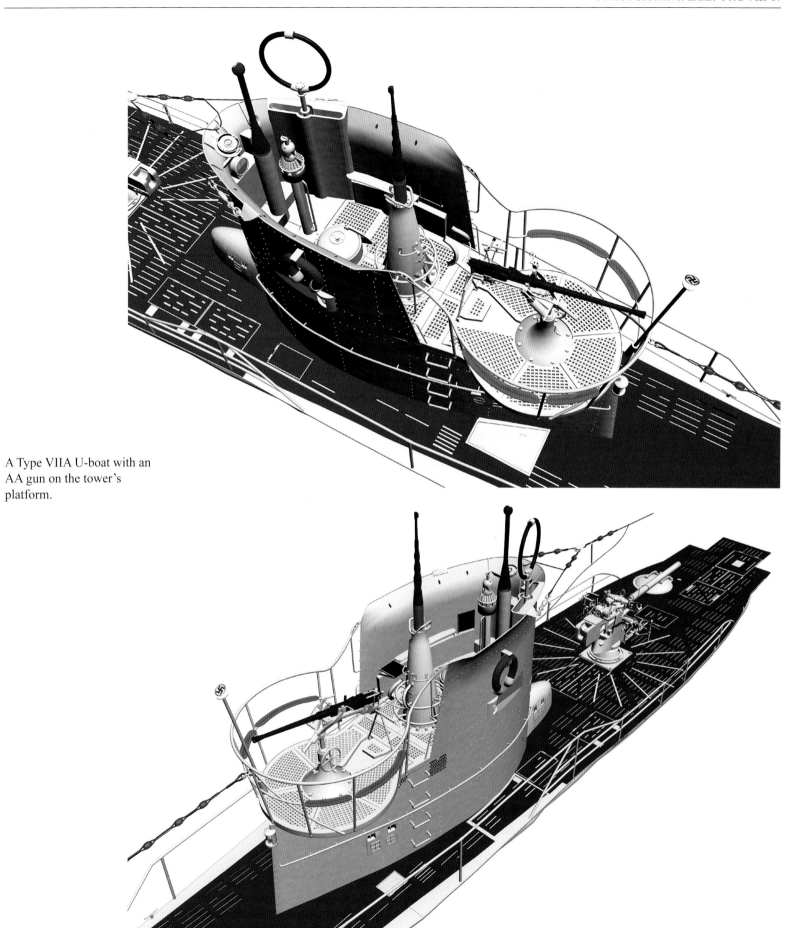

A Type VIIA U-boat with an AA gun on the tower's platform.

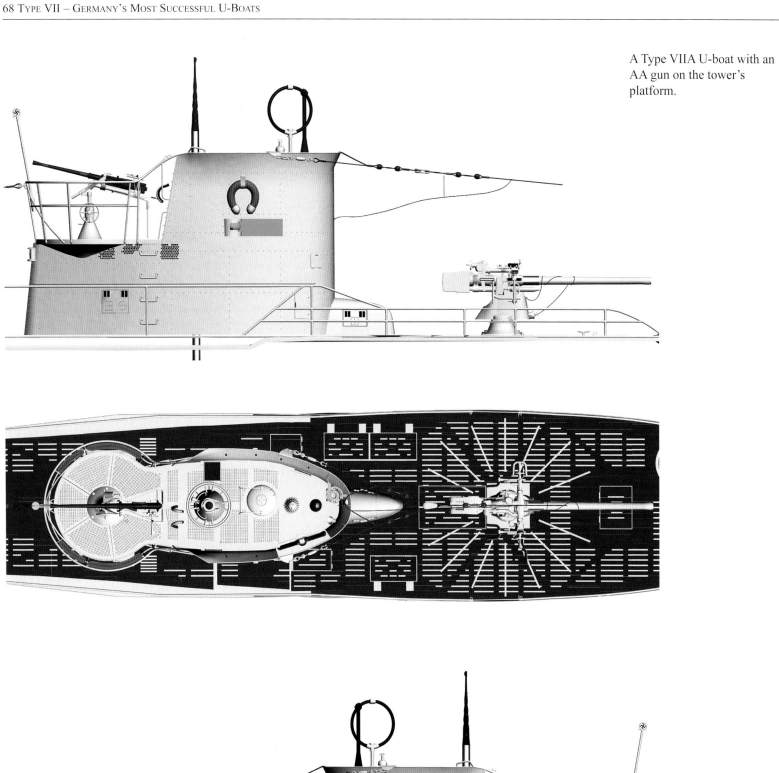

A Type VIIA U-boat with an AA gun on the tower's platform.

A Type VIIB – note the
additional ventilation duct on
the tower used on this U-boat
type.

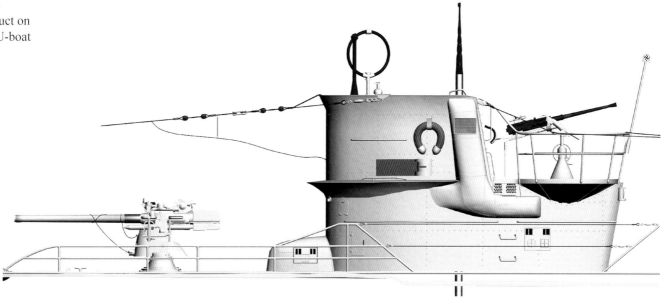

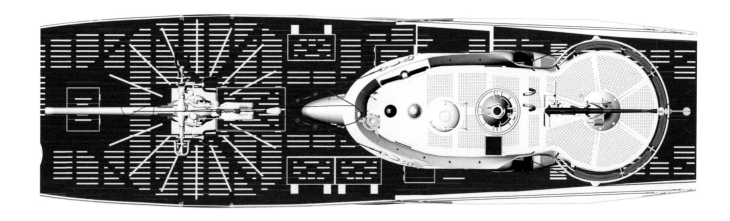

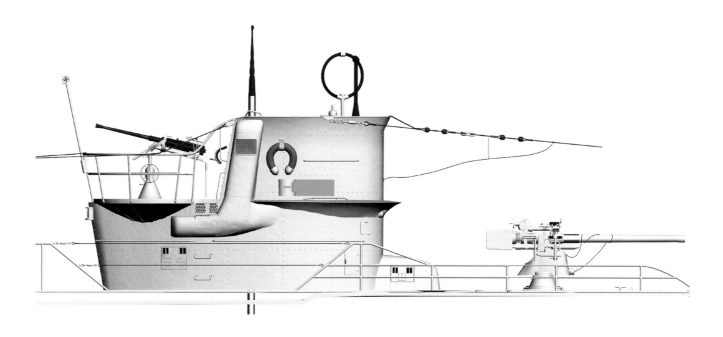

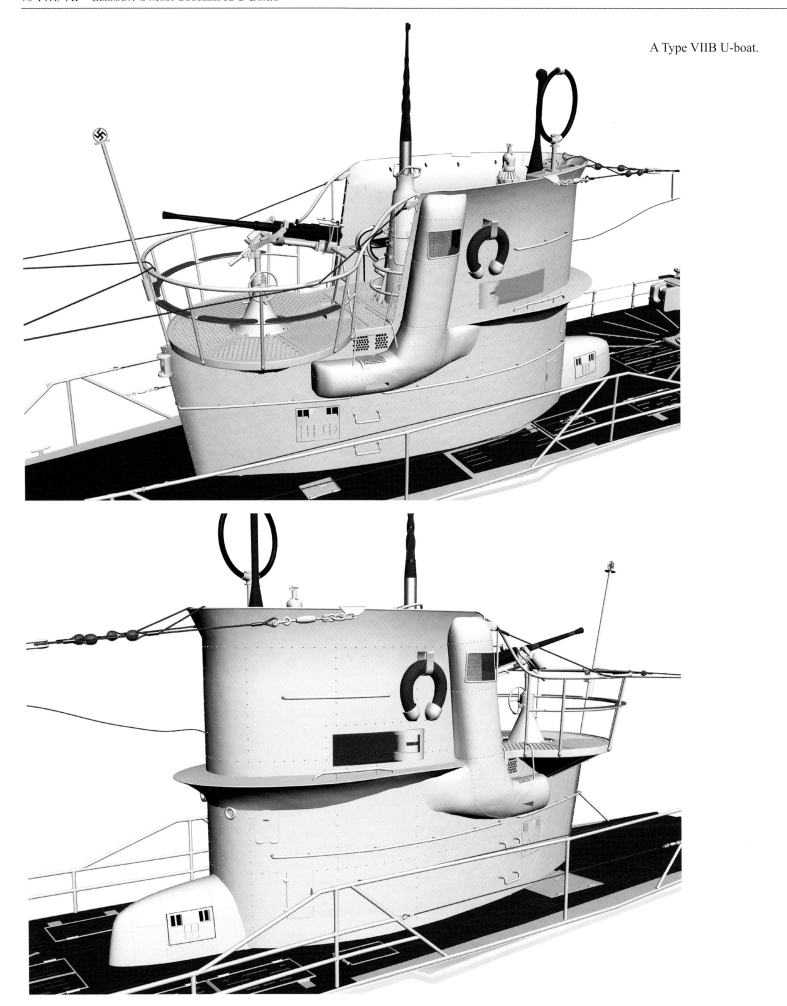

A Type VIIB U-boat.

A Type VIIC U-boat.

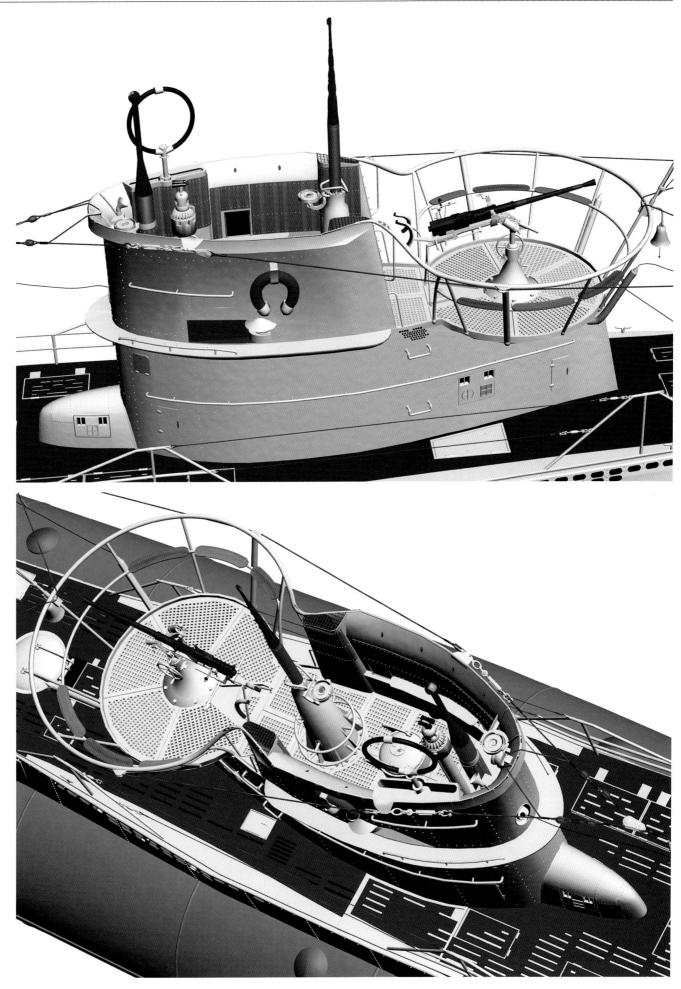

A Type VIIC U-boat.

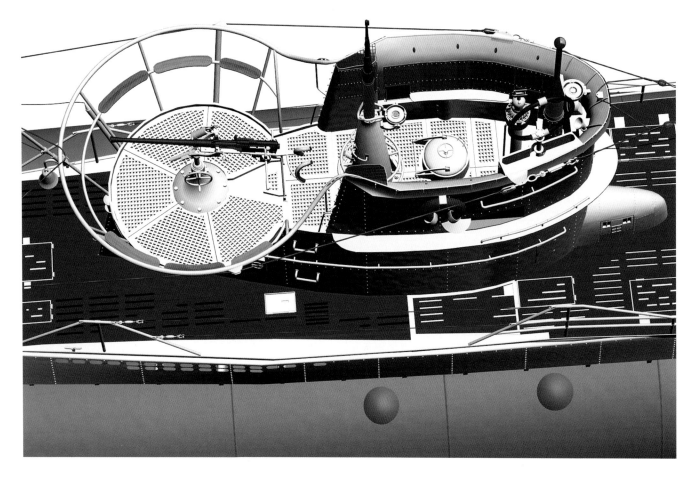

A Type VIIC U-boat.

A Type VIIC U-boat.

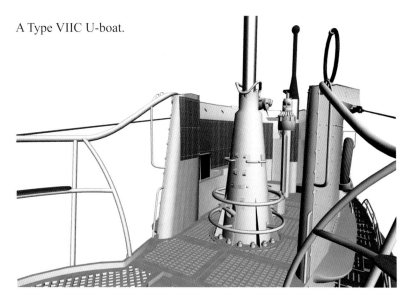

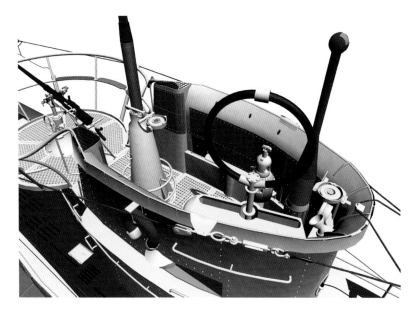

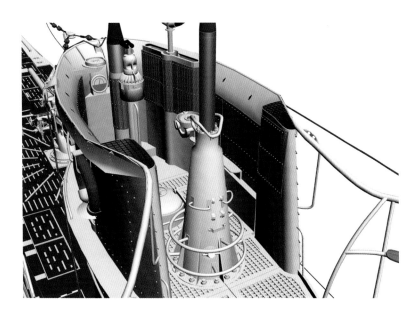
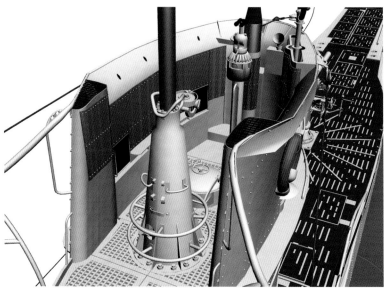

A Type VIIC U-boat.

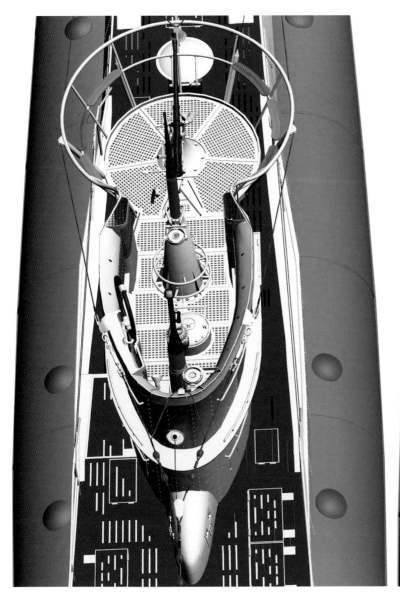
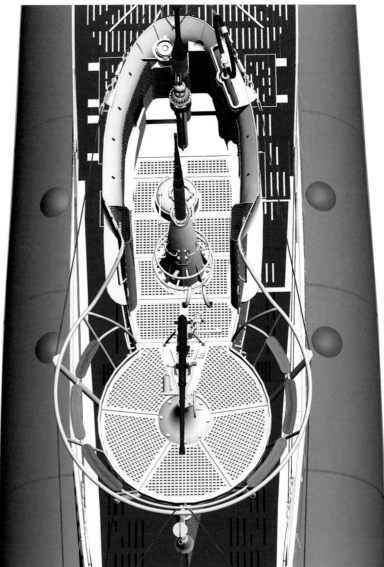

A Type VIIC U-boat.

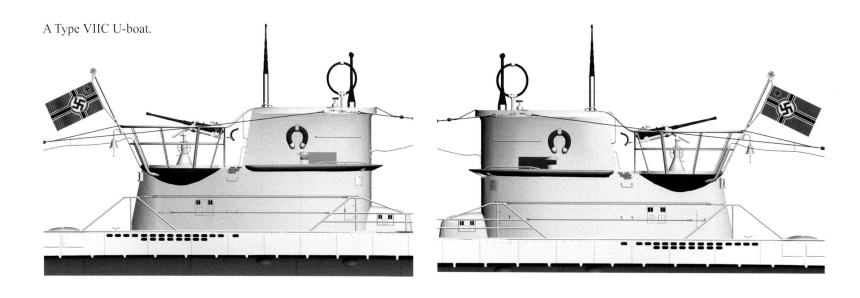

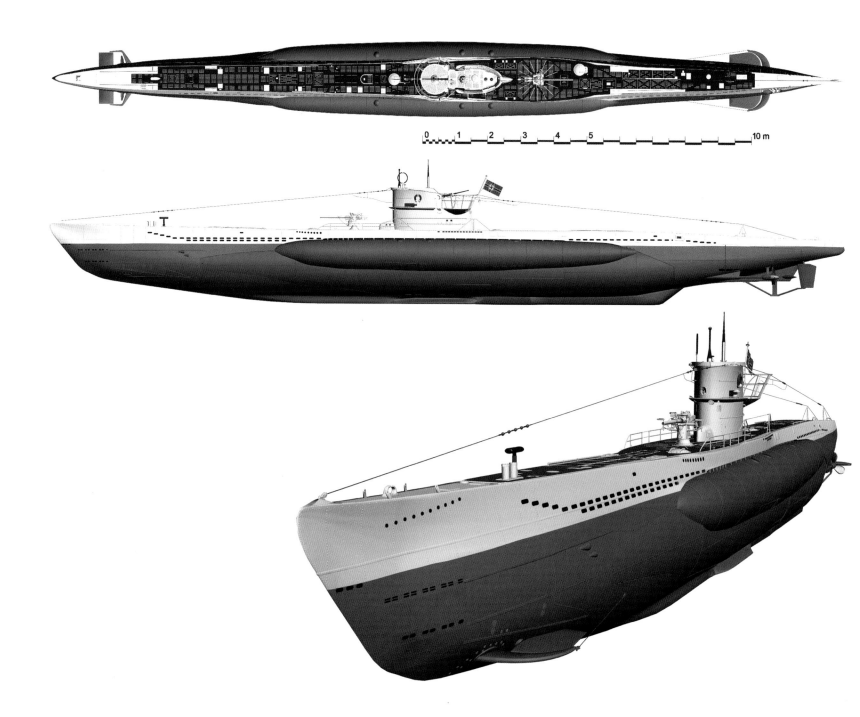

A Type VIIC U-boat.

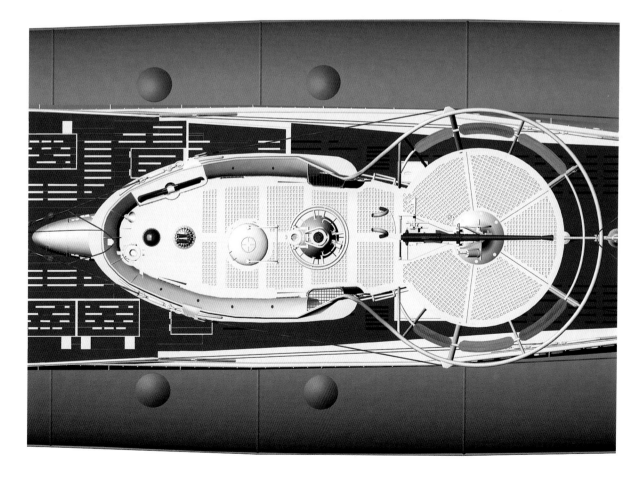

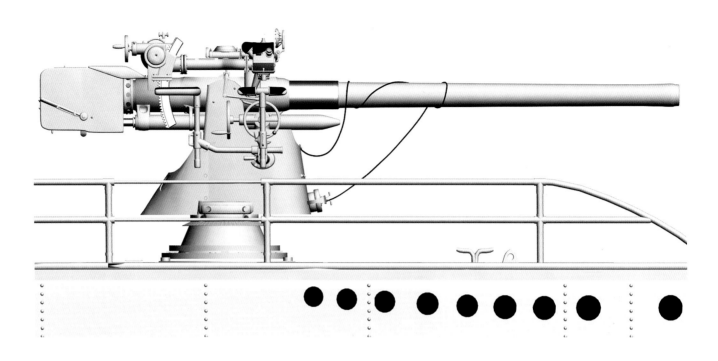

An 88mm SK C/35 deck gun on the Ubts.L. C/35 carriage.

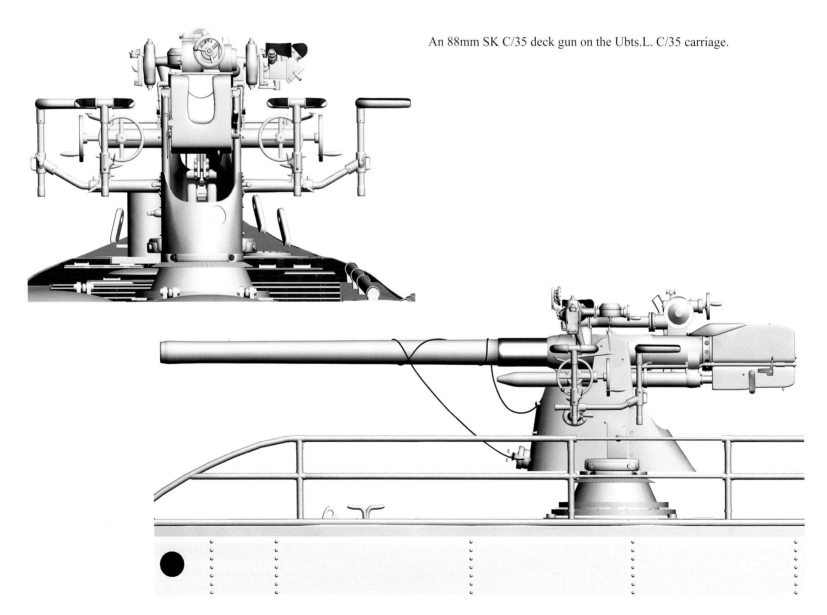

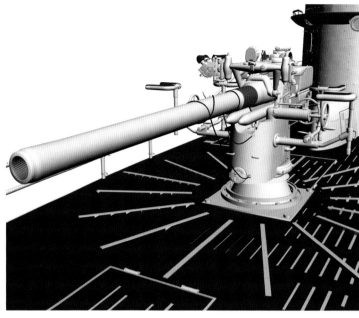

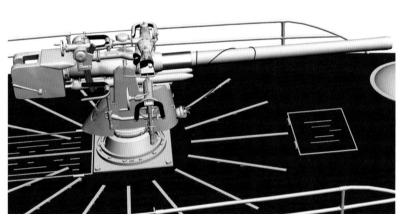

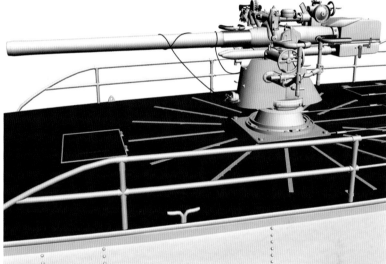

An 88mm SK C/35 deck gun on the Ubts.L. C/35 carriage.

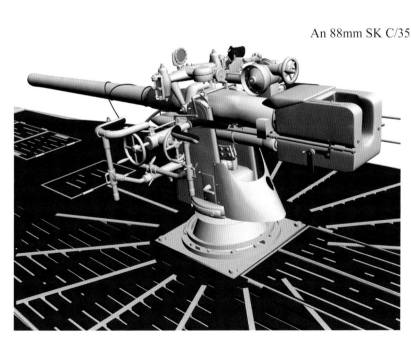

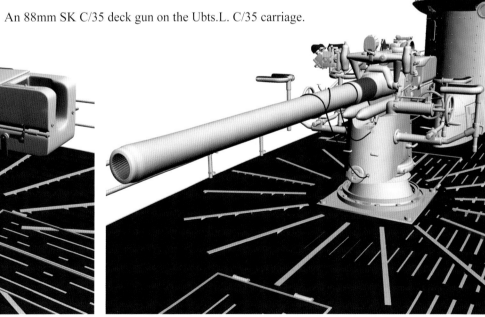

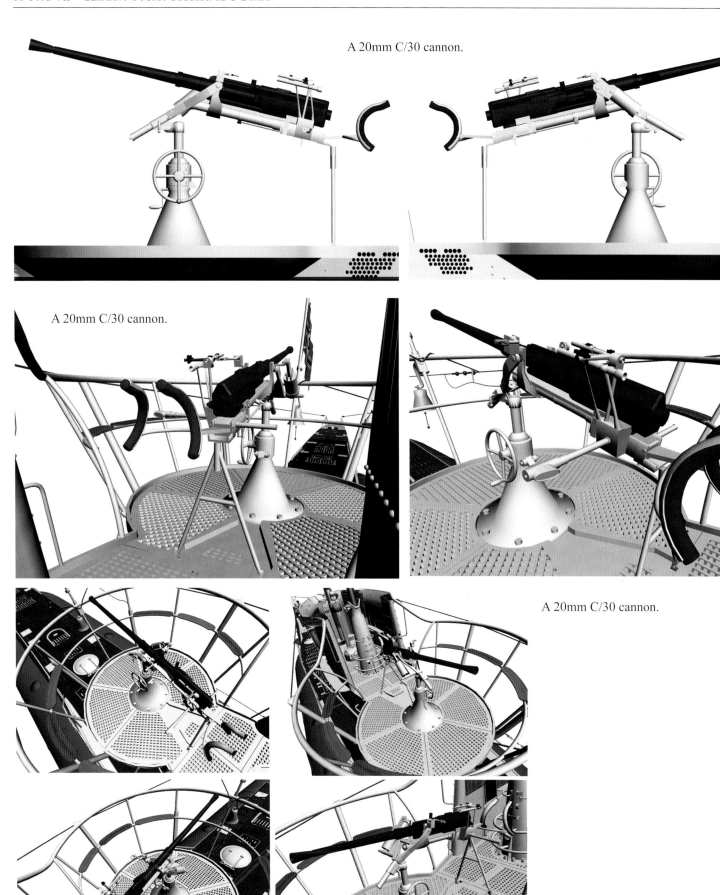

A 20mm C/30 cannon.

A 20mm C/30 cannon.

A 20mm C/30 cannon.

▶ A torpedo being loaded aboard a U-boat inside a pen in a base on the French coast. (CAW)

The principal torpedo issued to U-boats at the outbreak of the War was the G7a with contact fuses or Pi–2 magnetic fuses. These were advanced for their times but, as we know, far from perfect. Another improvement was the introduction of new programmable mechanisms like the Federapparat (FAT I) instead of the traditional gyroscope. An FAT I-equipped torpedo ran straight ahead to a pre-set distance of n × 100m and then it started an asymmetrical zigzag, with longer legs of 1492m (4895ft) and shorter ones of 820m (2690ft). A clockwork device determined the distance travelled by counting propeller shaft revolutions and thus executed the turns at the proper intervals. FAT I's successor, the FAT II, allowed both zigzagging and circling, further increasing the chances of a hit. An interesting member of this family of devices was the LUT (Lageunabhangiger), which initially propelled the torpedo to one side of the U-boat, and then started zigzagging it towards the target, thus concealing the attacking submarine's position.

The electrically-driven torpedo's electric, developed in the 1920s, was another significant achievement by German

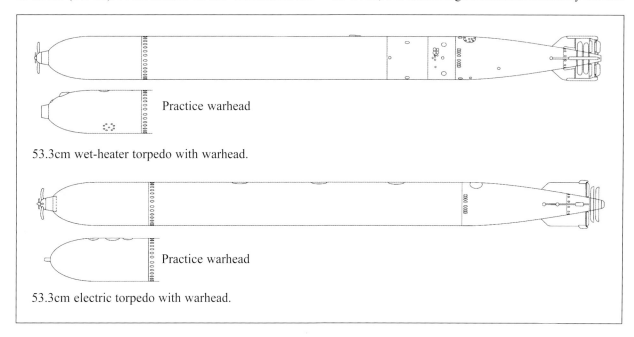

Practice warhead

53.3cm wet-heater torpedo with warhead.

Practice warhead

53.3cm electric torpedo with warhead.

Torpedo	Calibre/length [mm]/[mm (in)]	Weight [kg (lbs)]	Range [km (nm)]	Warhead weight [kg (lbs)]	Engine type
G7a TI	534.6/7163 (282.01)	1538 (3391)	7.5/12 (4.0/6.5)	280 (617)	Piston, 4-cyl.
G7e TII	534.6/7163 (282.01)	1608 (3545)	5.0 (2.7)	280 (617)	Electric 2 × 13T
G7e TIII	534.6/7163 (282.01)	1620 (3571)	5.0 (2.7)	280 (617)	Electric 2 × 13T
G7e TIIIa	534.6/7163 (282.01)	1760 (3880)	7.5 (4.0)	280 (617)	Electric 2 × 17T
G7es TIV Falke	534.6/7163 (282.01)	1400 (3086)	7.5 (4.0)	274 (604)	Electric 2 × 13T
G7es TVb Zaunkönig	534.6/7163 (282.01)	1495 (3296)	8 (4.3)	274 (604)	Electric 1 × 17T
G7ut. TVII Steinbarsch	534.6/7163 (282.01)	1730 (3814)	8 (4.3)	280 (617)	Walter turbine

engineers. The first model of the electric torpedo was propelled by a series, eight-pole 231:75 motor with a stationary field coil and a rotor with attached transmission gear. Power was provided by fifty-two 13 T–210 90 volt acid storage cells of 105 Ah capacity. During the War the solid cells were constantly improved and different kinds of acid batteries were used; the most common types were 13 T, 17 T and 9 T. In 1943 Zn-PbO2 cells were introduced. They allowed a longer range, up to 9000m (9843yds) at 30 knots. The later Mg-C battery proved to be outstanding, giving a range of 22,000m (24,059yds) at the same speed, although the War ended before it could be introduced into service. In the same year the first torpedo with an acoustic fuse was introduced, which very dangerous to escorting warships. To complete the list of German achievements in this discipline it is necessary to mention experiments with the Walter engine. That motor was powered with the gases generated by the combustion of decalin – a special kind of fuel – in an oxidizing agent (hydrogen peroxide was used) and did not produce any fumes, giving a high speed to the torpedo.

The table above includes only the torpedoes which were most commonly used on Type VII U-boats, not the other – often experimental – models such as Mondfisch, Klipfisch, Zaunbutt and K-butt.

▼ The following pages show the process of loading and stowing what the U-boat crews called 'Eels' – it was not an easy task. However, loading them in a base was relatively simple, as the crew could make full use of shore facilities. (CAW).

Engine output [kW]	Speed [kts]	Fuse	Notes
257/187	40.0/30.0	Pi, Pi2, cont. T23	With and without FAT and LUT devices
74	30.0	Pi, Pi2	
74	30.0	Pi2	FAT II device
74	30.0	Pi2	FAT II device
24	20.0	Pi4a	Acoustic, guided
30	21.5	TZ5, Pi4c	Acoustic, guided
316	45.0	TZ2, TZ6	With LUT II device

► Torpedo transfer on the high seas was not so easy. It had to be provided with floats and towed across from the supply submarine ('Milch Cow') to the U-boat. The boat being rearmed had to partly submerge in order to get the torpedo on deck. (CAW)

► Preparations for loading the torpedo into the U-boat. The loading hatch to the forward torpedo room is open and the torpedomen set the special cradle at the proper angle for transferring the torpedo into the boat. (CAW)

◄ ◄ Making the space for the torpedo under the deck. (CAW)

◄ A torpedo lowered onto the deck by a shoreside crane. (CAW)

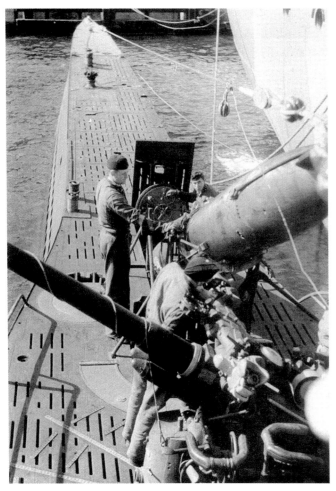

◄ The successive stages of loading a torpedo aboard a U-boat. The 'Eel', destined for the forward tubes, is lowered through a hatch leading to the forward compartment. (CAW)

▶ Another view of the loading of a G7e (T2) electric torpedo aboard *U 55*. The deck gun has been trained to port to keep it out of the way. (CAW)

▶ This torpedo is being loaded propellers-first, indicating that it is for the stern tube. Once aboard, it had to be transferred to the after compartment through the control room.

▶ ▶ Loading the stern tube was easier aboard a Type VIIA as the tube was outside the pressure hull and above the waterline, so the whole procedure could be done from the upper deck.

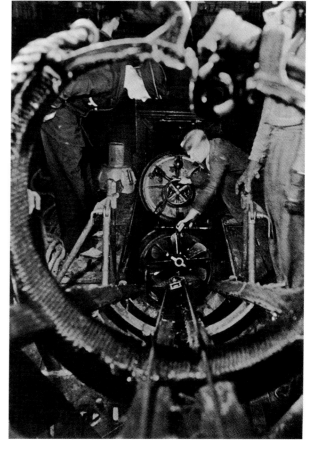

◄ Manhandling a 1600kg (3528lb) torpedo inside a U-boat was no easy task. The German Navy built this mock-up of a forward compartment, fully equipped for loading torpedoes, for its shore training establishment, but the cramped conditions aboard a real submarine meant the reality was far more difficult. (CAW)

◄ Loading a torpedo in a Type VII. (CAW)

► The lifting gear
('flaschenzuge') . . . (CAW)

► . . . and the loading rails.
(CAW)

◄ Actually getting the torpedo into the tube was, relatively speaking, the easiest part of the job. The torpedo slid part-way into the tube still on the rail. (CAW)

◄ Once the tube had 'got hold' of the torpedo, it was uncoupled from the pulley . . . (CAW)

▶ . . . and pushed inside. (CAW)

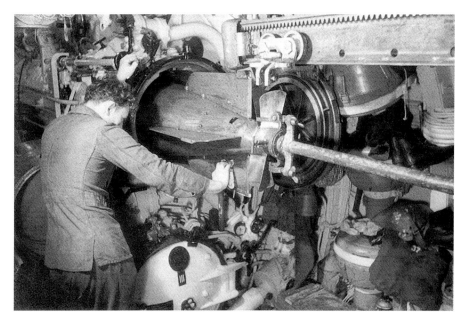

▼ Finally, the torpedo was loaded. (CAW)

▶ All that remained was to close the door of the tube. (CAW)

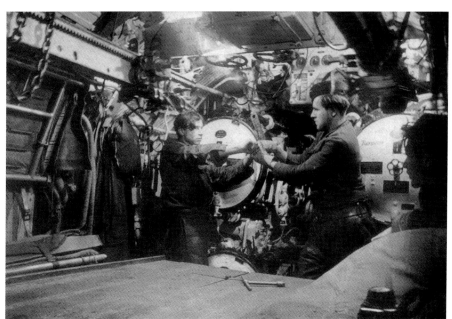

4. Operational Service

GERMANY BEGAN THE WAR with a relatively small number of U-boats – almost all of the major navies of the world, including the other Axis powers Japan and Italy, had more submarines in service. The Kriegsmarine had only fifty-seven U-boats and of course not all of these could be on patrol at any one time. Up to the end of the war a total of 1153 U-boats of all types were built – ranging from the Type II to the advanced Types XVII, XXI and XXIII, and also seven experimental boats with Walther engines. A further 1394 boats were ordered and approximately half of them were actually laid down, but were never launched. The U-boats completed almost 3000 patrols in all theatres of war, sinking 3500 ships totalling 18.3 million tonnes. Although the British figures published after the war are somewhat different – 2452 ships totalling 12.8 million tonnes – this was by any standards an impressive achievement. Apart from merchant vessels the U-boats also sank 175 Allied warships, including two battleships, three aircraft carriers, forty-eight destroyers, thirty-seven smaller escorts and five submarines. Furthermore ten auxiliary cruisers converted from merchantmen and eighteen ships operating under Allied control were also sunk. Nevertheless this impressive record, which had a significant impact on the course of the

war, came at a very high price. The combat was fierce from the very beginning; during the final stages of the war the U-boats operated against overwhelming ASW forces and were finally defeated. Six hundred and thirty-three U-boats were sunk by enemy action at sea, sixty-three were destroyed in air raids in harbour and eighty-five were lost to other causes. Two hundred and eighteen were scuttled by their own crews at the end of the war and 154 were surrendered to the Allies after the war was over. Of 40,000 officers and sailors serving aboard U-boats 28,000 were killed. The others kept fighting until the end with determination and courage, maintaining discipline and high morale until the last days of the war. The Type VII U-boats played a significant role in all operations and together with the larger Type IX they formed the backbone of the U-bootwaffe. Designed as relatively small vessels (larger variants only entered service later) for relatively short-ranged operations, as the war went on they came to operate practically everywhere, including the Atlantic, the Arctic Ocean and the Mediterranean. The time they could actually spend on patrol significantly increased after the Germans conquered France and Norway and established bases in occupied territories, and was further boosted by the introduction of replenishment at sea – which at first

◄ *U 47* is saluted by the crew of the light cruiser *Emden* on its return from sinking the battleship HMS *Royal Oak* in Scapa Flow. (A Jarski collection)

► A new Type VII boat leaves port for sea trials in late 1940. Note that the background has been removed from the photograph by the censor so the location cannot be identified. (CAW)

► In anticipation of the outbreak of war, the Germans had already deployed their U-boats to the shipping lanes in August 1939. This is a Type VIIA boat with a modified tower, most probably *U 33*, preparing to sail. (CAW)

involved standard Type IX boats, then their enlarged variants, and finally the specialised Type XIV supply U-boats, the famous 'Milch Cows'.

When beginning their war in defence of shipping, the British had to recall the lessons learnt against the U-boats in the previous conflict. The submarine offensives of 1915 and 1917 had almost starved Great Britain into surrender. The Admiralty had only defeated this threat by the reintroduction of an old tactic – convoys. This did limit losses of tonnage, but its adoption was in a way a small victory for the U-bootwaffe itself. Plenty of time was wasted – first the ships had to wait for a convoy to be formed, then the convoy followed a route which was often inconvenient for some of its ships, and finally congestion in harbours increased resulting in longer unloading times. This effectively reduced the capacity of the British merchant fleet by one-third, at a time when every ton of cargo was vital for the war effort. After defeating the German surface raiders and neutralising the threat from mines and aviation, the U-boats were all the British had left to deal with. But

this would not be easy. Dönitz had developed a doctrine of submarine warfare based on two concepts: wolfpacks and tonnage war. Since during the early days of the War Dönitz had insufficient U-boats to send organised groups into battle, the only possible tactic was to attack tonnage. This route was followed from the very beginning. The German commander assumed – quite correctly – that when his boat sank an enemy ship, not only would the enemy lose the vessel, cargo and possibly also it crew – all elements that could be sooner or later be replaced – but first of all he would be prevented from using the same ship for transporting further cargoes to the various theatres of war. Therefore the main point of this type of warfare was to sink more ships than enemy could construct, eventually starving Britain, bringing it to its knees, and enabling German victory. This was vital for the Germans as any Allied invasion of the Continent could only be launched from the British Isles, The fall of Britain would terminate all hopes for any 'Normandy' and an Allied victory in the war.

1939–40

Just before the outbreak of war, the U-boats were deployed around the British Isles, so immediately after the start of combat operations they could attack Allied shipping. Up to March 1940, i.e. until the German invasion of Norway, the U-boats sank 222 ships. At that time the submarines mainly targeted vessels sailing alone, leaving the convoys undisturbed. Their operations were also hindered by constantly changing orders from Hitler himself. The reason for those changes were political, for example for some time the German leader prohibited attacks on French vessels, as he hoped to influence France into leaving the anti-German coalition.

Some of the most spectacular successes during the initial phase of war occurred accidentally. One of such cases happened when Oberleutnant Otto Schuhart, in command of the Type VII *U 29*, managed to sink the British aircraft carrier HMS *Courageous* in an impressive attack south-west of Ireland on 17 September 1939. The British warship capsized after being hit by two of the three torpedoes launched and 518 of her crew were lost. The *Courageous* was the first Royal Navy warship sunk during the war, and also the first fleet aircraft carrier lost in action.

Kapitänleutnant Günther Prien, commanding another Type VII boat – *U 47* – achieved another success, though this one was thoroughly planned. Almost miraculously, he managed to slip into Scapa Flow – the most heavily-defended British naval base. This had been attempted twice during the First World War, but both missions ended tragically for the Germans, as the defences proved too strong. Nevertheless Dönitz needed a big success – not so much to deliver an effective blow against the enemy, but

▲ One of the first Type VII U-boats (later referred to as Type VIIAs), most probably *U 33*, leaving its base. Note the layout of the drainage slots in the fore part of the outer casing, different from those on later boats. The tower has already been modified, with ventilation ducts on the sides. On the outbreak of war *U 33* was commanded by Kptlt. Hans-Wilhelm von Dresky, who perished along with his boat on 12 February 1940. By then he had conducted three patrols, sinking ten mostly small vessels, with a total tonnage of 19,261 GRT, and participated in the destruction of one more 3670 GRT vessel. (CAW)

▼ A Type VII following a Kriegsmarine auxiliary vessel off the German coast. (CAW)

▲ The first victim of the U-boats in the Second World War – the liner *Athenia*, sunk on 3 September 1939, the first day of the war in the West. Her sinking caused an uproar all over the world, particularly in the USA, as there had been American citizens on board. The perpetrator, Kptlt. Fritz-Julius Lemp commanding of *U 30*, claimed that he had mistaken the ship for an auxiliary cruiser (though in fact at that time no British auxiliary cruisers were ready for operations and the Germans knew it). (CAW)

rather to boost the reputation of the U-bootwaffe in the eyes of his own superiors. The risky mission was entrusted to Kptlt. Prien, who was a bit older than his fellow U-boat commanders, but also more experienced, as a former merchant officer. Prien accepted the mission without hesitation. A strong desire to participate in an attack against the main British base was expressed in a short conversation between the First Officer of the *U 47* (and later one of the U-bootwaffe's aces) Oblt.z.S. Engelbert Endrass and his opposite number from another boat. When Endrass mentioned that *U 47* would soon depart for a secret mission, his colleague guessed its objective. He only asked 'Emelsman?'. Emelsman had been the commander who was killed during the same mission during the previous war. After surmounting numerous navigational obstacles, Prien managed to get inside the base unnoticed and torpedoed the only battleship present, HMS *Royal Oak*. *U 47* safely returned to base several days later. It was a massive propaganda victory.

After conquering Norway, the Netherlands and France the Germans had the use of their ports, allowing them to establish new naval bases with direct access to the Atlantic. This shortened the distance U-boats had to travel to their operational areas by 450nm, increasing their effective time on patrol. Aircraft and light surface forces were also deployed to these bases, effectively closing the Thames to merchant traffic. On the other side, the British informally occupied Iceland and acquired fifty old American destroyers, boosting its ASW assets. Along with the

'Flower' class corvettes, these ships would play a major role in the war against the U-boats.

As early as June 1940, the Germans launched a major campaign against British shipping lanes from their new bases, and despite the relatively small number of U-boats available, the British losses were massive. The U-boats' targets were now the merchant ships bringing vital cargos to the British Isles, either in convoy or sailing alone. The shortage of escort vessels meant that convoys could only be escorted to a point some 200 miles off the west coast of Ireland, where the warships would meet incoming convoys and escort them into port. Further out, the merchant ships were on their own, but there, 700 miles out into the Atlantic, the U-boats were waiting. Losses increased as Dönitz introduced new tactics in September 1940. When he had been in command of his own submarine in the previous

▼ Two Type VIIAs that became famous in the early days of the war: *U 29* (left) commanded by Kptlt. Otto Schuchart (lower left, in the white cap) sank the aircraft carrier HMS *Courageous* on 17 September 1939; *U 30* (right) under Kptlt. Lemp (upper right, talking to Schuchart) sank the liner *Athenia*. Lemp also hit HMS *Barham* for the first time – on 28 December 1939 – but the British battleship was only damaged. Less than two years later she would be sunk by Kptlt. Freiherr Hans-Diedrich von Tiesenhausen in *U 331*. Before his death on 9 May 1941 aboard *U 110* Lemp had sunk nineteen merchant ships totalling 96,314 GRT (including one neutral Swedish vessel), a single Royal Navy auxiliary of 325 GRT, and damaged three merchantmen totalling 14,317 GRT and one 31,000-ton battleship. This photograph was most probably taken on 4 May 1940, when both boats returned from their fifth patrols. (CAW)

▶ Another view of the same scene. Note the emblem of *U 30* while the boat was under Lemp's command. (CAW)

war, Dönitz had discovered that at night a U-boat was very hard to spot on the surface. Attacking on the surface meant the boat was faster, and once it had slipped through the escort screen it would be at the centre of the convoy and free to torpedo the surrounding vessels, the escorts being hampered by the presence of their own ships. As the autumn nights lengthened, Dönitz implemented 'die Rudeltaktik' – wolfpack tactics. Controlled from head-quarters ashore, groups of several U-boats were deployed in picket lines across the expected route of a convoy and began to search for it. If a boat spotted a convoy, it sent a contact report to HQ and shadowed the convoy without attacking, while other boats were ordered to close in. Despite the fact that there were at this time even fewer U-boats available than in September 1939, these tactics proved extremely effective. This was the beginning of

▶ Three Type VII U-boats, among other German vessels, put to sea. (CAW)

◀ An unidentified Type VIIC photographed from a low-flying aircraft. Note the fully-manned guns. (CAW)

what the U-boat crews called the 'Happy Time'. Between June and October 1940, the U-boats sank 274 ships totalling 14,000,000 GRT, one-fifth of the British merchant fleet in 1939 and the equivalent of five years' peacetime shipyard production. At this rate, Britain would lose the Battle of the Atlantic.

The Royal Navy traditionally followed the doctrine of decisive battles fought by large surface vessels. An officer's career normally began with a period of service aboard a battleship or a cruiser. In the worst case a young officer could start in destroyers, but preferably those which were part of screening forces for capital ships. Assignment to smaller escort destroyers, frigates or corvettes – which were the anti-submarine assets – was considered second-class and was in fact left to reserve officers in time of war. This way of thinking was followed by the Royal Navy's high command so the budget for escort vessel construction was traditionally kept low. There was no great focus on the development of ASW assets, so it was significantly restricted as the budget was mostly spent on the construc-tion of capital ships. The development of the secret ASDIC system, which was gaining momentum at the end of the First World War, all but halted during the inter-war period. The British also learned almost no lessons from the previous German submarine offensives, the only exception being convoys escorted by those few warships available. 'Die Rudeltaktik' therefore took them by surprise. Initially the Royal Navy attempted to solve this problem with its traditional offensive attitude, by deploying special anti-submarine search groups, but this approach was unsuccess-ful in the early stages of the war. Only two years later would such tactics start to be effective and force the U-boats to engage Allied warships, something they initially avoided, and it would ultimately lead to the defeat of the U-bootwaffe. In 1940 it was much too early for such an offensive attitude. A submarine which spotted an approaching task force simply dived and waited until it sailed away, and then attacked defenceless merchant vessels without opposition.

The first attack against a convoy during the Second World War occurred on 15–16 September 1939. The target was the Convoy OB 4, sailing from Liverpool to North America. Kapitänleutnant Johannes Habekost, commanding officer of *U 31* – one of the first Type VII boats, later known as the Type VIIA – spotted enemy ships on 15 September. On the following morning, at 08.15, he positioned his boat for an attack and launched torpedoes, sinking the British ship *Aviemore* (4060 GRT). This was the only vessel lost by OB 4. *U 31* safely returned to base at Wilhelmshaven on 2 October. The further history of this boat was quite interesting, as it had 'two lives'. It sailed under the command of three officers: Kptlt. Rolf Dau, Kptlt. Johannes Habekost and Kptlt. Wilfried Prellberg. On 11 March 1940, during trials, *U 31* was attacked and sunk in the Jade Estuary by a Bristol Blenheim Mk IV aircraft of 82 Squadron RAF. The boat was lost with all hands – forty-eight crewmembers and ten civilian experts. Raised on 24 March 1940, it was restored to serviceable condition and re-commissioned on 30 July 1940, but in November it was depth-charged by the destroyer HMS *Antelope* north-east of Ireland, and this time sank for good with two of its crewmembers. During its double life the U-boat carried out seven combat patrols, sinking eleven ships (totalling 27,751 GRT), two auxiliary warships (160 tonnes) and damaged one 33,950-tonne battleship.

The harsh winter of 1939/1940 reduced the tempo of U-boat operations. The number of submarines in active service had already dropped significantly due to necessary repairs and also losses suffered during the first months of this war. This also decreased the rate of British tonnage losses.

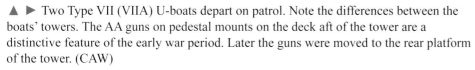
▲ ▶ Two Type VII (VIIA) U-boats depart on patrol. Note the differences between the boats' towers. The AA guns on pedestal mounts on the deck aft of the tower are a distinctive feature of the early war period. Later the guns were moved to the rear platform of the tower. (CAW)

▶ A ship comes alongside a Type VII off the Baltic coast, May 1942. (CAW)

On 24 August 1940 three U-boats – *U 48*, *U 57* and *U 124* – patrolling near the Hebrides, spotted and attacked Convoy HX 65 and after it Convoy HX 65A, both heading from Halifax and New York to Great Britain. The battle took two days and ended on 26 August. Only the Type VII *U 48*, commanded by Korvettenkapitän Hans-Rudolf Rösing (later a flotilla commander) conducted a successful torpedo attack, which sank the *La Brea* (6666 GRT). The same convoy was later also attacked by Luftwaffe aircraft – four He 115s and eight Ju 88s managed to sink a further two ships totalling 16,472 tonnes on 25 August. As has already been said, after their initial attacks the same boats spotted Convoy HX 65A following exactly the same route, and on the following day managed to sink four large ships and damage another. Two of them (*Athelcrest* of 6825 GRT and *Empire Merlin* of 2763 GRT) were sunk by Rösing's *U 48*. Again the destruction was continued by the Luftwaffe which sank two more merchantmen on the following day. *U 48* conducted a total of twelve patrols, sinking fifty-one merchant ships (306,875 GRT) and a single warship, and damaging a further three ships. Withdrawn from service in 1941 after being damaged by the explosion of a ship it had just torpedoed, *U 48* was eventually scuttled by its own crew on 3 May 1945.

The unplanned convoy battles fought thus far had been the first true successes of the German submarine force, which hit the British at exactly the right spot. Although there were attempts to form 'wolfpacks' from the outbreak of war, the shortage of available boats meant that this correct tactic was as yet ineffective. The first, formed on 1 October 1939, was the 'Hartmann' group, which owed its

◄ Lookouts on the bridge. Note the anti-aircraft machine guns. (CAW)

◄ Another view of the bridge of a U-boat on patrol in the Atlantic. On the right is the DF antenna retracted into its housing. (CAW)

▶ When a U-boat was on the surface, there were always four or five lookouts on the bridge, scanning the horizon all round. Both of these photographs were taken in the Mediterranean in the first quarter of 1942. (CAW)

name to its commander, the captain of *U 37*. Six boats left their base, but only three reached the patrol area. The other three had to abort for various reasons, so the entire idea of a joint operation failed completely. The next attempt was made in November and involved *U 38*, *U 41*, *U 43*, *U 47* (Kptlt. Günther Prien) and *U 49* (Kptlt. Kurt von Glosser), of which only the last two were Type VIIs. However, this time they turned out to be quite poor representatives of their type: *U 47* was not ready on time and did not leave its base and *U 49* failed to make contact with the enemy. The groups were searching and attacking targets on their own, but general guidance against detected convoys was conducted personally by Dönitz from his HQ on shore. This ensured better command cohesion and increased the combat effectiveness of the wolfpacks. From June to August 1940 several groups were sent out on patrol. The 'Rösing' group with the Type VIIs *U 48* (Kptlt. Hans-Rudolf Rösing), *U 29* (Kptlt. Otto Schuhart), *U 46* (Kptlt. Engelbert Endrass) and *U 101* (Kptlt. Fritz Frauenheim) unsuccessfully attacked Convoy US 3 west of Spain. Group 'Prien', comprising the Type VIIs *U 47* (Kptlt. Günther Prien), *U 28* (Kptlt. Günther Kuhnke), *U 30* (Kptlt. Fritz-Julius Lemp), *U 32* (Oblt.z.S. Hans Jenisch) and *U 51* (Kptlt. Dietrich Knorr), as well as *U 25* (Type I) and *U 38* (Type IX) operated between 12 and 15 June against Convoy HX 48 south of Ireland, but to no effect. An unnamed group consisting of *U 38* and two Type VIIs – *U 46* and *U 48* – searched for an HX convoy in the same area between 13 and 16 August. Some success was only achieved by another unnamed group composed of *U 65* and the Type VIIs *U 29* (Kptlt. Otto Schuchart), *U 47* (Kptlt. Günther Prien), *U 101* (Kptlt. Fritz Frauenheim) and *U 99* (Kptlt. Otto Kretschmer). It intercepted Convoy SC 2 west of Ireland and between 30 August and 9 September sank five ships – all by Type VIIs (four by *U 46*, one by *U 28*). On 27 September Prien in his *U 47* spotted a convoy west of Ireland. It was HX 72 heading from Halifax and New York for Great Britain and consisted of forty-one ships escorted by the sloop HMS *Lowestoft*, the destroyer HMS *Shikari* and the corvettes HMS *La Malouine*, HMS *Calendula* and HMS *Heartsease*. Upon receiving Prien's report headquarters began to form a group (unnamed) and vector it in on the detected target. Prien, whose boat was at that time assigned to report weather conditions and only had a single torpedo left, tracked the convoy and reported its movements. The first hunter to reach the convoy was the famous Kptlt. Otto Kretschmer in *U 99* who during the night of the 20th/21st sank three ships in consecutive attacks: *Baron Blythswood* (368 GRT), *Elmbank* (5156 GRT, previously damaged by Prien), and *Invershannon* (9154 GRT). The other boats soon followed: the Type IXs *U 32*, *U 46* and *U 65* and several Type VIIs: *U 29* commanded by Otto Schuhart, famous for sinking HMS *Courageous*, *U 46* commanded by Engelbert Endrass, who had been Prien's First Officer at the time of the Scapa Flow raid, Kptlt. Heinrich Bleichrodt's *U 48* and Kptlt. Joachim Schepke's *U 100*. On 21 September Bleichrodt sank the *Blairangus* (4409 GRT) and damaged the

Broompark (5136 GRT). Prien managed to damage the *Elmbank* with his last torpedo – she was later finished off by Kretschmer. Joachim Schepke in *U 100* had the best results, on 21 September managing to sink *Canonesa* (8286 GRT), *Dalcairn* (4606 GRT) and *Torinia* (10,364 GRT), followed on the 22nd by *Empire Airman* (6586 GRT), *Frederick S. Fales* (10,525 GRT), *Scholar* (3940 GRT) and *Simla* (6031 BRT). The last of those sailed under Norwegian colours. To top all that *Collegian* (7886 GRT) was damaged by Hans Jenisch (*U 32*). The hard-working escorts under Captain Knapp were unable to prevent this massacre, despite being reinforced on the 22nd by the destroyers HMS *Scimitar* and HMS *Skate*.

Another convoy battle occurred less than a month later. This time the target was SC 7 heading from Sydney to Great Britain, escorted by three sloops and two corvettes. There were thirty merchant ships. The battle occurred west of Ireland between 16 and 19 October. An unnamed German group, consisting of the Type VIIs *U 48* (Kptlt. Heinrich Bleichrodt), *U 101* (Kptlt. Fritz Frauenheim), *U 46* (Kptlt. Engelbert Endrass), *U 99* (Kptlt. Otto Kretschmer) and *U 100* (Kptlt. Joachim Schepke), and the Type IXs *U 38* and *U 123*, detected the convoy on 16 October. During the first day only the Canadian ship *Trevisa* (1813 GRT) was sunk by the Type IX *U 124*, which joined the operation for a short period, but on following days a genuine massacre took place. On 17 October *U 38* attacked and sank the Greek ship *Aenos* (3554 GRT), and Bleichrodt's *U 48* sank the *Languedoc* (9512 GRT) and *Scoresby* (3843 GRT). The next two days brought kills for the U-boat aces Schepke and Kretschmer. The former damaged two ships: the Dutch *Boeckelo* (2118 GRT) and the British *Shekatika* (5458 GRT), but he had to 'share' them with Karl-Heinz Moehle of *U 123* (a Type IX) who finished them off on 19 October. On 18 October *U 101*'s torpedoes found their way to two British ships: *Creekirk* (3917 GRT) and *Blairsprey* (4155 GRT). The latter ship actually proved a very tough nut to crack. Torpedoed twice – first by *U 101*, then by Schepke's *U 100* on 19 October – she kept going and eventually made it to port! Endrass in *U 46* sank the British ship *Beatus* (4885 GRT) and two Swedish vessels: *Convallaria* (1996 GRT) and *Gunborg* (1572 GRT). A further three casualties were inflicted by Kretschmer (*U 99*) – *Empire Miniver* (6055 GRT) and *Fiscus* (4815 GRT), both British, and one more Greek ship, the *Niritos* (3854 GRT). During the last day of the battle – 19 October – *U 123* finished off the *Boekelo* and *Shekatika* previously damaged by Schepke, as well as the *Clinton* (3106 GRT) and *Sedgepool* damaged by Kretschmer. Kretschmer himself, after damaging the *Clinton*, sank a further three

▶ Rather different clothing for lookouts in the Atlantic – here oilskins were the norm, as waves frequently broke over the bridge. Both photographs were taken in late 1941 or early 1942. The upper one shows *U 96* on its eighth patrol, commanded by Kptlt. Heinrich Lehmann-Willenbrock. (CAW)

merchant vessels: the British *Empire Brigade* (5154 GRT), the Norwegian *Snefjeld* (1643 GRT) and the Greek *Thalia* (5875 GRT). On this day the battle ended. The tactics employed by the U-bootwaffe was now proving effective. The German skippers were starting to master them, despite the rising effectiveness of the enemy. Just after the battle against SC 7, on 19 October, Prien's *U 47* located another formation of forty-nine ships in the same area. This was Convoy HX 79. As all the HX-series, it was heading from Halifax and New York to Great Britain, and was escorted by a quite powerful force consisting of two destroyers, five corvettes, three armed trawlers, a minesweeper and the submarine *O-14*. As soon as they received Prien's report the U-bootwaffe command immediately dispatched its nearest boats to deal with the enemy. This time the group – again unnamed – consisted of Type VIIs only. All the best skippers – Schepke, Prien, Endrass and Bleichrodt – were included. Moreover the battle involved – temporarily – Kptlt. Heinrich Liebe in *U 38* (Type IX) and Kptlt. Günther Kuhnke in *U 28* (Type VII). During the attack, which began on 19 October and continued the following day, twelve ships were sunk and one more was damaged. Liebe sank two, while all the other losses were inflicted by the aces. Endrass (*U 46*) destroyed the British *Ruperra* (3548 GRT) on 19 October and the Swedish *Janus* (9965 GRT) on the 20th. The highest 'score' was achieved by Prien (*U 47*) who on the 19th sank the *Uganda* (4966 GRT), the *Wandby* (4947 GRT) and damaged the *Shirak* (6023 GRT), and on the following day destroyed *La Estancia* (5185 GRT) and *Whitford Point* (5026 GRT), also damaging the *Athelmonarch* (8995 GRT). On the second day of the battle the damaged *Shirak* was finished off by Bleichrodt (*U 48*). Schepke in *U 100* 'scored' on three British ships: *Caprella* (8230 GRT), *Loch Lomond* (5452 GRT) and *Sitala* (6218 GRT).

The last convoy battle of 1940, which for the first time involved a 'wolfpack', occurred between 1 and 3 December. The target was Convoy HX 90. At this moment three convoys were closing in on the Western Approaches: one from Gibraltar (HG 47), another from Cape Breto (SC 13) and finally the aforementioned HX 90. According to the plan the ocean-going escort force was to leave the convoy at a specified location, to be replaced by the warships that had been escorting yet another convoy, OB 251. Due to bad weather in the area, however, the latter force failed to arrive on time, and there was a group of U-boats operating in the area. It consisted of one Type IX, Kptlt. Wolfgang Lüth's *U 43*, six Type VIIs – *U 47* (Kptlt. Günther Prien), *U 52* (Kptlt. Otto Salman), *U 94* (Kptlt. Herbert Kuppisch), *U 95* (Kptlt. Gerd Schreiber), *U 99* (Kptlt. Otto Kretschmer) and *U 101* (Kptlt. Ernst Mengersen) – and also three Italian submarines: the *Argo*, *Reginaldo Giuliani* and *Capittano Tarantini*. *U 101* located

◀ U-boats would frequently attack lone ships on the surface. The threat of the 88mm gun forced the ship to stop. (CAW)

◄ The ship's master would then be ordered to report aboard the U-boat with the ship's papers – the right-hand photograph shows this – after which the ship was usually sunk. These photographs were probably taken in the South Atlantic in late 1942. (CAW)

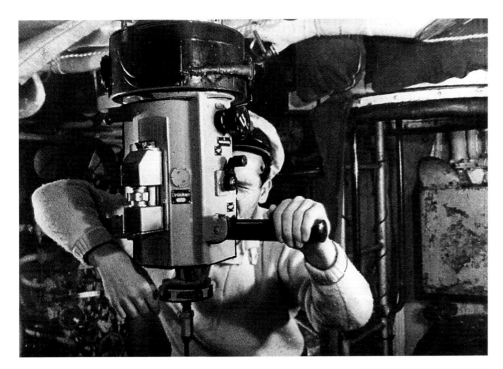

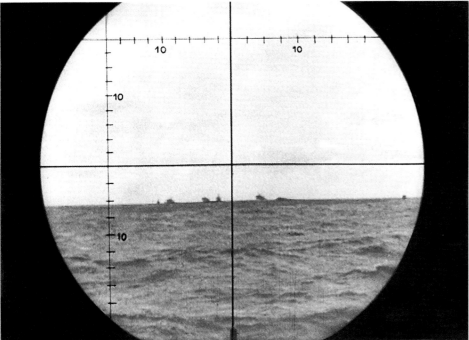

▲ An explosion sealing the fate of the targeted merchant ship. (CAW)

▲ The situation was completely different if a convoy was encountered. The U-boat would get ahead of the convoy on the surface, keeping out of visual range; it then dived in the convoy's path, trying to get into the best possible attack position using the periscope. The upper photograph shows a U-boat commander at his periscope, the lower one the view through it. (CAW)

HX 90 when it had already been left by the original escorts, but not yet met by the escorts coming from OB 251 – they would be unable to catch up with the convoy until the evening – so forty-nine ships loaded with war material were left without any protection. The first to attack were *U 47*, *U 52* and *U 101*. During a dark December day and with rough seas the U-boats easily penetrated the convoy. In the evening of 1 December *U 101* sank the British ship *Appalachee* (8826 GRT) and damaged *Loch Ranza* (4958 GRT). After midnight *U 47* destroyed the Belgian ship *Ville d'Arlon* (7555 GRT) and damaged the British ships *Conch* (8376 GRT) and *Dunsley* (3862 GRT). At the same time *U 52* sank the *Goodleigh* (5448 GRT) and *Tasso* (1586 GRT). Before dawn on 2 December *U 101* attacked

again and torpedoed the *Kavak* (2782 GRT), while *U 95* hit the already damaged *Conch*. The latter target proved really tough – again she did not sink immediately, finally going down on the following day. Otto Kretschmer was doing his best to get to the convoy and participate in the hunting, but his boat was intercepted by the armed merchant cruiser HMS *Forfar* with the rest of the escorting force, or rather what remained of it. Originally it consisted also of two destroyers, but HMCS *St. Laurent* had detached and set off to search for HX 90. Kretschmer decided to engage the warships and, after two hours of manoeuvring and at a cost of five torpedoes, he managed to sink the *Forfar* (16,402 GRT). Then he continued towards the decimated convoy, which did not reach until the morning of

◄ The first spectacular success of the U-bootwaffe: the aircraft carrier HMS *Courageous* sinking on 17 September 1939 after being hit by torpedoes from *U 29* (Type VIIA). (CAW)

◄ Kptlt. Otto Schuchart (left) and his crew accept congratulations aboard *U 29* for sinking the *Courageous*. (CAW)

◄ After returning from the patrol during which the *Courageous* was sunk, *U 29* was visited by Adolf Hitler. (CAW)

► Schuhart accepts congratulations from the Commander-in-Chief of the Kriegsmarine, Grossadmiral Raeder. In all Schuhart sank twelve merchant ships with a total tonnage of 67,277 GRT and a 22,500-ton aircraft carrier. He remained on combat patrols until the end of 1940, when he was transferred to training and staff duties. Appointed commander of the 21st Flotilla in June 1943, he survived the war. (CAW)

3 December, and finally dealt with the *Conch*, previously damaged by Prien and Schreiber (*U 95*). Also on the 2nd Kuppisch in *U 94* sank the *Stirlingshire* (6022 GRT) and *Wilhemina* (6725 GRT). All attacks performed by the Italian submarine *Argo* failed. Another Italian boat – *Tarantini* – became the first submarine to be chased from the convoy by the delayed escorts which finally managed to catch up. Roughly at the same time *U 43* established contact with OB 251 – the escorting force of which was supposed to pass to HX 90 – and sank two of its ships. *U 43*, *U 53*, *U 94* and *U 99* tried to find yet another convoy, SC 13, but it changed course to avoid the bad weather and luckily also avoided the German U-boats. The only submarine to succeed against this formation was the Italian *Argo*, which managed to find it and sink one ship. The battle finally came to an end on 3 December with the sinking of one more ship from HX 90, but this time it was done by the Luftwaffe.

▼ A propaganda photograph intended to encourage young men to join the U-bootwaffe: a submarine leaves its base on patrol. Note the censor's intervention – the lighthouse at the harbour entrance has been painted over to make the base impossible to identify. (CAW)

◀ Less than a month after Schuhart's success, on 14 October 1939 *U 47* (Type VIIB) commanded by Kptlt. Günther Prien slipped into the Home Fleet's base at Scapa Flow, sank the battleship HMS *Royal Oak* and escaped unharmed. This was a major blow to British pride. (CAW)

◀ Prien's exploit delighted the Germans and significantly boosted the prestige of the U-bootwaffe. Prien became famous and was the first U-boat commander to be awarded the Knight's Cross of the Iron Cross. He was lost with *U 47* and all hands in unexplained circumstances in the North Atlantic some time after 7 March 1941. By then he had sunk thirty merchant ships totalling 162,769 GRT and the 29,150-ton *Royal Oak*. The photograph shows Prien surrounded by his crew on the bridge of *U 47*. (CAW)

▲ Prien on the bridge of *U 47*. The boat's charging bull emblem, adopted after the Scapa Flow raid, can be seen on the lower left. This gave Prien his nickname of 'Der Stier von Scapa Flow' (The Bull of Scapa Flow), and soon appeared on the other boats of the 7th Flotilla. The emblem was apparently the idea of Prien's first officer, the then Oberleutnant zur See Engelbert Endrass. (CAW)

▲ Two photographs of Prien at propaganda events, meeting the German people. He has had a shave by now, and is wearing the regulation black cap. The distinctive commander's white cap was only worn aboard ship. (CAW)

1941

1941 saw an increase in the intensity of U-boat operations and a resulting increase in Allied tonnage losses, but also saw an increase in the strength of the convoy escort forces, which inflicted heavier losses on the U-bootwaffe: the price of their victories was starting to rise. Both the Royal Navy and the Royal Canadian Navy were growing stronger, and were dispatching their escorts further west and east into the Atlantic respectively, until in May an eastbound convoy was escorted for the entire length of its transatlantic voyage for the first time. The first westbound convoy was so escorted in June, closing the 'black hole' in the middle of

the ocean where the merchant ships were unprotected and the U-boats could attack them with impunity. Furthermore, as there were US-flagged ships in the convoys, at the same time the United States Navy began to conduct anti-submarine patrols near the North American coast with three destroyer flotilla and two squadrons of seaplanes. The Germans were informed of these patrols through diplomatic channels and were told to withdraw their U-boats from these areas. Although the US ships were forbidden to engage U-boats (except of course in self-defence), these patrols did have an effect and reduced the demands on British escort forces which no longer had to worry about American coastal waters. In May, the

Americans established a base in Canada and another one a month later in Iceland. Finally, in September the US Navy took over full responsibility for escorting convoys containing US ships in the Western Atlantic.

Also in 1941 the British began to fit radar and special star shell launchers on some of their ships, increasing their effectiveness in night-time ASW and going some way to depriving the U-boats of one of their major advantages, making it more dangerous for them to attack on the surface under cover of darkness. These upgraded ships, now with better-trained and more experienced crews, began to achieve more and more successes, and the tactic of convoys also guaranteed that the U-boats would be drawn to them, making them easier to find than when they had been ranging the oceans individually hunting for ships sailing alone. Searching for individual boats in the whole ocean with special task forces had been futile and was abandoned, until more capable ships came into service. Ideally, escort forces should be split into two types: the close screening forces which formed a dense barrier around the convoy, and mobile support groups, which could reinforce the close escort when necessary. Detecting a U-boat stalking merchant ships was significantly facilitated by the use of radar, but this did not yet guarantee success. In theory, all the escort had to do to destroy a submarine was force it to crash-dive, tracking it with ASDIC and then attack it accurately with depth charges, but this was easier said than done. First of all, a depth charge had to explode very close to its target in order to sink it, and secondly the charges were dropped or thrown from the stern of the attacking ship, after she had passed over the target and lost ASDIC contact. The U-boat therefore had the chance to execute a last-minute evasive manoeuvre, such as diving deeper or making a sudden turn, getting out of the depth charges' lethal radius. This problem was only solved by the introduction of forward-throwing launchers such as 'Hedgehog', which allowed the ship to attack a submarine while it still had it on sonar. With traditional depth charges, if the first attack failed, all the escorts could do was to repeat their attack runs and try to keep the U-boat down deep and away from the convoy. If the U-boat could be kept down long enough (36–48 hours), its batteries would be exhausted and it would be forced to surface. But keeping the escorts tied up with one attack for such a long time would make the convoy vulnerable to other U-boats'. This is exactly why the second type of escorting force – a mobile group – was needed. It could hunt and destroy U-boats, while the ships of the close screen stayed with the merchant ships. But the full application of this scheme would only come towards the end of the war.

Both the British and the Germans made mistakes in the early years of the war. The former failed to reassign more ships – particularly destroyers – from other theatres of operations and escort forces for capital ships, while the latter, hoping for a peace agreement with Great Britain, stopped the U-bootwaffe development programme. When production was finally increased and accelerated it was already too late – thanks to this mistake the Allies were

given some of the time they so badly needed to get their second wind. Even though by April 1941 the Germans had constructed 230 new U-boats, they could only deploy thirty-two of them on patrol at any one time. In 1941 the U-boats sank a total of 432 ships – less than in 1940 although the total tonnage was the same at two million GRT – for the loss of twenty-seven of their own number. This was no longer the 'Happy Time'. There were nine major convoy battles involving Type VIIs in 1941. The numbers of this class of boat were growing, with the Type VII now outnumbering the Type IX by three to one. This was because the Germans had noted that the smaller boats

▲ *U 47* prior to leaving for its ninth patrol. Prien – then at the peak of his fame – is still on the pier, saying his farewells. He is wearing a forage cap, grey jacket and a black scarf. Lorient, 3 November 1940. (CAW)

► The U-bootwaffe's greatest ace – Kptlt. Otto Kretschmer, sometimes known as the 'Tonnage King'. During his career Kretschmer commanded three U-boats: *U 35* (Type VIIA, before the war), *U 23* (Type VIIB, eight patrols, eight ships sunk) and *U 99* (Type VIIB, also eight patrols). He enjoyed his greatest successes in *U 99*. In total he sank forty merchant ships totalling 208,954 GRT, three auxiliary cruisers totalling 46,440 GRT and one 1375-ton destroyer, captured one 2136-GRT ship and damaged eight merchantmen totalling 37,965 GRT. Two more merchant vessels – total 15,513 GRT – were considered lost. On 17 December 1939 Kretschmer received the Iron Cross, 1st Class, on 4 August 1940 the Knight's Cross, on 4 November 1940 the Knight's Cross with Oak Leaves, and on 26 December 1941 the Knight's Cross with Oak Leaves and Swords. The last of those decorations was awarded when Kretschmer was already a prisoner of war. He was captured on 17 March 1941 when *U 99* was sunk south-east of Iceland by the British destroyer *Walker.* In the POW camp Kretschmer, known as 'Silent Otto', established an intelligence network. After the war he served in the Bundesmarine, and between 1965 and 1969 he was Chief of Staff of the NATO command COMNAVBALTAP (Allied Forces Baltic Approaches).

were more resistant to depth-charge damage than their larger brothers.

The first convoy attacked by U-boats in 1941 was SC 26, consisting of twenty-two ships heading from Sydney to Great Britain. On 1 April *U 76* – a Type VII commanded by Oblt.z.S. Friedrich von Hippel – spotted the ships escorted by the armed merchant cruiser HMS *Worcestershire*, the destroyers HMS *Wolverine* (soon to become a famous U-boat killer) and HMS *Havelock*, the sloop HMS *Scarborough* and the corvette HMS *Arbutus*. Following von Hippel's sighting report the German command immediately established a patrol line on the expected route of the convoy. It consisted exclusively of Type VIIs, which were *U 46* (Kptlt. Engelbert Endrass), *U 69* (Kptlt. Jost Metzler), *U 73* (Kptlt. Helmut Rosenbaum), *U 74* (Kptlt. Eitel-Friedrich Kentrat), *U 76* – which was shadowing the convoy – *U 97* (Kptlt. Udo Heilmann), *U 98* (Kptlt. Robert Gysae) and *U 101* (Kptlt. Ernst Mengersen). But *U 76* lost contact with the convoy and it was not picked up again until the evening of the next day by *U 74*. Its report attracted the closest U-boats in the line: *U 46*, *U 69* and *U 73*. On this day Endrass sank the *British Reliance* (7000 GRT), and on 3 April he destroyed *British Viscount* (6895 GRT) and the Belgian ships *Indie* (5409 GRT) and *Westpool* (5724 GRT), and also damaged *Alderpool* (4313 GRT), which was later finished off by Rosenbaum's *U 73*. *U 74* damaged HMS *Worcestershire* (11,402 GRT) and sank the Greek ship *Leonidas Z. Cambanis* (4274 GRT). After these attacks the convoy was ordered to scatter by its commodore, but *U 94* (Kptlt. Herbert Kuppisch) managed to find the largest group of ships that night and vectored *U 98* on to it. *U 94* itself sank the British ship *Harbledown* (5414 GRT), while *U 98* destroyed the Norwegian ship *Helle* (2467 GRT) and the British *Welcombe* (5122 GRT). *U 76* also took its turn, attacking and sinking the British ship *Athenic* (5351 GRT), but on 5 April it became a target itself after being spotted while surfaced, charging its batteries, by the destroyer HMS *Wolverine*. The U-boat crash-dived and tried to evade, but an accurately-aimed depth charge damaged it heavily. Another accurate pattern of depth charges dropped by the sloop HMS *Scarborough* finished *U 76* off. The submarine managed to surface for a short time, allowing its crew to abandon ship. The corvette HMS *Arbutus* picked up all but one of the survivors.

A month later – on 7 May – *U 94* intercepted Convoy OB 318 heading from Liverpool to North America. It consisted of thirty-eight ships protected by the 7th Escort Group – three destroyers, five corvettes, a sloop and an armed trawler. In mid-Atlantic the 7th Group was supposed to hand the convoy over to the 3rd Escort Group, which consisted of the armed merchant cruiser HMS *Ranpura*, three destroyers, four corvettes and two armed trawlers, returning from the west. After British intelligence managed to intercept the wireless message from *U 95*, which reported the detection of Convoy SC 29 further to the west, the Admiralty ordered OB 318 to alter its heading to avoid the expected ambush. However, this change of course sent the ships straight towards the patrolling *U 94*. The

convoy was spotted by the U-boat while it was expecting to swap escort groups. Part of the 7th Escort Group stayed with the ships throughout the next day. *U 94* (Kptlt. Kuppisch) which shadowed the formation from astern, attacked and sank the Norwegian ship *Eastern Star* (5668 GRT) and the British *Ixion* (10,263 GRT). Soon it was joined by *U 201* (Oblt.z.S. Adalbert Schnee) and *U 556* (Kptlt. Herbert Wohlfarth) – both Type VIIs – and one Type IX, *U 110* (Kptlt. Lemp). During the attack, the destroyers HMS *Bulldog* and HMS *Amazon* spotted *U 94*'s periscope and managed to damage the boat. On 8 May the escorts were joined by the four corvettes and a trawler of the 3rd Group; the remaining ships of the 7th Group departed. In the evening of the same day *U 110* established contact with OB 318 and vectored *U 201* onto the target. On the morning of 9 May, after agreeing upon tactics, both skippers attacked the convoy. *U 110* managed to sink two British ships, *Bengore Head* (2609 GRT) and *Esmond* (4976 GRT), while *U 201* damaged *Empire Cloud* (5969 GRT) and sank *Gregalia* (5802 GRT), both also British ships. During this engagement, an amazing event took place. Two accurate depth-charge patterns from the corvette HMS *Aubretia* forced *U 110* to surface very close to the destroyers HMS *Bulldog* and HMS *Broadway*. Instead of ramming it, the latter destroyer sent a boarding party to the enemy submarine and captured it. This was kept secret practically until the end of the war, so the Germans could not learn that their codes – which fell into Allied hands – had been compromised. In the meantime, *U 201* was also depth-charged by HMS *Amazon* which attacked together with the corvettes. After five hours of repeated attacks Schnee managed to finally escape his pursuers and

◀ Two photographs taken in early 1941 showing the Type VIIB *U 101*, commanded by Kptlt. Ernst Mengersen, who took the boat over from Kptlt. Fritz Frauenheim in November 1940. The boat is approaching a Sperrbrecher pathfinder ship. (Top: CAW. Bottom: A Jarski collection)

► The Type VIIC's very low freeboard left its decks frequently awash, even in moderate seas. (CAW)

▼ Two U-boats rendezvous at sea, far from any shipping lanes. Only in such areas would the crews dare to use a dinghy. Nonetheless the gun crews are closed up. (CAW)

continued with his patrol, despite his boat being damaged. On the night of 10 May *U 556* damaged the British ship *Aelybryn* (4986 GRT) and sank the Belgian *Gand* (5086 GRT) and the British *Empire Caribou* (4861 GRT).

On 19–20 May a fairly large group of U-boats encountered Convoy HX 126 which had a weak escort, consisting only of the armed merchant cruiser HMS *Aurania* and the submarine HMS *Tribune*. The attacking group consisted of two Type IXs (*U 111* and *U 56*) and the following Type VIIs: *U 94* (Kptlt. Kuppisch) which located the convoy and torpedoed two ships – the Norwegian *John P. Pedersen* (6128 GRT) and British *Norman Monarch* (4718 GRT) – and then lost contact; *U 556* (Kptlt. Wohlfarth), which after establishing contact on 20 May sank three British ships – *Cockaponset* (5995 GRT), *Darlington Court* (4974 GRT) and *British Security* (8470 GRT); *U 98* (Kptlt. Gysae) which sank the British *Rothermere* (5356 GRT); and *U 93* (Kptlt. Claus Korth) which engaged on 20 May together with the returning *U 94* and *U 46*. On 22 May *U 557* (Kptlt. Ottokar Paulssen) and *U 74* (Kptlt. Eitel-Friedrich Kentrat) also arrived, but they did not sink any Allied ships. In all the convoy lost nine ships with a total tonnage of 51,862 GRT.

On 26 July *U 68*, the only Type IX in the group, located Convoy OG 69 heading from Great Britain to Gibraltar. It should be noted that this convoy had already been tracked by the B-Dienst (the German signals intelligence service) and spotted by aircraft. U-bootwaffe command immediately dispatched eight of its boats to the area, sending six more to intercept another convoy detected on the same day – SL 80. However, the latter managed to out-

◄ The U-boats' principal targets were merchant ships, but it was attacks on warships that made the best propaganda for the German public. On 4 July 1940 a press release was distributed claiming that Kptlt. Engelbert Endrass (pictured) in *U 46* had torpedoed the new British aircraft carrier HMS *Illustrious*, but there are no records of any such attack in British archives. (CAW)

◄ Endrass had been First Officer aboard *U 47* during the Scapa Flow attack, and in May 1940 he was appointed commander of the Type VIIB *U 46*. On his first patrol he sank five ships, one of which was the auxiliary cruiser HMS *Carinthia*, and another five on his second patrol, including another auxiliary cruiser, HMS *Dunvegan Castle*, but his boat was damaged. On his return he was awarded the Knight's Cross, and five patrols later got the Oak Leaves. In September 1941 he left *U 46* and a month later took command of the Type VIIC *U 567*. On 21 December 1941, on its second patrol, *U 567* was sunk with all hands in depth-charge attacks by the British sloop *Deptford* and the corvette *Sapphire* off the Azores. The boat went down with all hands. By then Endrass had destroyed nineteen merchant vessels (81,164 GRT) and two auxiliary cruisers (35,284 GRT). (CAW)

manoeuvre the Germans and the attack was cancelled, but OG 69 was not so lucky. *U 68*, guided by an aircraft, established visual contact with the ships at 17.45. Between 19.30 and 20.40 the convoy was engaged by the Type VIIs *U 74* (Kptlt. Wolfgang Kaufman), *U 71* (Kptlt. Walter Flaschsenberg), *U 561* (Kptlt. Robert Bartels), *U 562* (Oblt.z.S. Herwig Collmann) and *U 331* (Kptlt. Freiherr Hans-Diedrich von Tiesenhausen), but all of them were chased off by the escorts. Before midnight two more boats arrived: *U 203* (Type VII, Kptlt. Rolf Mützelburg) and *U 126* (Type IX). The attacking U-boats launched a total of twenty-five torpedoes and sank seven ships (11,303 GRT in all). In return *U 79*, *U 203* and *U 562* were depth-charged. *U 562* was seriously damaged and had to return to base. Two ships were sunk by *U 126*. Mützelburg in *U 203* got three: the British *Hawkinge* (2475 GRT) and *Lapland* (1330 GRT) and the Swedish *Noria* (1516 GRT). Kauffman (*U 79*) sank the *Kellwyn* (1459 GRT) and Bartels (*U 561*) the *Wrotham* (1884 GRT). On 28 July the battle concluded with *U 203*'s attack.

On 17 August the Type VII *U 201*, commanded by Schnee, located the twenty-seven ships of Convoy OG 71, sailing from Great Britain to Gibraltar, escorted by a destroyer, six corvettes, a sloop and an armed trawler. On 20 August the escort was reinforced by two more destroyers and by yet another the next day. *U 106*, the only Type IX in the force, after taking over shadowing the convoy from *U 201*, lost contact in the late evening of 19 August, after being chased off by the escorts. After two days of searching the convoy was sighted again by Schnee,

OPERATIONAL SERVICE 1941 113

▶ *U 46* returning to St Nazaire after its second patrol under Endrass (on the left, in the white cap), on 21 September 1940. Note the damage suffered on 27 August, after attacking the auxiliary cruiser *Dunvegan Castle*. (CAW)

▼ Endrass and *U 46* welcomed back to Kiel on 26 August 1941 after his eighth 32-day patrol. (CAW)

guided by an aircraft. During the battle, which lasted until 23 August, eight ships were sunk together with two of the escorts. On the 19th Schnee (*U 201*) sank *Aguila* (3235 GRT) and *Ciscar* (1809 GRT), Kptlt. Hans Heidtmann (*U 559*) sank the *Alva* (1584 GRT) and *U 204* commanded by Kptlt. Walter Kell sank the Norwegian destroyer KNM *Bath*. On 22 August Oblt.z.S. Reinhard 'Teddy' Suhren (*U 564*) sank the Irish ship *Clonlara* (1209 GRT), the British *Empire Oak* (484 GRT) and the corvette HMS *Ziania* (900 tons), and Schnee destroyed the British ships *Aldergrove* (1974 GRT) and *Stork* (787 GRT). On the same day Oblt.z.S. Topp in *U 552* sank one more vessel – the Norwegian merchant ship *Spind* (2129 GRT).

The next major engagement took place in September. On the 28th the 'Markgraf' group commenced operations on the convoy routes south-east of Iceland. It consisted of four Type IXs – *U 38*, *U 43*, *U 105* and *U 501* – and eleven Type VIIs: *U 81* (Kptlt. Friedrich Guggenberger, a Bavarian who would become famous after sinking HMS *Ark Royal*), *U 82* (Kptlt. Siegfrid Rollmann), *U 84* (Kptlt. Horst Uphoff), *U 85* (Oblt.z.S. Eberhard Greger), *U 202* (Kptlt. Hans Linder), *U 207* (Oblt.z.S. Fritz Meyer), *U 432* (Kptlt. Heinz-Otto Schultze), *U 433* (Oblt.z.S. Hans Ey), *U 569* (Kptlt. Hans-Peter Hinsch) and *U 652* (Oblt.z.S. Georg-Werner Fraatz). Later on the group was joined by more Type VIIs: *U 372* (Kptlt. Heinz-Joachim Neumann), *U 373* (Oblt.z.S. Paul-Karl Loeser), *U 552* (Kptlt. Erich Topp), *U 572* (Kptlt. Heinz Hirsacker) and *U 575* (Kptlt. Günther Heydemann). The British, who thanks to wireless

◄ After serving aboard *U 46*, Topp commanded *U 57* and then *U 552*, both Type VIICs, conducting four patrols in the former and eight in the latter. He sank thirty-five merchant ships totalling 197,460 GRT and one warship, the destroyer USS *Reuben James*, attacked on 31 October 1941 when the USA was still technically neutral. Topp survived the war, later rising to the rank of Konteradmiral in the Bundesmarine. He was the third most effective U-boat commander, after Otto Kretschmer and Wolfgang Lüth. (CAW)

▲ Two friends: Kptlt. Erich Topp (left, then CO of *U 57*) and Endrass. Their friendship dated back to when Topp had been Endrass' First Officer aboard *U 46*. (CAW)

▼ *U 552*, commanded by Topp, leaves St-Nazaire for its fourth combat patrol, 25 May 1941. (CAW)

► Late 1941 saw several spectacular successes by U-boats, which were fully exploited by German propaganda. On 13 November the aircraft carrier HMS *Ark Royal* was torpedoed off Gibraltar and sank some hours later. The submarine was *U 81*, commanded by Kptlt. Friedrich Guggenberger on his third combat patrol. (CAW)

► Guggenberger (on the left, in service cap). *Ark Royal* was his third kill. In all he sank fifteen merchant ships with a total tonnage of 43,098 GRT (five of them in command of the Type IX *U 513*), one auxiliary Free French warship of 1150 GRT and a British aircraft carrier of 22,600 tons. In 1943, after his *U 513* had been sunk, Guggenberger was captured by the Allies and survived the war. On the right is Kptlt. Heinz Schomburg, who by contrast only managed to sink one 39-ton vessel during his six Mediterranean patrols in *U 561* (Type VIIC). (CAW)

intercepts knew about the prepared ambush, ordered Convoys ON 10, ON 11, SC 41, HX 146 and HX 147 to alter their routes in order to avoid the area patrolled by the enemy submarines. The German command in turn soon realised that no enemy vessels were appearing where 'Markgraf' was concentrated, so it ordered the boats to disperse over a wider area. This was the right decision. Convoy SC 42 fell into the enlarged trap – it could not alter course any further due to stormy weather as well as the edge of the pack ice. It was a large convoy, with sixty-four merchant ships protected by the Canadian escort group EG 24, which consisted of the destroyer HMCS *Skeena* and three corvettes. On 9 September *U 85* spotted and immediately attacked the convoy, but its torpedoes missed. More U-boats closed on the convoy during the night. *U 81*, *U 82* and *U 432* sank one ship each – *U 81* while it was still 9 September. *U 652* damaged the British ships *Baron Pentland* (which would be finished off by the Type VII *U 372* nine days later) and *Tahchee* (6508 GRT) which was subsequently towed to port by one of the escorts. On 10 September *U 432* took over shadowing the convoy and sank three ships. *U 85* attacked twice and sank one ship in daylight, but then it was depth-charged by the escorts and suffered extensive damage. *U 501* was sunk by the corvettes HMCS *Moosejaw* and HMCS *Chambly*, which arrived to reinforce the escorting force. On 11 September further Allied reinforcements arrived – these were warships previously escorting convoys which had reached their destinations: three corvettes and a minesweeper from HX 147 and British Group EG 2 of five destroyers from ON 13.

Also British aircraft appeared providing aerial cover to the embattled convoy. As a result *U 207* was lost during the attack. During the night the skilful escorts managed to keep the Germans away from their charges. Only two boats – *U 43* and *U 84* – managed to penetrate the screen, but their attacks proved ineffective. Extraordinarily bad weather helped the Allies, making further attacks by the U-boats impossible. Eventually the battle ended on 14 September, although on 16 and 19 September *U 98* and *U 372* sank two more stragglers. The overall result was sixteen ships lost from SC 42 (68,259 GRT) at a price of

two U-boats – *U 207* (Type VII) and *U 501* (Type IX). The ship sunk by *U 98* on 16 September had not been part of the convoy. All the Allied merchant ships lost were sunk by Type VIIs:

- On 9 September *U 81* sank *Empire Springbuck* (5591 GRT).
- On 10 September *U 432* sank the British *Muneric* (5229 GRT), the Norwegian *Stargard* (1113 GRT) and the Dutch *Winterswijk* (3205 GRT), *U 652* damaged the British ships *Baron Pentland* (3410 GRT), finished off by *U 372* on 19 September, and *Tahchee* (6508 GRT) later towed into port by the corvette HMCS *Orillia*, *U 81* sank the British *Sally Mærsk* (3252 GRT), *U 82* sank the British *Empire Hudson* (7465 GRT), and *U 85* the British *Thistleglen* (4748 GRT).
- On 11 September *U 82* sank three British ships, *Bulysses* (7519 GRT), *Empire Crossbill* (5463 GRT) and *Gypsum Queen* (3915 GRT), and damaged the Swedish *Scania* (1999 GRT) later finished off by *U 202*, *U 207* sank two British merchant vessels, *Berury* (4924 GRT) and *Stoepool* (4803 GRT), *U 432* sank the Swedish ship *Garm* (1231 GRT), and *U 433* damaged the Norwegian *Bestum*
- On 16 September *U 98* sank *Jedmoor*, a British ship from another convoy which had the bad luck to steer too close to the action.
- On 19 September *U 372* finished off *Baron Pentland*, previously damaged by *U 652*.

On 19 September 1941 an Italian submarine and a Luftwaffe aircraft located Convoy HG 73 and began to shadow it. The convoy consisted of twenty-five ships heading from Gibraltar to Great Britain and had a relatively strong escort consisting of a destroyer, two destroyer escorts, a sloop, eight corvettes and a fighter-catapult ship. An aircraft tracking the convoy directed *U 124* (Type IX) and *U 203* (Type VIIC) onto it during the night. In consecutive attacks they managed to sink seven ships: *U 124* one on 25 September and three on the 26th and *U 203* – commanded by Kptlt. Rolf Mützelburg – two

▲ HMS *Barham* and her killer – Kptlt. Freiherr Hans-Diedrich von Tiesenhausen, CO of *U 331* (Type VIIC). *Barham* was the first ship sunk by von Tiesenhausen, who later also managed to destroy an American auxiliary warship during Operation 'Torch'. (CAW)

▲ HMS *Audacity* – the world's first escort carrier – was sunk on 21 December 1941 after a short but surprisingly effective career by *U 751* (Type VIIC, Kptlt. Gerhard Bigalk), which hit the ship with three torpedoes, while she was escorting Convoy HG 76. The carrier sank in just ten minutes, 500 miles west of Cape Finisterre. (FAA Museum)

◄ Artist's impression of *Barham* sinking. The battleship was hit by three torpedoes on 25 November 1941, fired from a range of less than 700m (766 yards) so they all hit in close proximity to each other. The battleship immediately took on a list, while the U-boat fled, pursued by the escorts. Then *Barham*'s magazines suddenly exploded and she sank, taking 861 men with her. However, von Tiesenhausen was not aware he had sunk the ship, and the British did not publicise their loss, so the news did not get out for another two months. (CAW)

British ships, *Avoceta* (3442 GRT) and *Lapwing* (1348 GRT), and the Norwegian *Varangberg* (2842 GRT). Before that Schnee in *U 201* had sunk the British *Margareta* (3103 GRT), the Norwegian *Siremalm* (2468 GRT) and the fighter-catapult ship HMS *Springbank* (5155 GRT). *U 371* (a Type VIIC) which had been the first to spot the convoy, failed to get into a good attacking position and did not sink any vessels in this battle. On 28 September the Germans disengaged as they had run out of torpedoes.

A month later, on 15 October, a two-day battle commenced against Convoy SC 48 with fifty-two ships heading from Sidney for Great Britain. It was escorted by the Canadian EG 4.1.15 group commanded by Lt Cdr Davis with the destroyer HMCS *Columbia*, the British corvette HMS *Gladiolus*, a Free French vessel of the same type – the *Mimosa* – and five more Canadian corvettes. On the German side twelve U-boats took part: two Type IXs – *U 103* and *U 502* – and ten Type VIIs: *U 77* (Kptlt. Heinrich Schonder), *U 101* (Kptlt. Ernst Mengersen), *U 208* (Oblt.z.S. Alfred Schlieper), *U 374* (Oblt.z.S. Unno von Fischel), *U 432* (Kptlt. Heinz-Otto Schultze), *U 553* (Kptlt. Karl Thurmann), *U 558* (Kptlt. Gunther Krech), *U 568* (Kptlt. Joachim Preuss), *U 573* (Kptlt. Heinrich Heinsohn) and *U 751* (Kptlt. Gerhard Bigalk). At this time the British were using wireless intercepts very effectively to detect U-boats. Simultaneously the US Navy – technically still neutral – started to actively participate in escorting convoys in the North Atlantic. American warships would take over escorting ships from the Canadians and protect them until they rendezvoused with British forces. In this case the radio intercepts had already revealed the position of the German boats on 9 October, allowing SC 48 to be re-routed away from the enemy. The patrol line which the Allies tried to outmanoeuvre consisted of *U 109*, *U 208*, *U 374*, *U 502*, *U 553*, *U 568* and *U 573*. Nevertheless soon

▲ Bigalk (left) and another U-boat commander talk with the commander of the 7th Submarine Flotilla (7. Unterseebootsflotille), KKpt. Herbert Sohler. Bigalk was killed on 17 July 1942 when *U 751* was sunk with all hands by a British aircraft in the Atlantic, south-west of Cape Ortegal. By then Bigalk had sunk five merchant ships totalling 21,412 GRT and the 11,000-ton HMS *Audacity*. (CAW)

▲ *U 751* enters St-Nazaire upon its return from its fourth patrol, which only lasted eleven days, 16 December 1941. That same day, Bigalk received the Iron Class 1st Class and the Knight's Cross for sinking HMS *Audacity*. Curiously, HMS *Audacity* had previously been the German cargo liner *Hannover*, taken over by the British in the Caribbean in 1939. (CAW)

more German submarines arrived in the area – *U 73*, *U 77*, *U 101*, *U 432*, *U 558* and *U 751*. This allowed the line deployed across the anticipated convoy route to be extended considerably. Thanks to this, during the night of 15 October the Type VII *U 568* located the Allied convoy. Immediately after spotting the enemy ships, Kptlt. Thurmann in *U 553* attacked and sank the Norwegian merchant vessel *Ila* (1583 GRT) and the British *Silvercedar* (4354 GRT). Then he guided more U-boats to the convoy.

◀ In order to increase the time they could spend on patrol, U-boats were replenished with fuel, food and torpedoes at sea, at rendezvous points well away from the shipping lanes and out of range of Allied aircraft. While waiting for the supply ship, the crew of this Type VIIC amuse themselves with a swimming competition. (CAW)

U 553 was, however, discovered while taking up position for another attack and was driven away by the destroyer HMCS *Columbia*, but *U 568* took over shadowing the convoy. The Admiralty reacted promptly to the discovered threat and ordered the British group EG 3 – scheduled to relieve the Canadians on 17 October – to get to the convoy as soon as possible. Two corvettes from the escort of Convoy ON 25 and three destroyers relieving the escorts of TC 14 were also dispatched to assist. But as the battle against SC 48 had already begun and all the reinforcements were still quite far away, the British decided to order the nearby Convoy SC 24 to scatter and sent its escorts to assist the embattled SC 48. There were also some American destroyers present, but their inexperienced commanders proved unable to prevent German attacks, despite several attempts. To make things worse they took position too close to the convoy and fired star shell, illuminating the targets for the U-boat commanders. Nine ships were sunk. On 16 October *U 568* sank the British *Empire Heron* (6023 GRT). On 17 October *U 432* sank the Norwegian *Barfonn* (9739 GRT) and the Greek *Evros* (5283 GRT), *U 553* the Panamanian *Bold Venture* (3222 GRT) and *U 558* sank the Norwegian ships *Erviken* (6595 GRT) and *Rym* (1369 GRT), the British *W.C. Teagle* (5283 GRT) and the corvette HMS *Gladiolus* (925 tonnes). *U 568* damaged the destroyer USS *Kerarny*, the first American warship to be hit by a U-boat in the Second World War. On 18 October, when the battle had practically ended and British aircraft had arrived, *U 73*, *U 77*, *U 101* and *U 751* tried to attack once again, but only the torpedoes launched by *U 101* (Type IX) found a target, sinking the destroyer HMS *Broadwater* (1190 tonnes).

The end of 1941 saw one more convoy battle involving the 'Seerauber' group, consisting of one Type VII – *U 434* (Kptlt. Wolfgang Heyda) – and four Type IXs – *U 67*, *U 131*, *U 107* and *U 108*. Later the group was joined by the Type IX *U 125* and the Type VIIs *U 71* (Kptlt. Flaschenberg), *U 567* (Kptlt. Endrass), *U 574* (Oblt.z.S.

Gangelbach) and *U 751* (Kptlt. Bigalk). Their target was Convoy HG 76 heading from Gibraltar to Britain. It consisted of thirty-two ships protected by the 36th Escort Group commanded by the famous 'U-boat killer' Cdr Walker, whose health unfortunately collapsed under the strain of his duties, leading to his early death. In this battle he commanded two sloops and seven corvettes Warships under his command in this battle were two sloops and seven corvettes. There was also a support group consisting of the first escort carrier HMS *Audacity* and three destroyer escorts.

The Germans knew the departure date of HG 76 from their spies so the U-bootwaffe command set up the 'Seerauber' patrol line. Nevertheless the convoy initially managed to mislead the enemy by heading south and 'disappeared'. Then it stayed far from the coast, out of range

▼ One of the fans of swimming was Kptlt. Rolf Mützelburg (in the white cap), Commanding Officer of *U 203* (Type VIIC) – and this led to his death. On 11 September 1942 he jumped into the water from his boat's conning tower, but struck his head on the ballast tank. The crew pulled him back on board, but he died of his injuries a few hours later. Between 18 February 1941 and 11 September 1942 Mützelburg conducted seven patrols in his *U 203*, sinking nineteen merchantmen totalling 81,987 GRT and damaging three more (17,052 GRT). (CAW)

▶ For his achievements Kptlt. Rolf Mützelburg was decorated with the Knight's Cross (November 1941) and then the Oak Leaves. (July 1942). (CAW)

▶ ▶ Mützelburg (left), with the tower of *U 203* in the background. (CAW)

of Luftwaffe aircraft. It was only located on 16 December in the afternoon by an Fw 200 patrol aircraft. Its crew directed the Type IXs *U 67*, *U 108* and *U 131* to the target. They managed to intercept the convoy, but their initial attacks were repelled by the escorts. Further attempts on the same day by *U 107*, *U 108* and *U 131* also failed. *U 131* was attacked by aircraft from HMS *Audacity* and so badly damaged that it had to be scuttled. The whole crew were taken prisoner. During the night of 17/18 December *U 434* kept tracking the convoy, reporting its position, but in the morning the U-boat was detected and sunk by the escorts. During the day Walker's force again managed to repel all the U-boat attacks. Only on the morning of 19 December was *U 574* (Type VII) able to penetrate the defensive ring and torpedo the destroyer escort HMS *Stanley* (1190 tonnes). Walker, however, proved his skills again – after each attack he fired star shell to illuminate the surfaced U-boat, forced it to dive, tracked it with ASDIC and attacked with depth charges. These tactics proved fatal to *U 574*. Illuminated, forced to dive and depth-charged it managed to surface for a brief moment, but was immediately rammed by the sloop HMS *Stork*. But the U-boat commanders were not willing to give up. On the following day the Type VIIs *U 71*, *U 57* (Oblt.z.S. Wilhelm Eisele) and *U 751* attacked furiously, but Walker was still alert. The British commander was well aware that at least six U-boats were operating around his convoy and decided to use deception. While simulating repelling an attack, he ordered the entire convoy to execute a sharp turn. The ruse failed, however, after one of the ships accidentally fired a star shell, clearly illuminating the ships on their new

heading. *U 567* managed to regain contact which had been lost just after the ships turned, and immediately attacked, sinking one ship. Bigalk's *U 751* attacked from the other side and delivered a serious blow to the escorts by sinking the carrier HMS *Audacity*. Torpedoes launched by yet another attacking U-boat – the Type IX *U 67* – missed, and the sloop HMS *Depthford* destroyed *U 567*. On 23 September the two sides disengaged. All in all a quite numerous U-boat force only managed to inflict light losses on the convoy. The determined attitude of the escorts as well as the excellent command skills and courage displayed by Walker allowed the Allies to actually win the engagement. The Germans only managed to sink four Allied vessels. On 19 December *U 108* (Type IX) sank one British ship and *U 574* (Gengelbach) sank the sloop HMS *Stanley*. On 21 December Endrass in *U 567* sank the Norwegian *Annavore* (3324 GRT) but the U-bootwaffe's first ace was then killed in a depth-charge attack.

1942

The outcome of the Battle of the Atlantic in 1941 was a stalemate. Once the Americans entered the war, Allied resources increased immensely, laying the foundations for eventual victory, but the immediate result of the US declaration of war was another 'Happy Time' for the U-boats off the American coast. The US Navy was far from ready for war, and in order not to cause panic amongst the civilian population, no blackout was imposed along the coast. The lights of houses, street lamps and passing cars ashore perfectly silhouetted ships proceeding along the coast, making them perfect targets for German torpedoes. Also, the blinking lights of buoys made navigation easy for the U-boats. The results of this negligent attitude by Admiral King, commander of the US Atlantic Fleet, were disastrous. The U-boats operating in this area – on average eight at any one time – took a heavy toll of the defenceless ships which were still sailing singly, not in convoy. The British offered assistance and advice, but this was ignored. The Americans decided to use the tactics that had already failed in the U-boat war – active anti-submarine patrols by only a small number of ASW ships. In the first three months of their war, therefore, the US Navy sank no U-boats. British ships, which had fought their way across the Atlantic, were being sunk just off the cheerfully illuminated US coast. This second 'Happy Time' lasted until May 1942 and 362 Allied ships were sunk – a total tonnage equalling that of all the ships sunk the previous year. Finally, the convoy system was adopted, and the number of ships lost fell, while more U-boats were being sunk, forcing the Germans to operate further out at sea, away from the coast.

However, the number of operational U-boats continued to increase. By October Dönitz had 196 boats at his disposal, compared to 100 at the beginning of the year, and began to deploy them back into the North Atlantic. For the first time, he was able to conduct large-scale operations with stronger wolfpacks. The convoy battles increased in intensity, especially in the 'Air Gap' in the mid-Atlantic

where Allied air cover could not reach, and even the onset of winter did not reduce the ferocity of the action. In the second half of 1942, the U-boats sank 575 ships totalling 3,000,000 GRT, giving a total for the whole year of 1160 ships sunk (6,000,000 GRT).

The Allies, however, were making good use of signals intelligence and their excellent HF/DF ('Huff-Duff') radio direction finders. The Germans' wolfpack tactics required a large volume of wireless traffic, with boats reporting convoy positions and headquarters setting up patrol lines to intercept them, as well as normal weather and situation reports. Coastal DF stations picked these transmissions up and got fixes on the position of assembling wolfpacks, allowing convoys to be rerouted away from them. 'Huff-Duff' sets were also installed aboard escort vessels, allowing them to track U-boats near the convoy. When coupled with radar, this gave the defenders a significant advantage.

Nonetheless, since the outbreak of war in 1939 the Allies had lost 14,000,000 GRT of shipping and were in fact losing the Battle of the Atlantic. On the other hand, the Germans lost sixty-six U-boats in the second half of 1942 alone. An increasing number of these losses were to aircraft, but the mid-Atlantic 'Gap' was still there and in it the U-boats took a heavy toll of merchant ships.

The first major convoy battle of 1942 began on 21 February. The target was Convoy ONS 67 and the attacking U-boats were the Type IXs *U 155*, *U 158* and *U 162* and the Type VIIs *U 558* and *U 587*. They managed to sink eight ships, the Type VIIs accounting for three of them. Kptlt. Günther Krech in command of *U 558* damaged the British *Anadara* and sank the Norwegian *Eidanger* (9432 GRT) and the British *Inverader* (5578 GRT). On the same day – 24 February – *Anadara* (8009 GRT) was finished off by *U 587*, commanded by Kptlt. Ulrich Borcherdt.

On 11 May the 'Hecht' group composed of a single Type IX, *U 124* (Kptlt. Mohr) and five Type VIIs, *U 94* (Oblt.z.S. Otto Ites), *U 96* (Oblt.z.S. Hans-Jürgen

▲ *U 46* (Type VIIB) commanded by Kptlt. Herbert Schultze triumphantly returns to its base flying pennants denoting ships sunk, probably on 27 July 1941 after its eighth and last patrol under this commander. Schultze sank twenty-six ships totalling 169,709 GRT and damaged one more (9456 GRT). He received the Knight's Cross. (CAW)

◄ Schultze after returning from his fourth patrol in *U 46* on 26 February 1940. By that time he had already sunk sixteen ships, two of them neutral – one Swedish and one Finnish. (CAW)

▶ Kapitänleutnant Herbert Wohlfarth, CO of *U 556* (Type VIIC), after receiving his Knight's Cross on his return to Lorient on 30 May 1941. The decoration was awarded on 15 May 1941 while Wohlfarth was still at sea on his eighth patrol (his first in *U 556* – previously he had commanded two other boats, one Type IIB, and one Type IID). During his nine patrols Wohlfarth sank twenty-one ships totalling 66,032 GRT (six of them with his Type VII boat during the eighth patrol), damaged two more (9903 GRT, one with *U 556*) and also damaged one auxiliary cruiser of 10,552 GRT. While returning from his eighth patrol, when he was already in the Bay of Biscay he received an order to assist the battleship *Bismarck*, which was being pursued by the Royal Navy, either to help her in combat or at least recover her logbook.

Wohlfarth had no torpedoes and little fuel left, but nevertheless he proceeded as ordered, but the need to conserve fuel restricted his speed and by the time he reached the agreed rendezvous *Bismarck* was already deeper than *U 556* could ever dive. This was a personal blow for Wohlfarth, whose crew had many friends aboard the battleship. These friendships dated back to the day of *U 556*'s commissioning, when Wohlfarth went to see the *Bismarck*'s captain, Ernst Lindemann, and asked to borrow the battleship's band for the ceremony, as of course the U-boat did not have one of its own. In return, Wohlfarth promised that his boat would always protect the *Bismarck*. Lindemann agreed and a special 'contract' was drawn up. On another occasion, *Bismarck* and *U 556* were conducting gunnery exercises, and Lindemann courteously allowed his 'protector' to fire at the target first. But ten rounds from the U-boat's 88mm gun wrecked the target and *Bismarck* was unable to use it that day. *U 556* was sunk on its ninth patrol, nine days out of Lorient, on 27 June 1941. Wohlfarth was captured and spent more than six years as a prisoner of war. (CAW)

Hellriegel), *U 406* (Kptlt. Horst Dietrichs), *U 569* (Kptlt. Hans-Peter Hinsch) and *U 590* (Kptlt. Heinrich Müller-Edzards) engaged Convoy ONS 92 which was made up of forty-one ships. It was escorted by the American group A 3 comprising the destroyer USS *Gleaves*, the cutter USS *Ingram* and four Canadian corvettes. *U 569* located the convoy on 11 May and directed *U 94* and *U 124* onto it. All the boats attacked immediately after closing on the convoy. As a result five ships went down – four sunk by *U 124* and one by *U 94*. *U 569* scored only a non-fatal hit, and further attacks were prevented by bad weather. During the night that followed, despite repeated attacks, only *U 94* managed to sink two ships. The battle finally ended due to the bad

weather. Apart from the four ships destroyed by *U 124*, only one Type VII – *U 94* – sank two ships: the Panamanian *Cocle* (5630 GRT) and the British *Batna* (4399 GRT).

On 8 June the same 'Hecht' group, refuelling from the Type XB *U 116*, located Convoy ONS 94 and later ONS 96, but were unable to attack, because for a variety of reasons all the U-boats lost contact with the Allied ships. In the evening *U 124* spotted Convoy ONS 100 and attacked several times during the night, but was repelled each time by the Canadian escort group C 1 composed of a Canadian destroyer, two British and two French corvettes and a rescue ship. Eventually the German commander succeeded and sank the corvette *Mimosa*. On the following day other the boats of the wolfpack – except for *U 406* and *U 590*, which had engine trouble – caught up with the convoy. That night *U 94* sank two ships, but then the convoy was lost in fog which had suddenly appeared. On 11 June *U 96* regained contact and directed *U 94* and *U 569* onto the target. Those two boats jointly sank one ship. In the meantime the escorts were reinforced by two Canadian corvettes, but nevertheless *U 124* managed to sink another ship. On 13 June more corvettes – this time from the Royal Navy – arrived and put an end to the engagement. The Type VIIs had sunk three ships. On 10 June *U 94* destroyed *Empire Clough* (6147 GRT) and *Ramsay*, and on the following day *U 569* damaged *Pontypridd* (4458 GRT), which was finished off later that day by *U 94*.

On 1 July the Germans located Convoy PQ 17 (PQ indicated heading for Russia, QP heading from Russia) composed of thirty-three ships escorted by four cruisers,

▼ Kptlt. Herbert Wohlfarth and Admiral Karl Dönitz – a commemorative photograph taken after the former had received his Knight's Cross, late May 1941. (CAW)

three destroyers and two submarines, which was heading for the Soviet Union, to the arctic port of Arkhangelsk. The ships were carrying war material necessary for the survival of their new ally – although previously Germany's ally. What followed was the most dramatic convoy battle of the Second World War.

The Arctic Ocean quickly became a new theatre of operations for the U-boats. Between August 1941 and the PQ 17 disaster twelve convoys made the voyage, with more than a hundred ships. Only one vessel was lost, sunk by the first U-boat deployed to that theatre, the Type VII *U 454* commanded by Kptlt. Burkhard Hackländer. The victim was the British destroyer HMS *Matabele*, which was lost on 17 January while escorting Convoy PQ 8. The PQ and QP convoys had to sail quite close to the northern Norwegian coast, within range of Luftwaffe air bases. And indeed German aircraft managed to sink four ships of PQ 16, which preceded the ill-fated PQ 17. PQ 17 itself left Iceland on 27 June. Its thirty-five ships carried enough equipment of to equip four or five Soviet divisions. Two merchant vessels had to leave the convoy soon after departure – the *Richard Bland* was damaged after running aground and the *Exford* suffered damage from ice. After British intelligence informed the convoy commander that heavy German surface units, including the battleship *Tirpitz*, had sortied from their Norwegian bases, the British command made the tragic – and premature – decision to scatter the convoy. The Germans had indeed commenced an operation codenamed 'Rösselsprung' and the *Tirpitz* had left her base on the evening of 2 July, followed by the 'pocket battleships' *Lützow* and *Admiral Scheer* at noon on the following day, but the surface force soon returned to port. Meanwhile the defenceless Allied merchant ships continued on their own. Because of the ice present in the north they had to stay close to the Norwegian coast where they were decimated by U-boats and the Luftwaffe. In total during almost two weeks of attacks the Germans sank twenty-four ships with 153 men, 430 tanks, 3000 other military vehicles and 210 bomber aircraft aboard. The convoy was first spotted by the Type VII *U 255* (Kptlt. Reinhart Reche). The first seven ships were sunk while the convoy was still together, and further casualties were inflicted by submarines and aircraft after it had scattered.

The Luftwaffe carried out 202 combat sorties and sank eight ships for the loss of five aircraft. The successes of the U-boats – all Type VIIs – were as follows. On 4 July *U 334* (Kptlt. Hilmar Siemon) sank the American ship *William Hooper* (7177 GRT), and *U 457* (KKpt. Karl Brandenburg) the American *Christopher Newport* (7191 GRT). On 5 July *U 334* sank the British *Earlston* (7195 GRT) and *U 456* (Kptlt. Max-Martin Teichert) the American *Honomu* (6977 GRT), *U 703* (Kptlt. Heinz Bielfeld) sank two British ships, the *Empire Byron* (6645 GRT) and the *River Afton* (5479 GRT), and *U 88* (Kptlt. Heino Bohmann) sank the American *Carlton* (5127 GRT) and *Daniel Morgan* (7177 GRT). On 6 July the US ship *John Witherspoon* (7191 GRT) was sunk by *U 255* (Kptlt. Reche). On the following day the same U-boat

destroyed another American ship, *Alcoa Ranger* (5116 GRT), *U 355* (Kptlt. Günther La Baume) sank the British *Hartlebury* (5082 GRT) and *U 457* the *Aldersdale* (8402 GRT). On 8 July *U 255* sank the American ship *Olopana* (6069 GRT). July 10th saw the destruction of a further two vessels: the Panamanian *El Capitan* (5255 GRT) sunk by *U 251* (Kptlt. Heinrich Timm) and the American *Hoosier* (5060 GRT), the victim of *U 376* (Kptlt. Frederick-Karl Marks). On 13 July *U 255* sank the Dutch *Paulus Potter* (7168 GRT). Of the eleven ships which survived this slaughter, three were sunk while returning from Russia in the next convoy – among them was *Silver Sword*, torpedoed by *U 255*.

The next convoy – PQ 18 – also suffered heavily, losing thirteen out of its forty ships. Three of these were victims

▲ Swimming for U-boat crewmen was not always for fun. Aboard this Type VIIC somewhere in the Atlantic in mid-1943, one crewman is carrying out repairs while the other holds on to the safety line. (CAW)

▲ A similar scene on the afterdeck of a Type VIIC U-boat, 1943. (CAW)

group consisted of *U 164*, *U 217*, *U 511*, and two Type VIIs, *U 210* (KKpt. Rudolf Lemcke) and *U 553* (KKpt. Karl Thurmann). The other group was codenamed 'Wolf' and consisted of *U 43*, *U 71* and five Type VIIs: *U 454* (Kptlt. Burkhard Hackländer), *U 552* (Kptlt. Erich Topp), *U 597* (Kptlt. Eberhard Bopst), *U 607* (Kptlt. Ernst Mengersen) and *U 704* (Kptlt. Horst Kessler). *U 210*, which was the first to locate the convoy, guided *U 164*, *U 217*, *U 511*, *U 553* and *U 588* on the target. The German submarines launched a series of unsuccessful attacks during the next two days, losing *U 588* (which was not assigned to either group), sunk by the destroyer HMCS *Skeena*. Shortly afterwards the destroyers of the escort group had to leave the convoy as their fuel was low, but on 2 August two other destroyers, accompanied by one more corvette, reinforced the convoy.

U 552 managed to regain contact with the convoy after it had been lost in poor visibility. Despite the efforts of the convoy's commodore, which by the way introduced some chaos into the formation with one column being detached from the main force, the U-boats attacked successfully, sinking three ships and damaging one more. On 3 August Erich Topp in *U 552* damaged the British merchant ship *G.S. Walden* (10,627 GRT) and sank another, the *Lochkatrine* (9419 GRT). Karl Thurmann in *U 553* damaged the Belgian ship *Belgian Soldier* (7167 GRT), which was finished off by Ernst Mengersen in *U 607* the following day. The third ship lost was the British *Arletta* (4870 GRT), which sank after being hit by *U 458* commanded by Kptlt. Kurt Diggins.

On 5 August Kptlt. Gerd Kebling in the Type VII *U 593* located Convoy SC 94 heading from Sydney for Great Britain, composed of thirty ships and escorted by the Canadian group C 1: a destroyer and five corvettes – two Canadian and three British. The convoy was attacked by the 'Steinbrick' group, made up of *U 210* (KKpt. Rudolf Lemcke), *U 379* (Kptlt. Paul-Hugo Kettner), *U 454* (Kptlt. Burkhard Hackländer), *U 593* (Kptlt. Gerd Kelbling), *U 597* (Kptlt. Eberhard Bopst), *U 607* (Kptlt. Ernst Mengersen) and *U 704* (Kptlt. Horst Kessler) – all Type VIIs – as well as *U 71*. The group would be reinforced by more U-boats which were going out on patrol: *U 174*, *U 176*, *U 595* and six Type VIIs – *U 254* (Kptlt. Hans Gilardone), *U 256* (Kptlt. Odo Loewe), *U 438* (Kptlt. Rudolf Franzius), *U 605* (Kptlt. Herbert-Viktor Schütze), *U 660* (Kptlt. Götz Baur) and *U 705* (Kptlt. Karl-Horst Horn). The first attacks were carried out by *U 593* and *U 595*, but after sinking one ship they were chased off by the escorts. The single victim was the Dutch ship *Spar* (3616 GRT), sunk by *U 593*. On 6 August U-boats could not get at the convoy, thanks to the decisive actions of the escorts. *U 454* (Type VII) and *U 595* were heavily damaged and had to return to base and *U 210* (Type VII) was sunk by the destroyer HMCS *Assiniboine*. On 7 August the attacking force was reinforced by the U-boats originally not assigned to the group, listed above, which had been heading for their patrol areas. On 8 August *U 176* (Type IX) sank two ships, the British *Kelso* and the Greek *Mount Kassion*,

of the U-bootwaffe. The Type VII *U 408* (Kptlt. Reinhard von Hymmen) sank the American ship *Oliver Ellsworth* (7191 GRT), the Soviet *Stalingrad* (3559 GRT) and the British *Atheltemplar* (8939 GRT), which had been previously damaged by *U 457* (Brandenburg), though this was at a cost of three Type VIIs lost – *U 88*, *U 457* and *U 589*. Nevertheless after this battle the arctic convoys were suspended for almost half a year, despite protests from Stalin, who was not that bothered about casualties. Convoys to Russia were only resumed in December.

The next major convoy battle was fought between 29 July and 3 August 1942. The target was Convoy ON 115 composed of forty-one ships escorted by the Canadian group C 3 (Cdr Wallace) – two destroyers and four corvettes. The German were two wolfpacks. The 'Pirat'

◄ Rendezvous with a supply vessel in mid-Atlantic. As well as fuel and torpedoes, U-boats were also resupplied with food and received medical help. The photo shows a doctor returning from the U-boat. (CAW)

and *U 379* (Type VII) sank another two, the British *Anneberg* (2537 GRT) and the American *Kaimoku*. The crew of three ships panicked and abandoned their vessels; one of them, *Trehata*, was sunk – again by *U 176*. The escorts of were reinforced by two destroyers equipped with HF/DF equipment – the Polish ORP *Blyskawica* and the British HMS *Broke*. A corvette sank the Type VII *U 379*. Throughout 9 August U-boats tried to attack the convoy again, but only *U 176* managed to sink the *Radchurch*. On 10 August *U 438* (Type VII) sank two ships, the Greek *Condylis* (4439 GRT) and the British *Oregon* (6008 GRT), both previously damaged by *U 660*. *U 660* itself sank also two British ships on its own, the *Cape Race* (3807 GRT) and the *Empire Reindeer* (6259 GRT).

On 9 September the Type VII *U 584* sighted Convoy ON 127 composed of thirty-two merchant ships escorted by two destroyers and four corvettes of the Canadian group C 4, and another battle began. The German submarine, commanded by Kptlt. Joachim Deecke, was a part of the 'Vorwarts' group, which consisted of *U 218* (Type IX) and ten other Type VIIs, *U 91* (Kptlt. Heinz Walkerling), *U 92* (Oblt.z.S. Adolf Oerlich), *U 96* (Oblt.z.S. Hans Jür-gen Hellriegel), *U 211* (Kptlt. Karl Hause), *U 380* (Kptlt. Josef Rother), *U 404* (Kptlt. Otto von Bülow), *U 407* (Oblt.z.S. Ernst-Ulrich Brüller), *U 411* (Oblt.z.S. Gerhard Litterscheid), *U 594* (Oblt.z.S. Friedrich Mumm) and *U 608* (Oblt.z.S. Struckmeier). *U 584*, which shadowed the convoy, lost contact during the night, but it was restored at mid-day on 10 September by *U 96*, which immediately attacked, sinking two ships, the Belgian *Elisabeth van*

Belgie (4241 GRT) and the Norwegian *Sveve* (6313 GRT), and damaging the British tanker *F.J. Wolfe* (12,190 GRT). *U 659* (Type VII, Kptlt. Hans Stock), which joined the group, managed to damage the British ship *Empire Oil* (8029 GRT) after darkness fell. During the night the U-boats attacked several times and continued to do so throughout the next day. And so on 11 September *U 218* damaged one Norwegian tanker, the *Fjordaas*, and *U 404* (von Bülow) damaged another, *Marit II*. Deecke in *U 584* finished off the *Empire Oil* and sank the Norwegian ship *Hindanger* (4884 GRT). On 12 September *U 211* (Hause) damaged two British ships, the *Empire Moonbeam* (6849 GRT) and the *Hektoria* (13,797 GRT), both later finished-off by *U 608*, and *U 404* did the same to the Norwegian *Daghild* (9272 GRT). On 13 September *U 594* sank the Panamanian ship *Stone Street* (6131 GRT), and on the following day – the last of the battle – *U 91* destroyed the Canadian corvette HMCS *Ottawa* (1375 tonnes). Then, as the convoy was now in range of Newfoundland and Allied aircraft appeared overhead, the U-boats broke off the action.

On 18 September 1942 the American A 3 escort group, consisting of two cutters and seven Canadian and one British corvettes, fought a battle in defence of the twenty-four ships of Convoy SC 100 heading from Sydney to Britain. The formation was attacked by two wolfpacks. 'Lohs' consisted of nine U-boats: the Type IX *U 176* and eight Type VIIs, *U 135* (Kptlt. Freidrich Hermann Praetorius), *U 259* (Kptlt. Klaus Köpke), *U 373* (Kptlt. Paul-Karl Loeser), *U 410* (KKpt. Kurt Sturm), *U 432*

▶ In the cramped interior of a U-boat, cooking for over forty men was no easy task. (CAW)

(Kptlt. Heinz-Otto Schultze), *U 569* (Kptlt. Hans-Peter Hinsch), *U 599* (Kptlt. Wolfgang Breithaupt) and *U 755* (Kptlt. Walter Göing). The other was 'Pfeil' with eight

U-Boats: *U 216* (Type IX) and seven Type VIIs, *U 221* (Kptlt. Hans Trojer), *U 258* (Kptlt. Wilhelm von Mässenhausen), *U 356* (Kptlt. Georg Wallas), *U 595* (Kptlt. Jürgen

▶ Despite this, the cook was required to bake the traditional German cake, the Sonntagkuche, every Sunday. (CAW)

▶ ▶ Washing the dishes afterwards was not easy either. (CAW)

Quaet-Faslem), *U 607* (Kptlt. Ernst Mengersen), *U 615* (Kptlt. Ralph Kapitzky) and *U 617* (Kptlt. Albrecht Brandi). Attacks were often interrupted by bad weather – every now and then the German boats would lose contact with the convoy, only to regain it some time later. On 22 September the battle was suspended as some U-boats left to intercept Convoy RB 1 which had just been located, but during the following night the remaining submarines resumed their attacks. Nevertheless, bearing in mind the number of U-boats involved, the results were quite mediocre. Only five Allied ships were sunk. In most cases they were stragglers which had become separated from the convoy in bad weather. On 20 September *U 596* unsuccessfully attacked the escorts, but was able to sink the British merchant ship *Empire Harbeeste* (5676 GRT). The rest of the losses were the stragglers: the British *Athesultan* (8882 GRT) and *Tennessee* (2342 GRT), both hit by *U 617* on 23 September, the American *Pennmar* (5868 GRT), destroyed by *U 432*, and finally the Belgian *Roumanie* (3563 GRT) by *U 617* again. Both these ships perished on 24 September. On the day after that the Germans broke off the action.

Between 20 and 22 September a group of Type VII boats consisting of *U 251* (Kptlt. Heinrich Timm), *U 255*

(Kptlt. Reinhart Reche), *U 403* (Kptlt. Heinz Ehlert Clausen), *U 408* (Kptlt. Reinhard von Hymmen), *U 435* (Kptlt. Siegfried Strelow), *U 592* (Kptlt. Karl Borm) and *U 703* (Kptlt. Heinz Bielfeld) attacked the Arctic convoy QP 14 composed of fifteen merchantmen and defended by fourteen warships. On 20 September *U 255* sank the American ship *Silver Sword* (4937 GRT), *U 435* destroyed the minesweeper HMS *Leda* (835 tonnes), and *U 703* sank the British HMS *Somali* (1870 tonnes). On 22 September Strelow in his *U 435*, who definitely owned the day, sank the American ship *Bellingham* (5345 GRT) and two British merchantmen, *Grey Ranger* (3313 GRT) and *Ocean Voice* (7174 GRT).

Between 12 and 16 October another wolfpack codenamed 'Wotan' attacked Convoy SC 104 (Sydney – Great Britain). The pack consisted of *U 216* and nine Type VIIs, *U 221* (Kptlt. Trojer), *U 258* (Kptlt. Mässenhausen), *U 356* (Kptlt. Wallas), *U 410* (Kptlt. Sturm), *U 599* (Kptlt. Wolfgang Breithaupt), *U 607* (Kptlt. Mengersen), *U 615* (Kptlt. Kapitzky), *U 618* (Kptlt. Kurt Baberg) and *U 662* (KKpt. Wolfgang Hermann). The targeted convoy consisted of forty-eight ships escorted by the British group B 6: two destroyers and four Norwegian corvettes.

U 258 located the ships on 11 October, but was unable to attack until the next day. On the night of 12 October *U 221* managed to penetrate the escort screen and attack three times, sinking three ships. The escort group nonetheless proved quite effective, driving away other U-boats, but while tracking them it fell behind the convoy and failed to rejoin it before nightfall. The Germans took

◄ During a patrol the commanding officer would hardly ever get an opportunity to eat in the mess. This shows Kptlt. Günther Krech snatching a quick meal on the bridge of his *U 558* (Type VIIC) in the Atlantic, during his ninth patrol in early 1943. The partially-elevated antenna of the DF can be seen on the right, while the UZO is covered by a megaphone which happened to be available. Krech conducted a total of ten patrols, all aboard this boat. *U 558* was damaged on 20 July 1943 by an American Liberator of the 19th Anti-submarine Squadron in the Bay of Biscay while on the surface (and was eventually sunk by a British Halifax of 58 Sqn RAF). Only five (six, according to some sources) men who were on the boat's conning tower survived – among them the commanding officer, who spent the rest of the war in a POW camp. All the others did not manage to get out. During two years and almost two months of active service Krech sank seventeen merchant ships with a total capacity of 93,186 GRT and one 950-ton 'Flower' class corvette *Gladiolus*. He also damaged two ships totalling 15,070 GRT and caused the loss of yet another of 6672 GRT. On 17 September 1942 he received the Knight's Cross. (CAW)

◄ Life aboard a U-boat: after his watch, a sailor warms his soaked and frozen feet in a spent lube oil can filled with warm water. (CAW)

► An officer on the bridge of a Type VII taking a sun sight with a sextant. (CAW)

advantage of the situation and sank a number of ships on 14 October. On the same day the attackers were reinforced by another wolfpack codenamed 'Leopard', composed of *U 254* (Kptlt. Odo Loewe), *U 353* (Oblt.z.S. Wolfgang Römer), *U 382* (Kptlt. Herbert Juli), *U 437* (Kptlt. Werner Karl Schulz), *U 442* (KKpt. Hans-Joachim Hesse), *U 620* (Kptlt. Heinz Stein) – all Type VIIs – and a single Type IX, *U 661* (Oblt.z.S. von Lilienfeld). During the battle *U 353* was lost after being depth-charged by a destroyer, and *U 571* was damaged.

On 13 October Hans-Hartwig Trojer sank the British ship *Ashworth* (5227 GRT) and two Norwegian merchantmen, the *Fagersten* (2342 GRT) and the *Senta* (3785 GRT). On 14 October the same boat – *U 221* – destroyed the British ship *Southern Empress* (12,398 GRT) – which had aboard eleven small landing craft, nine larger LCMs and one LCT – and the American *Susana* (5929 GRT). *U 607* sank the Greek ship *Nellie* (4826 GRT), while *U 616* destroyed the British *Empire Mersey* (5791 GRT). The sole Type IX, *U 661*, sank the Yugoslavian ship *Nikodina Matkovic* (3672 GRT). After that increasingly strong aerial patrols forced the Germans to disengage.

The next major battle – against Convoy HX 212 – was an 'all Type VII' affair, fought between 26 and 29 October 1942. The target convoy was escorted by the group A 3 under Cdr Lewis and composed of a destroyer, a cutter and six corvettes. The attacking force was the 'Puma' group composed of *U 224* (Oblt.z.S. Hans-Karl Kosbadt), *U 301* (Kptlt. Willy-Roderich Körner), *U 383* (Kptlt. Horst

► Lookouts on the bridge of a Type VIIC, the North Atlantic, 1942. Note the partly-raised periscope. Normally they were kept lowered when the boat was on the surface, so the highest point above the water was the top of the lookout's head. (CAW)

◀ Parting of two Type VIICs which had met in the central Atlantic, 1942. The dinghy proves that there was a visit, perhaps to transfer mail. (CAW)

Kremser), *U 436* (Kptlt. Günther Seibicke), *U 441* (Kptlt. Klaus Hartmann), *U 443* (Oblt.z.S. Konstantin von Puttkamer), *U 563* (Kptlt. Götz von Hartmann), *U 602* (Kptlt. Philipp Schüler), *U 606* (Oblt.z.S. Hans Döhler), *U 621* (Kptlt. Horst Schünemann), *U 624* (Kptlt. Ulrich Graf von Soden-Fraunhofen), *U 753* (KKpt. Alfred Manhardt von Mannstein) and *U 757* (Kptlt. Friedrich Deetz). On 27 October torpedoes launched from *U 436* sank the British merchantman *Sourabaya* (10,107 GRT), which had aboard a 291-tonne LCT. The same boat also damaged two other ships, the Norwegian *Frontenac* (7350 GRT) and the American *Gurney E. Newlin* (8225 GRT). On 28 October *U 606* finished off the *Gurney E. Newlin* and damaged the Norwegian ship *Kosmos II* (16,966 GRT). On 29 October – the last day of this battle – *U 224* sank the Canadian ship *Bic Island* (3921 GRT), while *U 624* finished off the *Kosmos II*, which had three 291-tonne LCTs aboard.

▶ Another meeting of two Type VIICs in the North Atlantic, mid-1943. (CAW)

▼ A Type VIIC U-boat rendezvous with a Kriegsmarine surface ship. Warships usually escorted U-boats into and out of their bases. (CAW)

On 27 October *U 409* located the 37-ship Convoy SL 125. The 'Streitaxt' wolfpack consisted of ten U-boats – three Type IXs, *U 509*, *U 510* and *U 103*, and seven Type VIIs, *U 134* (Kptlt. Rudolf Schendel), *U 203* (Kptlt. Hermann Kottmann), *U 409* (Oblt.z.S. Hanns-Ferdinand Massmann), *U 440* (Oblt.z.S. Hans Geissler), *U 572* (Kptlt. Heinz Hirsacker), *U 604* (Kptlt. Horst Höltring) and *U 659* (Kptlt. Hans Stock). Dönitz deployed this group to the vicinity of Gibraltar, where the Allies had been building up their forces for some time. The battle lasted five days and at the end of it twelve ships totalling 80,005 GRT had been sunk, but during it the Allies had been able to get several convoys vital to Operation 'Torch', the invasion of North Africa, through the area 'Streitaxt' was operating in.

During the battle *U 509* (Witte) sank four ships and damaged three more. *U 510* damaged one Norwegian vessel, and *U 103* sank one ship. Other ships were lost to Type VIIs. On 27 October *U 604* sank the *Anglo Mærsk* (7705 GRT). On the 29th *U 203* destroyed the British vessel *Hopecastle* (5178 GRT), and on the following day damaged *Corinaldo* (7131 GRT). *U 409* did the same to *Bullmouth* (7519 GRT) and sank *Silverwillow* (6373 GRT), both British ships. Still on the same day *U 604* sank two more British ships, *Baron Vernon* (3642 GRT) and *President Doumer* (11,898 GRT), while *U 659* – like an executioner – finished off three damaged vessels, *Bullmouth*, *Corinaldo* and *Tasmania* (6405 GRT). *Corinaldo* was very unlucky, as she had already survived being torpedoed twice during the battle – by *U 509* and *U 203* – suffering only slight damages. Only *U 659* managed to

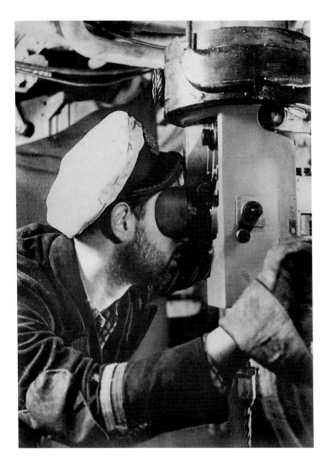

◄ U-boats spent much of their time on the surface when on patrol – but dived when a convoy was sighted. (CAW)

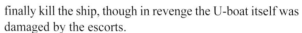

finally kill the ship, though in revenge the U-boat itself was damaged by the escorts.

On 24 October west of Newfoundland a wolfpack codenamed 'Veilchen' was formed. It consisted of thirteen U-boats, all Type VIIs: *U 71* (Oblt.z.S. Hardo Rodler von Roithberg), *U 84* (Kptlt. Horst Uphoff), *U 89* (Kptlt. Dietrich Lohmann), *U 132* (Kptlt. Ernst Vogelsang), *U 381* (Kptlt. Wilhelm Heinrich Graf von Pückler und Limburg), *U 402* (KKpt. Siegfried Freiherr von Forstner), *U 437* (Kptlt. Werner Karl Schulz), *U 438* (Kptlt. Rudolf Franzius), *U 442* (KKpt. Hans Joachim Hesse), *U 454* (Kptlt. Burkhard Hackländer), *U 571* (Kptlt. Helmut Möhlmann), *U 658* (Kptlt. Hans Senkel) and *U 704* (Kptlt. Horst Kessler). Three Type IXs, *U 520*, *U 521* and *U 522*, which were already operating south of Newfoundland, also took part in the subsequent engagement. Because the group had been ordered only to attack eastbound convoys, the westbound Convoy ON 140 was not attacked when it was sighted by *U 437* on the 28th. But when *U 522* sighted the eastbound SC 107 on the 30th, an unusually dramatic battle commenced which would last until 5 November. The increased wireless traffic from the German boats alerted the British command, which correctly identified the threat and dispatched reinforcements to the convoy. SC 107 had originally been escorted by the Canadian C 4 group consisting of one destroyer – HMCS *Restigouche* – and four corvettes. Now the Admiralty sent two more destroyers – HMS *Walker* and HMCS *Columbia* – to assist. These ships joined the convoy and stayed with it for some time. Aircraft were also dispatched, and on the 30th *U 520* and *U 658* were sunk in air attacks. *U 522* tried to take revenge by

◄ A U-boat was a very wet place, and not only on the bridge. The helmsman's position shown here was directly under the open hatch, so he could hear commands shouted down from the bridge. In heavy seas, it was almost permanently awash. (CAW)

attacking HMCS *Columbia*, but to no effect. But now the convoy, pursued by the U-boats, was entering the 'Gap' in mid-Atlantic. Out of range of air cover, the German submarines could now mount more daring attacks.

HMS *Walker* positioned herself at the rear of the convoy and made sweeps with her ASDIC, preventing any U-boat from shadowing the convoy. The Allies kept the Germans at bay until midnight, but after that the enemy took the initiative, and *U 402* sank the first merchant vessel. On the evening of 2 November thick fog came up and the U-boats had to suspend their attacks. During the following day the escorts again managed to keep the Germans away, but during night the attackers made their way through and sank two ships. One of them was loaded with ammunition and blew up after being hit by a torpedo. The explosion badly damaged *U 132*, which subsequently sank.

Some ships left the convoy and headed for Iceland unescorted, and 4 November rescue ships full of survivors from the sunken vessels also headed that way, while two destroyers and a cutter dispatched from Iceland arrive to reinforce the convoy. Nevertheless, *U 89* managed to attack successfully. On the following day, however, this boat was damaged by aerial bombs.

The convoy suffered its heaviest losses on 2 November. On that day alone Freiherr Siegfried von Forstner in *U 402* sank the British ships *Dalcroy* (4558 GRT), *Empire Antelope* (4945 GRT), *Empire Leopard* (5676 GRT) and the Greek *Rinos* (4649 GRT), and damaged the British *Empire Sunrise* (7459 GRT), which was later finished off by *U 84*. *U 438* damaged the British ship *Hartington*, which on the same day was again hit by a torpedo, this time from *U 522*, but only further torpedoes from *U 521* managed to finally sink her. As well as that tough ship, *U 522* also sank three more vessels during this battle. November 3rd saw the end of two merchant ships, one torpedoed by *U 521* and the other, *Jeypore* (5318 GRT), by *U 89*. On 4 November *U 132* sank *Empire Lynx* (6378 GRT) and the Dutch *Hobbema* (5507 GRT) and damaged the British *Hatimura* (6690 GRT), later finished off by *U 442*. The last loss was the British ship *Daleby* (4640 GRT), a victim of *U 89*.

After the majority of German submarines were dispatched to deal with the Allied naval force conducting Operation 'Torch', only one wolfpack remained in the North Atlantic. This was 'Kreuzoffer', consisting of three Type IXs, *U 184*, *U 521* and *U 522*, and ten Type VIIs, *U 84* (Kptlt. Horst Uphoff), *U 224* (Obtl.z.S. Hans Carl Kosbadt), *U 262* (Kptlt. Heinz Franke), *U 264* (Kptlt. Hartwig Looks), *U 383* (Kptlt. Horst Kremser), *U 454* (Kptlt. Burkhard Hackländer), *U 606* (Oblt.z.S. Hans Döhler), *U 611* (Kptlt. Nicolaus von Jacobs), *U 624* (Kptlt. Ulrich Graf von Soden-Fraunhofen), and *U 753* (KKpt. Alfred Manhardt von Mannstein). Between 15 and 21 November this group was engaged with the 33-ship Convoy ONS 144. On 17 November *U 184* and *U 264* sank one ship each: the former the British *Widestone* (3192 GRT), and the latter the Greek *Mount Taurus* (6696 GRT). On 18 November *U 264* sank the American

ship *Parismina* (4732 GRT) and the British *President Sergent* (5344 GRT), and also damaged the American merchantman *Yaka* (5432 GRT), later finished off by *U 522*. On the same day *U 262* destroyed the Norwegian corvette KNM *Montbretia* (K208) (925 tonnes). Of the German boats, *U 184* failed to return to base.

Between 15 and 21 December Convoy ON 153 with forty-three ships, escorted by the British group B 7 (two destroyers and four corvettes), was attacked by the 'Raufbold' group composed of thirteen U-boats, *U 135* (Oblt.z.S. Heinz Schütt), *U 203* (Kptlt. Hermann Kottmann), *U 211* (Kptlt. Karl Hause), *U 356* (Obltl.z.S. Günther Ruppelt), *U 409* (Oblt.z.S. Hanns-Ferdinand Massmann), *U 410* (KKpt. Kurt Sturm), *U 439* (Kptlt. Wolfgang Sporn), *U 600* (Kptlt. Bernhard Zurmühlen), *U 609* (Kptlt. Klaus Rudloff), *U 610* (Kptlt. Walter Freiherr von Freyberg-Eisenberg-Allmendingen), *U 621* (Kptlt. Horst Schünemann), *U 623* (Oblt.z.S. Hermann Schröder) and *U 664* (Oblt.z.S. Adolf Graef). On 16 December *U 610* sank the Norwegian ship *Bello* (6125 GRT) and damaged the British *Regent Lion* (9551 GRT), while *U 664* destroyed the British freighter *Emile Franqui* (5859 GRT). On 17 December *U 211* sank the destroyer HMS *Firedrake* (1350 tonnes). Finally, on 20 December *U 621* sank the British ship *Otina* (6217 GRT).

► Also, on surfacing not all the water might drain from the bridge, so the man who opened the hatch got a good shower. (CAW)

The following thirteen photographs illustrate one of the most unusual events of the U-boat war – the capture of *U 570* by an aircraft. *U 570* left Trondheim on 23 August 1941 for its first combat patrol, commanded by Kptlt. Hans-Joachim Rahmlow. On 27 August at 07.30 the boat surfaced, with an Allied aircraft – a Lockheed Hudson of No 269 Sqn based at Kaldaðarnes, Iceland – right overhead. Its pilot, F/Sgt Mitchell, immediately spotted the U-boat and attacked, but unfortunately his depth charges hung up on the rack and *U 570* crash-dived. Another Hudson from the same squadron on standby (V9028/S) was called to assist and immediately took off. Its crew consisted of S/Ldr J H Thompson (pilot), F/O W J O Coleman (navigator), and two gunners – Frederick J Drake and Douglas Strode. When the aircraft arrived in the area, *U 570* surfaced again. This time depth charges were successfully released and exploded near the hull. *U 570* managed to dive, but the explosions had damaged the batteries, which started to release large amounts of chlorine gas. Rahmlow ordered the boat to surface. The crew clambered out of the boat, choking on the poisonous gas. Thompson signalled by lamp that the crew should remain on deck or he would sink the boat. The gunners Drake and Strode fired short bursts near the boat on each pass, and the Germans hoisted a white sheet. Thompson called for assistance as he was running low on fuel. Diverted from a flight between Iceland to Scotland, another Hudson of 269 Sqn arrived on the scene

(P/O J G Owen-King, pilot, and F/O H H Eccles, navigator – those two airmen sometimes exchanged their duties, and usually it was Eccles in control of the aircraft). The photographs shown here were taken from that aircraft. On this page you can see the crew gathered around the conning tower and a British dinghy approaching the submarine. (RAF Museum)

At 11.00 a Catalina of No 209 Sqn (AH553/WQ-J, F/O Jewis) was scrambled from Reykjavik. It sighted *U 570* at 13.44. Surface ships were summoned to secure the prize. In the meantime further flying boats arrived. The first ship at the scene was the small anti-submarine trawler HMT *Northern Chief*, which arrived at 21.45 and after 13 hours of circling the Catalina could at last return to base. Later the destroyers HMS *Burwell* and HMCS *Niagara* came to assist. (RAF Museum)

The photographs on these two pages show *U 570* being examined by the British. The German crew had already been removed from the boat and transferred to the Allied ships, and a towline had been attached. At that point unexpected happened: a Northrop N3PB of No 330 Sqn dropped its small depth charges between the trawler and the U-boat and later opened fire on *Northern Chief*, which responded in kind. There were no casualties. (RAF Museum)

◀ A Lockheed Hudson from No 269 Squadron. Note the dorsal turret, occasionally used to fire on the U-boat; the other machine gun was installed in the nose. (RAF Museum)

◀ *U 570* in port, flying British colours. The boat was repaired and commissioned into the Royal Navy as HMS *Graph*. Kptlt. Rahmlow was accused of having handed his the boat to the enemy and was tried by an informal court martial organised in a POW camp and chaired by KKpt. Otto Kretschmer. With Kretschmer's full approval, the former First Officer of *U 570*, Bernhardt Berndt escaped from the camp – located close to the Barrow-in-Furness shipyard, where the boat was being repaired – intending to destroy the U-boat. The plan failed, Berndt was captured and shot while trying to escape. (IWM)

The very end of 1942 saw one more convoy battle, between 26 and 30 December. The target was Convoy ONS 154 with forty-five ships. It was escorted by the Canadian group C 1 (the destroyer HMCS *St. Laurent*, five corvettes and the rescue ship *Toward*). It was intercepted by two wolfpacks – 'Spitz' and 'Ungestum' – totalling nineteen U-boats, only one of them a Type IX. The former group consisted of the sole Type IX, *U 123*, and the Type VIIs *U 203* (Kptlt. Hermann Kottmann), *U 225* (Oblt.z.S. Wolfgang Leimkühler), *U 260* (Kptlt. Hubertus Purkhold), *U 356* (Oblt.z.S. Günther Ruppelt), *U 406* (Kptlt. Horst Dieterichs), *U 440* (Kptlt. Hans Geissler), *U 659* (Kptlt. Hans Stock), *U 662* (KKpt. Wolfgang Hermann) and *U 664* (Oblt.z.S. Adolf Graef). The other wolfpack was composed exclusively of Type VIIs, namely *U 336* (Kptlt. Hans Hunger), *U 373* (Kptlt. Paul-Karl Loeser), *U 409* (Oblt.z.S. Hans-Ferdinand Massmann), *U 435* (Kptlt. Siegfried Strelow), *U 441* (Kptlt. Klaus Hartmann), *U 455* (Kptlt. Hans-Martin Scheibe), *U 591* (Kptlt. Hans-Jürgen Zetzsche), *U 615* (Kptlt. Ralph Kapitzky) and *U 628* (Kptlt. Heinrich Hasenschar). On 27 December *U 225* damaged the British ship *Scottish Heather* (7078 GRT) while *U 356* sank three British vessels, *Empire Union* (5952 GRT), *King Edward* (5224 GRT) and *Melrose Abbey* (2473 GRT) and damaged the Dutch *Soekaboemi*, later finished off by *U 441*. On the following day, 28 December, determined U-boat attacks succeeded again, despite the significant efforts of the escorts. *U 225* sank one British ship, the *Melmore Head* (5373 GRT), and damaged two others, the *Empire Shackleton* (7068 GRT) and the *Ville de Rouen* (5598 GRT) as well as the Belgian *President Franqui* (4919 GRT). *U 260* destroyed yet another British ship – *Empire Wagtail* (4893 GRT). Later on the same day, *U 406* torpedoed and seriously damaged three British merchant ships: *Baron Cochrane* (3385 GRT), *Lynton Grange* (5024 GRT) and *Zarion* (4871 GRT). All these vessels were sunk on the following day: *Baron Cochrane* by *U 123*, *Lynton Grange* by *U 628* and *Zarion* by *U 591*. *U 123* managed to inflict further damage on the *Empire Shackleton*, but the ship survived this attack also. *U 336* sank the damaged *President Franqui* and *U 435* finally dealt with *Empire Shackleton*. The same U-boat also finished off the Norwegian *Norse King* (5701 GRT), which had also been damaged on the preceding day by *U 591*. *U 662* sank *Ville de Rouen*. During the last day of the battle Strelow in *U 435* sank the British destroyer HMS *Fidelity* (2456 tonnes), which had been already attacked by a number of U-boats the day before. Two landing craft – *LCV 752* and *LCV 754* (10 tonnes each) – were lost together with the destroyer which carried them.

Special operations

In 1942 a Type VII U-boat was assigned to carry out a special operation. On 25 April *U 213* (Type VIID), commanded by Oblt.z.S. Amelung von Varendorff, left Lorient and headed across the Atlantic towards Great Salmon, an uninhabited island off New Brunswick in Canada. The boat carried a special passenger, Oblt. M A

► A Type VIIA U-boat near its own base photographed from a Heinkel 115 maritime patrol seaplane. (CAW)

A Type VIIC on patrol in the Mediterranean. (CAW)

U 406 (Type VIIC) on patrol. Note the collapsible boat on deck. (CAW)

Langbein, a highly-trained Abwehr (German Military Intelligence) operative. His task was to observe and report on outgoing ship traffic from Halifax, one of the largest ports on the east coast of North America, posing as Mr Alfred Haskins of Toronto.

On 14 May, von Varnedorff landed his passenger safely and returned home. However, at this point the would-be spy seems to have changed his mind about his mission. He buried his radio transmitter and walked to the village of St Martins on the Bay of Fundy. Here he did some shopping and then hitch-hiked to St John. From here he took a train to Montreal and eventually settled in Ottawa. Using funds from the Reich he lived there peacefully until the end of 1944 when he turned himself in to the authorities, who, having realised that he had done no harm, brought no charges against him

Another special mission involving Type VIIs was Operation 'Pastorius'. A Nazi Party member who had lived in the USA for twelve years, Walter Kappe, recruited two groups of agents from German-Americans who had returned to fight for the Reich to conduct sabotage operations in the USA. Their list of targets included hydro-electric plants at Niagara Falls, Aluminum Company of America factories in Illinois, Tennessee, New York and Philadelphia, locks on the Ohio River between Louisville and Pittsburgh, the railway station at Newark, the famous Horseshoe Curve railway line in Altoona, Pennsylvania, together with other railway infrastructure, and the New York City water supply system. They were also expected to bomb Jewish-owned stores.

A 20mm MG C/30 cannon on the tower platform aboard a Type VIIC. (CAW)

► Two Type VIIC U-boats meet during their patrols, late autumn 1942. (CAW)

► Dusk, autumn 1941: a Type VIIC photographed from another vessel during a patrol. It can be clearly seen that the highest point of the boat is the top of the look-out's head. (CAW)

On 25 May 1942 *U 584*, commanded by Kptlt. Joachim Deecke, departed from Brest with one of the saboteur detachments aboard and headed towards the designated landing beach near Jacksonville, Florida. The other team boarded *U 202*, commanded by Kptlt. Hans-Heinz Linder, on 26 May. *U 202* was ordered to land its passengers on the southern coast of Long Island, near East Hampton. Both groups upon arrival were supposed to hide their equipment and then – posing as US citizens – meet in Cincinnati on 4 July. Each team was equipped with explosives, forged identity documents and genuine US currency. Kappe was supposed to join his agents later and coordinate their actions.

On 12 June *U 202*, after a stealthy journey across the Atlantic – submerging during the day and only travelling on the surface at night – approached the coast of Long Island. Armed sailors from the U-boat took the saboteurs

ashore in a rubber dinghy. Shortly after landing the agents encountered a Coast Guard patrol and attempted to bribe them, but without success. The Coast Guards searched the area and discovered all the saboteurs' equipment, although the agents themselves managed to flee. Several days later the other group successfully landed near Jacksonville. Nevertheless all the agents were betrayed by the commander of the first group, who had turned himself in, and were arrested by the FBI. Dasch and Burger, who had given themselves up, received long gaol sentences, although in 1948 they were deported to Germany. All the other agents went to the electric chair.

The next year to come – 1943 – would prove to be a turning point in the Battle of the Atlantic. Later that year all initiative was already in Allied hands and U-boats were forced to operate defensively.

▲ A U-boat cruising through calm Atlantic waters – quite an uncommon sight. Autumn 1942. (CAW)

► A Type VIIC photographed from a German aircraft while heading towards its patrol area, late summer 1941. (CAW)

▼ Two Type VIIC U-boats approaching their base, most probably La Spezia, in the Mediterranean. (CAW)

▲ Two U-boats head for their patrol areas in the Atlantic, summer 1941. (CAW)

▲ *U 404* of the 6th Flotilla returns to St-Nazaire from its third seventy-day patrol, 14 July 1942. The crew and the CO, Kptlt. Otto von Bülow, can be seen on the conning tower. During this patrol they sank seven ships, which are denoted by pennants on the periscope with the estimated tonnage of the targets written on them. (CAW)

▼ Kptlt. Otto von Bülow (left) and Oblt.z.S. Hans-Jürgen Hellriegel, then CO of *U 96*, beginning of the second half of 1942. (CAW)

▲ Kptlt. Otto von Bülow, from an aristocratic Mecklen - burg family, after his return from his sixth and last patrol aboard *U 404*. During this patrol, on 23 April 1943, von Bülow fired two FAT* torpedoes and two G7e electric torpedoes at an aircraft carrier identified as USS *Ranger*. In fact it was the much smaller British es - cort carrier HMS *Biter* and the torpedoes exploded either in her wake or at the end of their range. Nonetheless, von Bülow was confident he had sunk the ship and his alleged success was celebrated by the Nazi press … until the Americans demonstrated that USS *Ranger* was safe and sound. But von Bülow had already been deco- rated for his alleged success – on 26 April, still during the patrol (which ended on 3 May), he was awarded the Knight's Cross with Oak Leaves and on 1 June promot- ed to the rank of Korvettenkapitän. During his six com- bat patrols lasting 280 days he sank fourteen merchant ships with a total capacity of 71,450 GRT and one 1220- ton destroyer, and damaged two ships totalling 16,689 GRT. On 1 September 1943 he was appointed com- mander of the 23rd Flotilla in Danzig (Gdańsk). He sur- vived the war. (CAW)

Note: *German abbreviation of Flächen-Absuch- Torpedo, deployed for the first time in 1942. It was designed to attack convoys which were too heavily defended to be attacked with standard straight-running torpedoes. Due to their distinctive course FAT/LUT tor- pedoes are sometimes referred to as loop, pattern-run- ning or zig-zag torpedoes.

Details of the Type VIIC/41 U-boat.

**All artwork in colour section
by Waldemar Góralski**

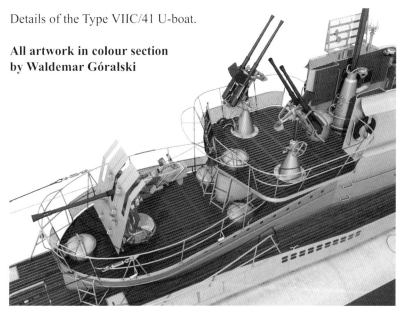

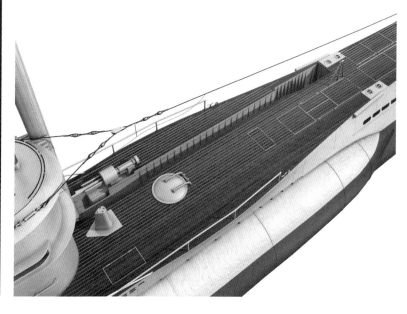

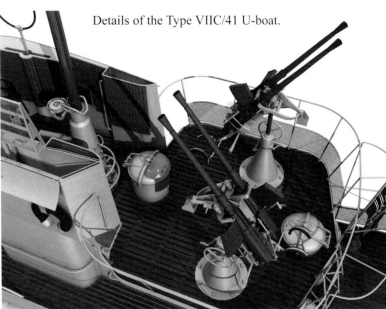

Details of the Type VIIC/41 U-boat.

Details of the Type VIIC/41 U-boat.

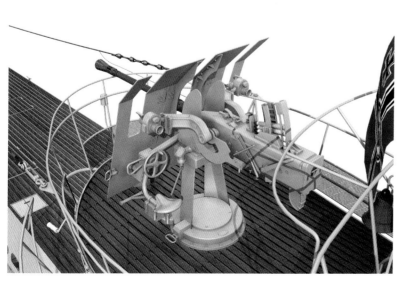

Details of the Type VIIC/41
U-boat.

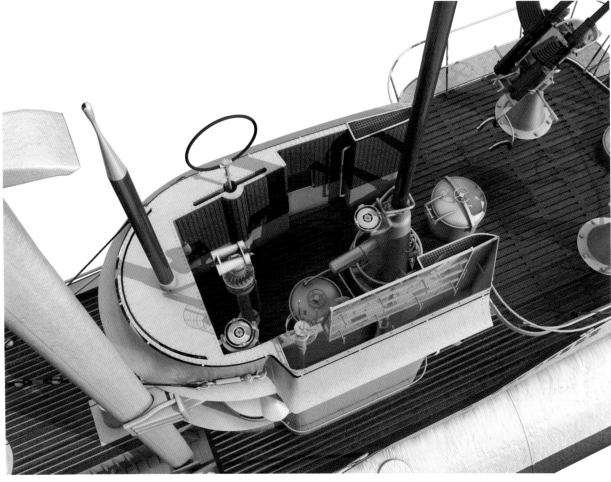

Details of the Type VIIC/41
U-boat.

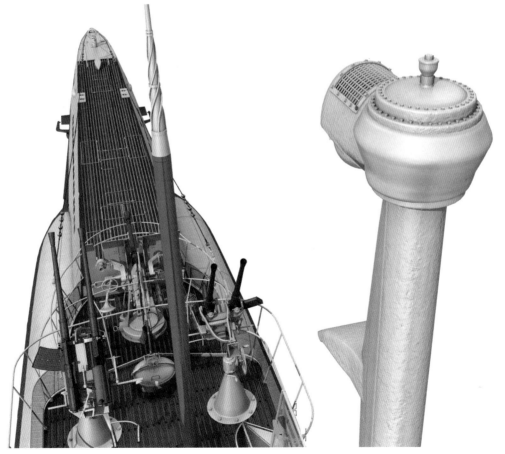

Details of the Type VIIC/41 U-boat.

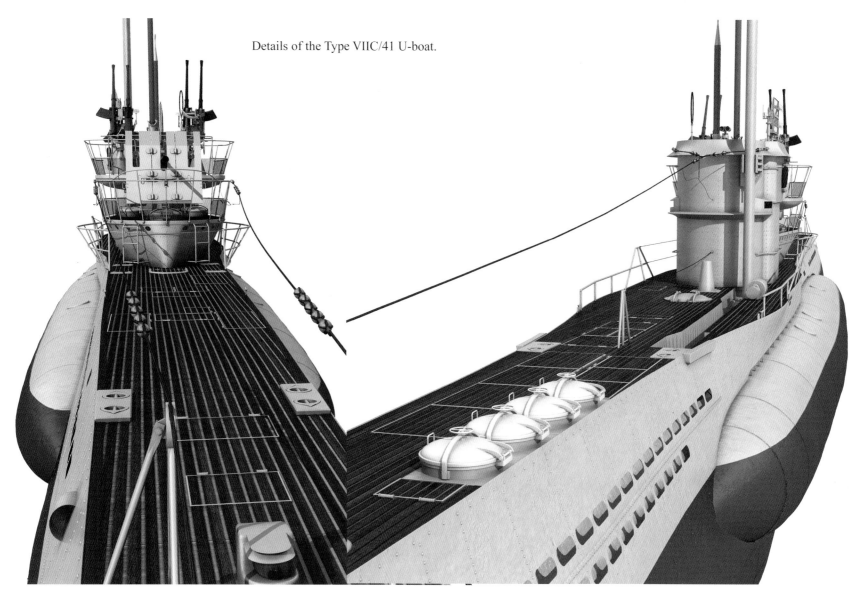

Details of the Type VIIC/41 U-boat.

Details of the Type VIIC/41 U-boat.

Details of the Type VIIC/41 U-boat.

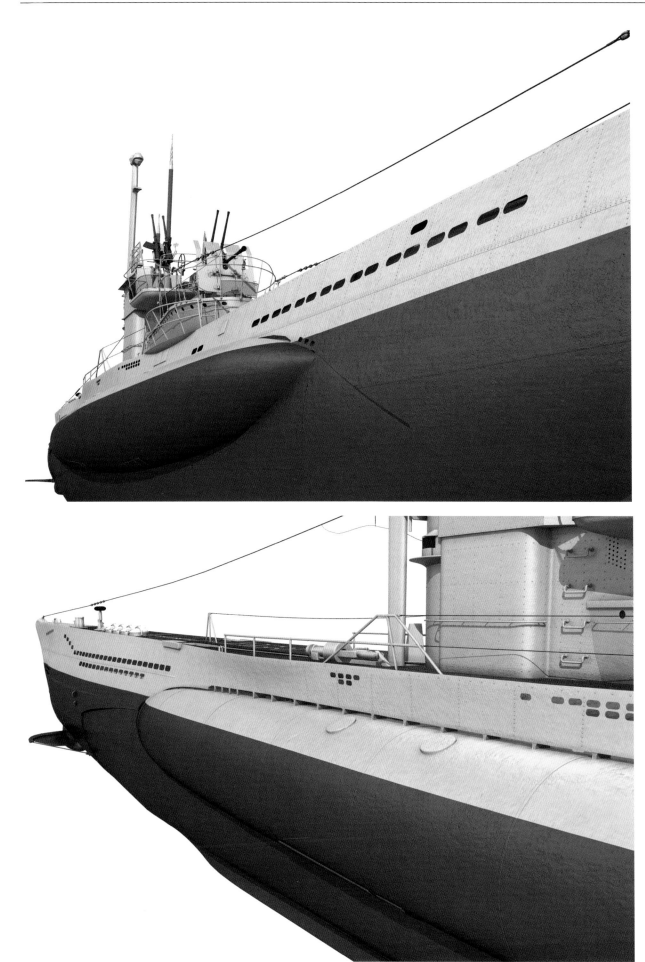

Details of the Type VIIC/41 U-boat.

A photographic tour of *U 995*, a Type VIIC/41 preserved at Labo

Key to the locations of the views on the following pages

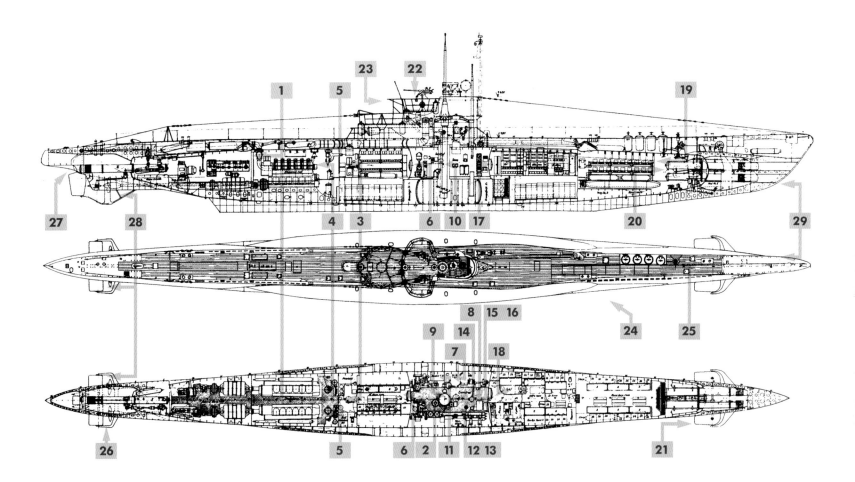

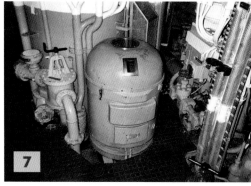

U 995 (Type VIIC/41 Type) exhibited in Laboe.

1. Aft compartment – motor room, main switchboards. On both sides of passageway there are two electric motors and in the background one can see the round hatch of aft torpedo tube.

2. Control room – right rear corner – air compressor. On the right, the circular after hatch is seen, above it there is the wheel shutting the aft starboard ballast tank valve. At the bottom: the venting and blowing valves of trim, regulation, auxiliary and fresh water tanks.

3. Engine room – looking forward. The hatch leading to the galley is visible in the background.

4. Engine room – looking aft. The round dials are the engine telegraph repeaters – red for the port engine, green for the starboard one. The black levers seen below are the clutch and engine revolution controls.

5. Galley.

6. After petty officers' mess. In the background the aft hatch to the engine room. By the lower bunk you can see the collapsible wooden tables.

7. The master gyrocompass.

8. The hydroplane controls. The wheels were used for manual steering; inside them there are the buttons, by means of which the planesmen operated the planes electrically. The large dial on the left is the famous Papenberg – the depth meter for small ranges. The upper dials are the engine telegraph repeaters for the port (red) and starboard (green) engines respectively. The indicator visible on the right is the rough depth reading gauge, in the centre – the vertical glass tube – the small precise depth meter used when working with the periscope (the drawing of the periscope is seen on the left edge of the meter) and to the right, the vertical indicator – a kind of weight balance (instrument showing the distribution of weight throughout the boat for 'putting on the trim'). The round dials seen above the hydroplanes wheels are indicators of the planes' positions: forward to the left and aft on the right.

9. Control room. On the left the attack periscope standard can be seen, to the right the chart table. The black wheel above opens and closes the vents from the port middle ballast tank.

10. Control room. On the right, one can see the attack periscope standard and the vertical ladder leading to conning tower. On the left, a part of the 'Christmas tree' – the valves controlling the medium-pressure compressed

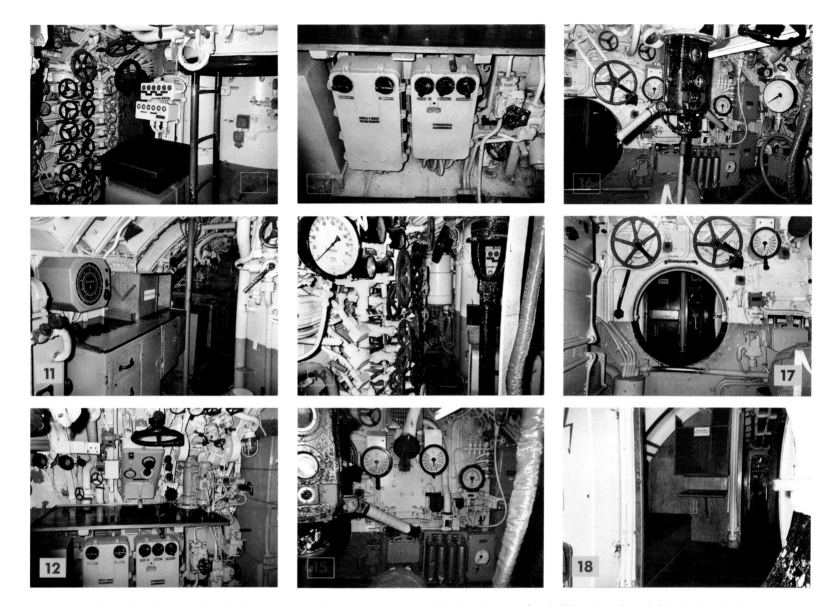

air tanks. On the right – the torpedo tubes' firing control lights.

11. Control room, port side looking forward. The chart table with the drawers for stowing the navigational charts, to the left the indicator of the echo sounder and the boxes for the sextants.

12. Control room, port side. The chart table, under it the steering and engine telegraph selectors.

13. Control room, port side. The steering and engine telegraph selectors under the chart table.

14. Control room, starboard side. The 'Christmas tree', the flooding and bilge valves. In the background the starboard-side air compressor is seen. The black vertical shaft is part of the remote control of the snorkel.

15. Control room, fore bulkhead, starboard side. On the left the search periscope with unfolded handles can be seen. In the middle, engine telegraphs and between them the voice pipe for communication with the bridge. On the right, there is the rudder position indicator. At the bottom are the rudder control and the CO_2 scrubbers.

16. Control room, fore bulkhead, starboard side. In the middle, the periscope is visible; below it the rudder control; next to it and to the left, the fore hatch with the ballast tank valve and engine telegraph.

17. Control room, fore bulkhead, the hatch leading to the captain's cabin; above the blue wheels controlling the fore ballast tank vents. Next to them you can see the port engine telegraph and below them the rudder control.

18. Captain's cabin, looking forward. The captain's 'cabin' is only a corner of the wardroom shut off by a thick curtain from the main passageway, giving the C/O an illusion of privacy.

Continued on next page

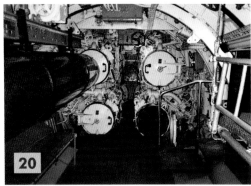

19. Forward compartment inhabited by seamen, looking aft. The spare torpedoes are stowed under the ratings' bunks. On the right, a torpedo slung from the rail, ready to be loaded.

20. Forward compartment, looking forward. Four torpedoes tubes are visible.

21. Fore hydroplane.

22. View of the 'Wintergarten' – 'bandstand' – the open platform at the aft end of the bridge.

23. Conning-tower of the U-boat seen from the rear.

24. A general view of the conning-tower. On the side one can see the side tanks, called 'the saddle tanks'.

25. A view of the boat's deck and it's conning-tower, looking aft. In the deck, alongside the conning tower, the folded-down snorkel is visible. Noticeable is the magnetic compass housing which projects in front of the tower.

26. The aft hydroplane and starboard propeller, looking aft.

27. The view of ship's stern. In it's characteristic recess the outer door of the stern torpedo tube is visible.

28. The aft hydroplane and starboard propeller.

29. *U 995* on display in Laboe. All the interior shots shown here were taken aboard this boat.

1943

Although 1943 began with successes for the Germans, this was the year the U-bootwaffe would be defeated, when it would begin to withdraw its boats from the Atlantic. Allied defences were becoming stronger and stronger: technical advances, the increasing use of aviation and the closing of the mid-Atlantic 'air gap', improving signals intelligence and the ever-tightening blockade of the Bay of Biscay were all having an effect. More effective independent hunter-killer groups were patrolling the convoy routes searching for U-boats, which they were able to attack on sight, as the convoys had their own close escorts which were themselves now more effective. Signals intelligence frequently allowed convoys to be re-routed to avoid the wolfpacks, which found themselves waiting in vain for targets which never appeared. Despite all this, however, final Allied victory was still some distance away.

The first engagement of 1943 was a clash with a small convoy, TM 1 of only nine ships, protected by the British group B 5 (a destroyer and three corvettes). The action began on 3 January, after the convoy had been spotted by *U 514* and the 'Dolphin' group was directed onto it. The wolfpack consisted of seven Type VIIs, *U 134* (Kptlt. Rudolf Schendel), *U 381* (Kptlt. Wilhelm-Heinrich Graf von Puckler und Limburg), *U 436* (Kptlt. Günther Seibicke), *U 442* (KKpt. Hans Hesse), *U 571* (Kptlt.

Helmut Moehlmann), *U 575* (Kptlt. Günther Heydemann) and *U 620* (Kptlt. Heinz Stein), and four Type IXs, *U 134*, *U 181*, *U 511* and *U 522*. During the engagement 'Dolphin' was reinforced by four more Type IXs, *U 105*, *U 124*, *U 125* and *U 514* which had spotted the convoy. After reporting its position, *U 514* torpedoed and damaged one of the ships of the convoy, a tanker, which was later finished off by *U 105*. When Dönitz learned of the presence of tankers carrying fuel for Allied forces in North Africa, he immediately cancelled all other operations and ordered the 'Dolphin' group to intercept the convoy. Unfortunately, the commodore of the convoy appears to have ignored Admiralty instructions to alter course and so sailed straight into the waiting U-boats.

On 8 January *U 381* also made contact with the convoy. In a series of attacks which lasted until the 12th, the Germans sank seven tankers, so that only two of them reached Gibraltar with their vital cargo, at the cost of two U-boats damaged, *U 134* and *U 436*. On 8 January the Norwegian tanker *Albert L. Ellsworth* (8309 GRT) and the British *Oltenia II* were both torpedoed by *U 436*, on 9 January the British *Empire Lytton* (9801 GRT) was destroyed by *U 442* and on 11 January *British Dominion* (6983 GRT) was finished off by *U 620*, after being damaged by *U 522*. This operation was considered a major strategic success.

Between 4 and 8 February the 'Pfeil' and 'Handegen' groups fought a fierce battle against the large convoy SC 118 (Sydney – Great Britain). The ships were escorted by the British group B 2 with three Royal Navy destroyers, three British and three Free French corvettes, and an American cutter. Among the convoy was the rescue ship

▼ It became the custom to hoist pennants representing ships sunk with the estimated tonnage on them when a boat returned to base. Some are being prepared here. (CAW)

▼ Painting a victory symbol on the door of the stern torpedo tube of an unidentified Type VII. In this case it is this silhouette of a destroyer. (CAW)

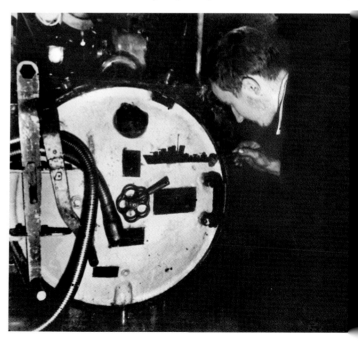

Toward, equipped with HF/DF, which would play a crucial role in the course of the battle. The Germans were lucky that B 2's commanding officer, the very successful U-boat killer Commander Donald Macintyre, was absent as his destroyer HMS *Hesperus* was in dock after ramming a U-boat on her previous voyage.

SC 118 was picked up by the B-Dienst almost from the moment it sailed, and signals intercepts allowed them to plot its route with considerable accuracy. This information was by chance confirmed by a survivor from the convoy HX 224 who had been picked up by the Germans.

Dönitz hastily deployed the U-boats of the 'Pfeil' group, the Type IX *U 187* and the Type VIIs *U 89* (KKpt. Dietrich Lohmann), *U 135* (Oblt.z.S. Heinz Schutt), *U 262* (Kptlt. Heinz Franke), *U 266* (Kptlt. Ralf von Jessen), *U 267* (Kptlt. Otto Tinschert), *U 402* (KKpt. Siegfried Freiherr von Forstner), *U 413* (Kptlt. Gustav Poel), *U 454* (Kptlt. Burkhard Hacklander), *U 465* (Kptlt. Heinz Wolf), *U 594* (Kptlt. Friedrich Mumm), *U 608* (Kptlt. Rolf Struckmeier) and *U 609* (Kptlt. Klaus Rudloff), across the anticipated route of the convoy.

◀ ▲ Keeping track of a U-boat's position was a significant challenge for the crew. As the boats only usually surfaced at night, taking a sun-sight at noon was not an option. Charts of the night sky, as seen here, were used, as well as dead reckoning based on heading, speed and predicted currents. (CAW)

Nevertheless, despite the fact that the convoy sailed practically right through the middle of the German patrol line, the U-boats failed to locate it. Only a star shell accidentally fired by one of the merchant ships revealed its position. It was spotted by *U 182*, but while transmitting its sighting report the boat was sunk by the destroyers HMS *Beverly* and HMS *Vimy*. But the prompt response of the escorts could not help the fact that the convoy's position had already been revealed to the Germans. After receiving the appropriate report Dönitz ordered five Type VIIs from the 'Handegen' group, *U 438* (Kptlt. Rudolf Franzius), *U 613* (Kptlt. Helmut Köppe), *U 624* (Kptlt. Ulrich Graf von Soden-Fraunhofen), *U 704* (Kptlt. Horst Keßler) and *U 752* (Kptlt. Karl Ernst Schroeter), as well as *U 456* (Kptlt. Max-Martin Teichert) and *U 614* (Kptlt. Wolfgang Sträter), to assist.

► The engine room aboard a U-boat. (CAW)

The U-boat commanders were much too talkative and practically swamped their HQ with reports. Their radio transmissions were tracked with the HF/DF equipment, revealing their positions to the convoy escorts. Knowing where the threat was, they were able to keep the situation under control and drive off the attackers. During the turn made in order to avoid the enemy, the convoy broke up. Three of the left-hand columns failed to make the turn, remaining on their original course and became separated from the other ships. The Germans immediately took advantage of this and most U-boats followed this detached group, but in vain. All their attacks failed again.

On 5 February, thanks to the efforts of the escorts, the convoy reunited. In deteriorating weather U-boats lost contact with their targets, and finally the escorting force was reinforced by three American ships coming from Iceland. On the following day the Germans regained contact and attacked again, the escorts counter-attacking just as fiercely. The heavily-damaged *U 465* had to disengage – the boat's position had been given away by its radio transmissions.

In the evening, after more intense attacks, *U 267*, heavily damaged by the destroyer HMS *Vimy*, broke off the action. *U 262* managed to get on the side of the convoy unprotected by the escorts and fired a salvo of torpedoes, but scored no hits. One torpedo from a second salvo hit and sank the small Polish merchant ship *Zagloba*, but *U 262* was in turn badly damaged by a corvette and had to return to base.

Up to now the escorts had had the upper hand, but *U 402* was about to change the course of the battle. Its commander repeated the achievement of his colleague in *U 262* and attacked from the other side of the convoy. Just after midnight he torpedoed two ships and withdrew to

▼ A U-boat's control room. Note the planesmen's stations and the depth gauges above them. (CAW)

reload his tubes. This might not seem that significant, but KKpt. Freiherr von Forstner's attack would have serious consequences for the convoy, because one of the ships he had sunk was the rescue ship *Toward*. Now the duty of picking up survivors would fall on the escorts, forcing them to leave their places in the escort screen. Furthermore, the HF/DF set was lost. As escorts fell out to pick up survivors, U-boats were able to penetrate the screen and attack. Several times the deadly-efficient *U 402* did this, spreading death and destruction at every opportunity. However, on occasions leaving the formation could have positive results. Whilst searching for survivors in the wake of the convoy, the Free French corvette *Lobella* sighted *U 609* on the surface and opened fire. The U-boat dived, only to be destroyed by depth charges.

At twilight contact was lost again. On 7 February the Germans located the target for a short time and *U 402* used its last torpedo to sink the seventh ship, although all the other attacking U-boats were chased away by the escorts. During these last attempts both *U 135* and *U 614* were damaged. It had been an extremely fierce battle, but the Germans could not be happy with the outcome. Twelve merchant ships sunk at the cost of *U 187* and the two Type VIIs *U 609* and *U 624* and *U 267*, *U 262*, *U 465*, *U 135* and *U 614* damaged was not a great achievement. Only two commanders, Franke in *U 262* and Freiherr von Forstner in *U 402*, had been able to get around the escort force, which despite the absence of Macintyre had been very efficient, making excellent use of the HF/DF and their radars. After analysing this engagement Dönitz decided to alter U-boat

◄ ▼ The motor room aboard *U 553* (Type VIIC), 1941. (CAW)

tactics: from then on the U-boats would be ordered to move away from the convoy in daylight, get ahead of it and only attack at night. Furthermore, these attacks were to be conducted submerged, not on the surface as before.

All the Allied ships sunk were victims of Type VIIs. The first casualty was the American *West Portal* (5576 GRT) torpedoed on 5 February by *U 413*. On 6 February two ships were lost: the Polish *Zagloba* (2864 GRT) sunk by *U 262* and the Greek *Polyktor* destroyed by *U 266*. Losses on 7 February were: the British *Afrika* (8597 GRT), the American *Henry R. Mallory* (6063 GRT), the Greek *Kalliopi* (4965 GRT), the American *Robert F. Hopkins* (6625 GRT) and the British *Toward* (1571 GRT). They were all victims of Freiherr von Forstner in *U 402*. The same boat also managed to damage the Norwegian ship *Daghild* (9272 GRT). The same day saw loss of one more ship – the British *Harmala* (5730 GRT) sunk by *U 614*. On 8 February *U 402* destroyed the British ship *Newton Ash* (4625 GRT), while *U 608* finished off *Daghild* which sank along with a landing craft, *LCT–2335* (291 tonnes), she had aboard.

On 21 February *U 604* located the 49-ship Convoy ON 166 which was escorted by the American group A 3 composed of the cutters USS *Spencer* and USCG *Campbell*, and one British and four Canadian corvettes. The battle was preceded by a contest between the signal intelligence teams of both sides, in which the Germans tried to determine the route of the Allied ships, while the Allies did their best to avoid the German ambushes.

The force dispatched to attack included the 'Ritter' group – *U 529*, *U 332* (Oblt.z.S. Eberhard Hüttemann), *U 377* (Kptlt. Otto Köhler), *U 454* (Kptlt. Burkhard Hackländer), *U 468* (Oblt.z.S. Klemens Schamong), *U 603*

(Oblt.z.S. Hans-Joachim Bertelsmann), *U 623* (Oblt.z.S. Hermann Schröder), *U 628* (Kptlt. Heinrich Hasenschar), *U 653* (Kptlt. Gerhard Feiler) and *U 753* (KKpt. Alfred Manhardt von Mannstein), all but the first being Type VIIs – and the 'Neptun' group. Initially the convoy managed to evade the German patrol line by altering course to the south, but the Germans were aware of this manoeuvre. However, the turn had taken the convoy out of range of the 'Neptun' group, so the 'Knappen' group was ordered to attack instead. It consisted of *U 91*, *U 92* and two Type VIIs, *U 600* (Kptlt. Bernhard Zurmühlen) and *U 604* (Kptlt. Horst Höltring). Several independent boats also took part in the engagement. These were *U 186* and the four

Type VIIs *U 223* (Kptlt. Karl-Jürg Wächter), *U 303* (Kptlt. Karl-Franz Heine), *U 621* (Oblt.z.S. Max Kruschka) and *U 707* (Oblt.z.S. Günther Gretschel).

The first day of the battle was not really successful for the Germans. *U 604*, which was shadowing the convoy, was detected and chased away by USS *Spencer* before the other U-boats managed to intercept the enemy ships. *U 603* and *U 332* jointly sank one ship, but the escorts not only managed to drive them away, but also began to inflict damage on the U-boat force. Cooperating Allied aircraft sank *U 623* and damaged *U 91*. *U 332*, *U 454* and *U 753* all failed to get through the ring of escorts. The escorts were further reinforced by the Polish destroyer ORP *Burza*. In the evening *U 91* torpedoed two ships, one of which proved to be too damaged to continue and was finished off by the *Burza*. The other one was scuttled by its own crew later on, but before that *U 753* and *U 92* unsuccessfully attempted to do the job themselves. *U 529* disappeared during further attack attempts. On 22 February no U-boat managed to carry out a successful daylight attack. Only after nightfall did Germans try again, but only *U 606* was successful, torpedoing three ships, two of which sank; the third one was finished off by *U 303*. In return *U 606* was lost in a counter-attack by USCG *Campbell,* ORP *Burza* and the corvette HMCS *Chilliwack*. However, *Campbell* was seriously damaged when she rammed the U-boat and had to make for Ireland, escorted part of the way by *Burza*. The Polish destroyer soon rejoined the convoy, but running low on fuel she had to leave for Newfoundland, together with one of the corvettes. *U 604* sank a rescue ship which

▲ One way to increase a lookout's field of view – raise him on the periscope. Note the grinning swordfish – most probably painted in red – on the conning tower. This symbol first appeared in green on *U 96* when it was commanded by Kptlt. Heinrich Lehmann-Willenbrock. During one of its patrols the boat carried a war correspondent aboard, Sonderführer-Leutnant Lothar-Günther Buchheim, who later wrote the famous novel *Das Boot*, the character of 'Der Alte' ('The Old Man') being modelled on Lehmann-Willenbrock. After being promoted to the rank of Korvettenkapitän, Lehmann-Willenbrock was appointed commander of the 9th Flotilla based in Brest, which adopted the symbol on most of its boats. (CAW)

▶ Lehmann-Willenbrock was one of the most effective U-boat commanders. He sank twenty-four ships (including one neutral Swedish ship) totalling 170,237 GRT, damaged two more of 15,864 GRT and caused the destruction of yet another of 8888 GRT. All those successes were achieved between December 1940 and March 1942, when he commanded *U 96* (Type VIIC). On 31 December he received the Knight's Cross with Oak Leaves. (CAW)

Date	Ship	GRT	Nationality
21 Feb 1943	*Stigstad* (damaged)	5964	Norwegian
21 Feb 1943	*Stigstad*	5964	Norwegian
21 Feb 1943	*Empire Trader*	9990	British
22 Feb 1943	*Chattanooga City*	5687	American
22 Feb 1943	*Empire Redshank*	6615	British
22 Feb 1943	*Expositor*	4959	American
22 Feb 1943	*Nielsen Alonso*	9348	Norwegian
23 Feb 1943	*Eulima*	6207	British
23 Feb 1943	*Hastings*	5401	American
23 Feb 1943	*Winkler*	6907	Panamanian
23 Feb 1943	*Expositor*	4959	American
23 Feb 1943	*Glittore*	6409	Norwegian
23 Feb 1943	*Stockport*	1683	British
24 Feb 1943	*Ingria*	4391	Norwegian
24 Feb 1943	*Madoera* (damaged)	9382	Dutch
24 Feb 1943	*Jonathan Sturges*	7176	American
25 Feb 1943	*Manchester Merchant*	7264	British

got separated during the battle. On 23 February the weakened escorts, which now also had to pick up survivors, were no longer as effective as before and six ships were sunk with a further two being damaged. A change of course ordered by the commodore prevented further losses, and on 24 February aircraft from Newfoundland appeared over the convoy. During the battle the Germans lost two Type VIIs – *U 623* and *U 606* – and a Type IX – *U 529*. *U 91* was damaged and had to abort its patrol and return to base. The Allied losses were as shown in the table above.

Also between 22 and 25 February, the 'Rochen' group engaged Convoy UC 1. The group was composed of the Type VIIs *U 87* (Kptlt. Joachim Berger), *U 202* (Kptlt. Günter Poser) and *U 558* (Kptlt. Günther Krech) and the Type IXs *U 43* (Oblt.z.S. Hans-Joachim Schwantke), *U 66*, *U 218*, *U 504* and *U 521* and was further reinforced by another Type IX, *U 522* and the Type VIIs *U 382* (Kptlt.

Herbert Juli) and *U 569* (Oblt.z.S. Hans Jhannsen). UC 1 was escorted by the British group 44 with four sloops and two frigates and an American support group with four destroyers. In this action the Germans managed to sink three ships but lost *U 522*. *U 202* destroyed the American *Esso Baton Rouge* (7989 GRT) and also damaged *British Fortitude* (8482 GRT), the Dutch *Murena* (8252 GRT) and one more British ship – the *Empire Norseman* (9811 GRT). This last ship was later also hit by *U 382* and eventually sunk by *U 558*. *U 522*, the only Type IX to score in this battle, sank the British *Athelprincess* (8882 GRT).

Convoy SC 121, with fifty-nine ships escorted by the American group A 3 (a cutter, a destroyer and two British and two Canadian corvettes), cleverly outmanoeuvred the 'Burggraf' and 'Wildfang' groups which were positioned across its route, but on 6 March it was located by *U 405*, which duly reported its presence to headquarters. Because the U-boats which had been evaded by the convoy would

▼ Lehmann-Willenbrock (in the middle, seated) plays with the mascot of the 9th Flotilla, a suitably-uniformed goat. (CAW)

◀ *U 96* in the entrance channel of St-Nazaire on its return from a patrol. At that time the boat belonged to the 7th Flotilla commanded by Kptlt. Herbert Sohler (between May 1940 and February 1944) – hence the charging bull emblem on the port side of the tower. On the starboard side the boat displays the personal emblem of its CO, Kptlt. Heinrich Lehmann-Willenbrock.

▲ A Type VIIC cruising in calm seas. (CAW)

▲ KKpt. Heinrich Lehmann-Willenbrock commanded the 9th Flotilla stationed in Brest between May 1942 and September 1944, when it was disbanded. He was a popular commander and often personally met with his submarine crews. (CAW)

▼ ► Fixing a broken antenna cable on a Type VIIC. The photograph below shows the boat's commanding officer who has crawled from the bridge along the stays. (CAW)

not now be able to intercept it, Dönitz's staff decided to form two new patrol lines. The first was 'Westmark' with *U 523*, *U 526*, *U 527* and the following Type VIIs: *U 228* (Kptlt. Erwin Christophersen), *U 230* (Kptlt. Paul Siegmann), *U 332* (Oblt.z.S. Erberhard Hüttemann), *U 359* (Oblt.z.S. Heinz Förster), *U 405* (KKpt. Rolf-Heinrich Hopmann), *U 409* (Oblt.z.S. Hans-Ferdinand Massmann), *U 432* (Kptlt. Hermann Eckhardt), *U 448* (Oblt.z.S. Helmut Dauter), *U 566* (Kptlt. Hans Homkohl), *U 591* (Kptlt. Hans-Jürgen Zetsche), *U 616* (Oblt.z.S. Siegfried Koitschka), *U 634* (Oblt.z.S. Eberhard Dahlhaus), *U 659* (Kptlt. Hans Stock) and *U 709* (Oblt.z.S. Karl-Otto Weber). Because the convoy consisted of ships of different speeds, as the weather deteriorated the slower ships began to fall behind, the large number of stragglers providing easy prey for the U-boats. The escort group was also nearly exhausted from continuous operations and its ships all needed maintenance.

▲ *U 30*, a veteran Type VIIA, alongside a tender during maintenance, 1943. This was one of the first Type VII boats which had a different drainage slot hole layout in the outer casing near the hawse hole. It became famous when – commanded by Kptlt. Fritz-Julius Lemp – it executed the first attack against a ship during the Second World War, sinking the passenger liner *Athenia* without warning. On 1 December 1940 the boat was reassigned to the 24th Flotilla, a training unit, based at Memel (Klaipėda). (CAW)

◄ A Type VIIA from astern, showing the distinctive stern torpedo tube mounted outside the pressure hull, meaning it was a one-shot weapon while at sea. On later models the tube was mounted inside the pressure hull, with its outer door much lower down, between the rudders. (CAW)

► A sequence of photographs showing a Type VIIC U-boat being launched. Part of the pressure hull of another boat can be seen on the left. (CAW)

◀ The successes achieved by the U-bootwaffe from the beginning of the war combined with the poor performance of the surface warships meant that almost all shipbuilding efforts in Germany became concentrated on submarine construction. Two Type VIIC U-boats in the final stages of construction, 1944. (CAW)

On the night of 6/7 March *U 230* and *U 566* attacked. *U 230* sank the small British ship *Egyptian* (2868 GRT), its loss going completely unnoticed in the storm. The British *Empire Impala* (6116 GRT) managed to pick up survivors from the sunken ship, but in doing so she also fell behind the convoy. Before dawn she was torpedoed by *U 591* and sunk. On 7 March several U-boats tried to attack in daylight again, but with no result. On 8 March the weather improved slightly, so the German command hastily formed another group, 'Ostmark', with *U 198*, *U 530* and seven Type VIIs: *U 229* (Oblt.z.S. Robert Schetelig), *U 439* (Oblt.z.S. Helmut von Tippelskirch), *U 447* (Kptlt. Friedrich-Wilhelm Bothe), *U 618* (Kptlt. Kurt Baberg), *U 641* (Kptlt. Horst Rendtel), *U 642* (Kptlt. Herbert Brünning) and *U 665* (Oblt.z.S. Hans Jürgen Haupt). On that day *U 190* sank one ship and *U 527* sank two. *U 591* destroyed the Yugoslavian *Vojvoda Putnik* (5879 GRT), *U 633* sank the British *Guido* (3921 GRT), and *U 642* the British *Leadgate* (2125 GRT). On 9 March *U 405* sank the Norwegian ship *Bonneville* (4665 GRT) with the British landing craft *LCT 2341* (291 tonnes) aboard, and *U 409* destroyed the American *Malantic* (3837 GRT) and the British *Rosewood* (5989 GRT). The Type IX *U 530* destroyed the Swedish ship *Milos* (3058 GRT) on the same day. On 10 March, the last day of the battle, *U 229* sank the British *Nailsea Court* (4946 GRT) and damaged the British *Coulmore* (3670 GRT).

The mounting losses of merchant ships made many senior Royal Navy officers question the effectiveness of

◀ A Type VII enters a recently-completed U-boat pen on the Atlantic coast of occupied France. (ADM*)*

▲ A Type VIIC U-boat returns to base after a patrol. The boat is approaching its berth. (ADM)

▼ A happy U-boat crewman opens the hatch on his return from patrol. (CAW)

convoy tactics. Nonetheless, they were actually quite efficient as most ships that were sunk were stragglers – those that for whatever reason had fallen behind the escorts. Another cause of losses was the insufficient number of escorts. The crews of the often elderly ships were exhausted, having to fight both the U-boats and the elements. It was not until after the battles for Convoys SC 122 and HX 299 that Churchill finally assigned more ships to the escort forces, and thus won the Battle of the Atlantic. But this was yet to come.

For now the Allies' bad luck continued. On 10 March *U 336* found sixty ships protected by the British 3rd Escort Group of two British and two Polish (ORP *Burza* and ORP *Garland*) destroyers and two British and three French corvettes. This was Convoy HX 228 heading from New York to Great Britain. On 6 March, the escorting force had been reinforced by the American Support Group, the escort aircraft carrier USS *Bogue* and two destroyers. On the same day the Germans had formed the 'Neuland' group, composed entirely of Type VIIs: *U 86* (Kptlt. Walter Schug), *U 221* (Kptlt. Hans Trojer), *U 336* (Kptlt. Hans Hunger), *U 373* (Kptlt. Paul-Karl Loeser), *U 406* (Kptlt. Horst Dieterichs), *U 440* (Oblt.z.S. Hans Geissler), *U 441* (Kptlt. Klaus Hartmann), *U 444* (Oblt.z.S. Albert Langfeld), *U 448* (Oblt.z.S. Helmut Dauter), *U 590* (Kptlt. Heinrich Müller-Edzards), *U 608* (Kptlt. Rolf Struckmeier), *U 659* (Kptlt. Hans Stock) and *U 757* (Oblt.z.S. Friedrich Deetz). The group was further reinforced by *U 228* (Kptlt. Erwin Christophersen), *U 333* (Oblt.z.S. Werner Schwaff), *U 359* (Oblt.z.S. Heinz Förster), *U 405* (KKpt. Rolf-Heinrich Hopman), *U 432* (Kptlt. Hermann Eckhardt), and *U 566* (Kptlt. Hans Homkohl).

On 8 March the boats of the northern part of 'Neuland' were reassigned to 'Ostmark' in order to engage Convoy SC 121 as mentioned above. Because at about this time the U-boat command had changed its codebooks, the British could no longer read their wireless traffic and therefore could not get a clear picture of where the U-boats were lying in wait. The convoy's route was not changed and the ships fell into the German trap.

U 336, which had first located the convoy, was initially driven away by the escorts, but its place was soon taken by *U 444*, which – despite the efforts of USS *Bogue* and her aircraft – summoned other 'Neuland' boats to the area. During the night the Germans attacked. On 10 March, before midnight, *U 221* sank the American ship *Andrea F. Luckenbach* (6565 GRT) and the British *Tucurinca* (5412 GRT), and also the American merchant vessel *Lawton B. Evans* (7197 GRT). On 11 March *U 757* destroyed two vessels: the American ship *William C. Gorgas* (7197 GRT) and the landing craft *LCT 2398* (291 tonnes) aboard her, but the U-boat was damaged in the explosion of the ship's cargo of ammunition and had to disengage.

The escorts counter-attacked immediately. The destroyer HMS *Harvester* depth-charged *U 444*, forcing it to surface, and then rammed it. The two vessels remained locked together for some time, but *U 444* managed to break free and attempted to escape, but was rammed again and sunk by the Free French corvette *Aconit*. The damaged HMS *Harvester* tried to catch up with the convoy on her one serviceable shaft, but that too broke down and she had to stop. *U 432* took advantage of this and sank her with a well-aimed torpedo. But the U-boat's crew could not celebrate their victory for long, as the *Aconit*, returning after dealing with *U 444*, depth-charged *U 432* and forced it to surface. The French ship then opened fire and rammed the boat, destroying it. At the same time *U 590* damaged the British ship *Jamaica Producer* (5464 GRT), while *U 86* sank the Norwegian *Brant County* (5001 GRT).

Between 16 and 19 March 1943 one of the largest convoy battles of the war took place. The mid-Atlantic 'air gap' had not yet been closed, and numerous U-boats would hunt there, spaced some 15–16 miles apart, deployed across the route of convoys heading from New York and Halifax to Britain. In March there were as many as three patrol lines in that area. At the west edge of the 'gap' there was 'Raubgraf' made up entirely of Type VIIs: *U 84* (Kptlt. Horst Uphoff), *U 89* (Kptlt. Dietrich Lohmann), *U 91* (Kptlt. Heinz Walkering), *U 435* (Kptlt. Siegfried Strelow), *U 600* (Kptlt. Bernhard Zurmühlen), *U 603* (Oblt.z.S. Hans-Joachim Bertelsmann), *U 615* (Kptlt. Ralph Kapitzky), *U 653* (Kptlt. Gerhard Feiler), *U 664* (Oblt.z.S. Adolf Graef) and *U 758* (Kptlt. Helmut Manseck). The other two groups were deployed across the entire 'gap'. The first was 'Dranger' with *U 86* (Kptlt. Walter Schug), *U 221* (Oblt.z.S. Hans Trojer), *U 333* (Oblt.z.S. Werner Schwaff), *U 373* (Kptlt. Paul-Karl Loeser), *U 406* (Kptlt. Horst Dietrichs), *U 440* (Kptlt. Hans Geissler), *U 441* (Kptlt. Klaus Hartmann), *U 590* (Kptlt. Heinrich Müller-Edzards), *U 608* (Kptlt. Rolf Strukmeier) and *U 610* (Kptlt. Walter Freiherr von Freyberg-Eisenberg-Allmendingen), all Type VIIs. The other group, which extended the 'Dranger' line, was codenamed 'Sturmer': *U 523*, *U 526*, *U 527*, *U 530*, *U 190* and the Type VIIs *U 134* (Oblt.z.S. Hans-Gunther Brosin), *U 229* (Oblt.z.S. Robert Schetelig), *U 305* (Kptlt.

Rudolf Bahr), *U 338* (Kptlt. Manfred Kinzel), *U 384* (Oblt.z.S. Hans-Achin von Rosenberg-Gruszczynski), *U 439* (Oblt.z.S. Helmut von Tippelskirch), *U 598* (Kptlt. Gottfried Holtorf), *U 618* (Kptlt. Kurt Baberg), *U 631* (Oblt.z.S. Jürgen Krüger), *U 641* (Kptlt. Horst Randtel), *U 642* (Kptlt. Herbert Brünning), *U 665* (Oblt.z.S. Hans-Jürgen Haupt) and *U 666* (Oblt.z.S. Herbert Engel). There were more Type VIIs, acting independently, which also took part: *U 228* (Oblt.z.S. Erwin Christophersen), *U 230* (Kptlt. Paul Siegmann), *U 616* (Oblt.z.S. Siegfried Koitschka) and *U 663* (Kptlt. Heinrich Schmid). One of the two convoys which would a play central role in the events to come – SC 122 heading from Sydney to Great Britain – had passed through the position assigned to 'Raubgraf' the day before the U-boats got there. Also the other convoy – HX 229 – also eastbound, had managed to pass through the German line undetected during a storm. There might not have been a battle at all had it not been for an accident. The Type VII *U 653*, having lost crewmen washed overboard from the conning-tower, running low on fuel and with only one torpedo left, was ordered to return to base. The commander accordingly set course for France, unaware that he was in fact following the convoys. At 03.30 on 16 March *U 653* sighted Convoy HX 229, relatively close to the

▲ U-boats were often escorted in and out of base by surface ships, like this Type VII returning from a patrol between two escorts, December 1942. (CAW)

► A Type VII entering a U-boat pen at a French port in late February 1942. It has just been completed by the Organisation Todt – note the scaffolding still on the roof. These pens were intended to be bomb-proof. (CAW)

▼ A Type VIIC U-boat entering a pen. The berths are already numbered. (CAW)

'Raubgraf' line, which had already been passed unnoticed by the escorts. HX 229 had thirty-seven ships and was escorted by the group B 4. Due to a breakdown, its flagship, the destroyer HMS *Highlander*, was forced to turn back on 23 February with the group's CO, Commander Day, aboard, so now the escorting force was under Commander Luther. It consisted of the destroyers HMS *Volunteer*, HMS

Beverly and HMS *Mansfield* and two corvettes. HMS *Highlander* did not rejoin the force until 18 March and a day later and American destroyer USS *Babbitt* and a British corvette also arrived. Another chance event which determined the course of the battle was that HX 229 caught up *en route* with a slower convoy, SC 122. This latter was escorted by the group B 5 commanded by Cdr Boyle, which consisted of an American and a British destroyer, a frigate and five corvettes. A US Coast Guard cutter joined the force on 19 March.

After U 653 sent its sighting report, 'Raubgraf' was ordered to pursue HX 299 – the Germans were unaware of Convoy SC 122 – while 'Dranger' and 'Sturmer' were ordered to move to intercept it.

Seven 'Raubgraf' boats refuelled from the Type IXs U 119 and U 463 posted nearby, and then found their target. German submarines attacked at twilight and by morning torpedoed eight ships. Roughly at the same time the Type VII U 338 from 'Sturmer' spotted more ships some 120 miles ahead of the last reported position of HX 229 – these were the fifty merchant ships of Convoy SC 122.

U 338 launched a spread of torpedoes and hit four ships. A real slaughter ensued. The escorts were too few to protect the combined ships of both convoys from such a large number of U-boats, despite their best efforts. By 17 March, long-range Liberator aircraft based in Iceland and Northern Ireland were able to reach the convoys, but they were unable to prevent two more ships from HX 299 and three from SC 122 being sunk during the day. The Liberators flew again on the 18th but this time were unable to find HX 229, and the U-boats sank two more ships. On 19 March the escort forces were joined by the reinforcements described above, and larger numbers of aircraft also arrived, preventing further losses. Allied aircraft sank U 384 on that day and the rest of the U-boats were ordered to disengage.

In all HX 229 lost:

- On 16 March the Norwegian ship *Elin K.* (5214 GRT) sunk by U 603.
- On 17 March the British *Coracero* (7252 GRT) sunk by U 384, the American *William Eustis* (7196 GRT) sunk by U 435, the British *Southern Princess* (12,156 GRT) sunk by U 600, the American *Irénée Du Pont* (6125 GRT) and the British *Nariva* (8714 GRT), both damaged by U 600 and finished off by U 91, the Dutch *Terkoelei* sunk by U 631, the American *James Oglethorpe* (7176 GRT) and the Dutch *Zaanland* (6813 GRT), both sunk by U 758, and the American *Harry Luckenbach* (6366 GRT) sunk by U 91.
- On 18 March the British *Canadian Star* (8293 GRT) and American *Walter Q. Gresham* (7191 GRT) sunk by U 221.
- On 19 March the American ship *Mathew Luckenbach* was damaged by U 527 and finished off by U 523, both Type IX boats.

◄ The U-boat pens also provided repair facilities. These were more like an enlarged workshop than a full shipyard, but they could still restore boats to combat readiness. Almost every U-boat needed some repair work on return from a patrol, mainly due to failures of on-board equipment. The photograph shows the recommissioning of the 300th repaired U-boat in the summer of 1942. (CAW)

▼ The crew of a U-boat leaving on patrol being greeted by another crew which has just returned from a fruitful (as proven by the numerous pennants on the periscope) one off the US coast. The latter boat is *U 201* (Type VIIC) commanded by Kptlt. Adalbert Schnee – it returned from its 59-day tenth patrol on 21 May 1942. (CAW)

► *U 201* in Brest, 21 May 1942. It was a Type VIIC U-boat, at that time commanded by Kptlt. Adalbert Schnee. Note the camouflage pattern with wavy borders (usually these were straight or broken lines). On the conning-tower is the coat of arms of the town of Remscheid, patron of the boat, and a snowman – proof that the boat's CO had a sense of humour (Schnee means snow in German). (NARA)

▼ *U 201* entering Brest on 8 August 1942. The Commanding Officer, in the white cap, salutes the welcoming committee. This is the end of Kptlt. Schnee's eleventh patrol, his last one in this boat. The oak leaves were displayed on the tower to celebrate the fact that Schnee was awarded a Knight's Cross with Oak Leaves on 15 July. Note the slightly different shape of the snowman emblem. (NARA)

Convoy SC 122's losses were:

- On 17 March two British ships, *Port Auckland* (8789 GRT) and *Zouave* (4256), were sunk by *U 305*, three ships were sunk and one damaged by *U 338*'s devastating salvo, and one more was sunk by the same boat on the same day – the damaged ship was the British *Fort Cedar Lake* (7134 GRT), and the four vessels sunk were the Panamanian *Granville* (4071 GRT), the British *King Gruffydd* (5072 GRT) and *Kingsbury* (4898 GRT), and the Dutch *Alderamin* (7886 GRT). *Fort Cedar Lake* was finished off by *U 665*.
- On 18 March *Clarissa Redcliffe* (5754 GRT), a British ship which had left her position in the convoy and tried to flee on her own, was sunk by *U 663*
- On 19 March the Greek ship *Carras* (5234 GRT) was damaged by *U 666* and later finished off by *U 333*.

This was a major German victory. Shaken by the scale of their losses, the Allies finally reassessed their tactics, which would result in them winning the Battle of the Atlantic. After learning of the disaster, Churchill ordered that all available forces be concentrated in the area to

◄ ► Oblt.z.S. (later – after 1 March 1942 – Kptlt.) Adalbert Schnee at his periscope. The left-hand photo shows him at the beginning of a patrol, the other one some time later. Schnee began his career aboard *U 6* (Type IIA), and later commanded *U 60* (Type IID) in which he sank two small ships and damaged one large one of 15,434 GRT. (Left: NARA. Right: CAW)

◄ In October Schnee (left) was assigned to the BdU staff led by the then Vizeadmiral Dönitz (centre), where he organised anti-convoy operations. This was something he had considerable personal experience of – by then he had sunk twenty-one ships with a total tonnage of 90,189 GRT (including one neutral Swedish vessel), two auxiliary Royal Navy warships (including the first Fighter Catapult Ship, the 5155-GRT *Springbank*) and damaged three more ships (among them one neutral Argentinian), with a total tonnage of 28,820 GRT. Schnee remained at headquarters until September 1944 when he was appointed Commanding Officer of *U 2511* – the first and only Type XXI U-boat to be operationally deployed. He did not achieve any success in it, but survived the war. He was the son-in-law of Admiral Dönitz. (NARA)

◄ HMS *Springbank*, the first Fighter Catapult Ship (FCS) invented as a response for the threat posed by Fw 200 Kondor patrol aircraft. The ship was armed with anti-aircraft guns, but its main weapon was a fighter aircraft launched by a catapult installed amidships. The catapult itself had been removed from the cruiser HMS *Kent*. *Springbank* was sunk by *U 201* commanded by Oblt.z.S. Adalbert Schnee on 27 September 1941. This type of ship did not prove successful in action and was replaced by the Catapult Armed Merchantmen (CAM ships). (FAA Museum)

forty-two ships with escort group B 7 (two destroyers, a frigate, four corvettes, two rescue trawlers and a naval tanker). The convoy was therefore heading straight for the sixteen U-boats of 'Star': *U 192*, *U 528*, *U 531*, *U 532*, *U 533* and the Type VIIs *U 209* (Kptlt. Heinrich Brodda), *U 231* (Kptlt. Wolfgang Wenzel), *U 258* (Kptlt. Wilhelm von Mässenhausen), *U 378* (Kptlt. Erich Mäder), *U 381* (Kptlt. Wilhelm-Heinrich Graf von Pückler und Limburg), *U 386* (Oblt.z.S. Hans-Albrecht Kandler), *U 413* (Kptlt. Gustav Poel), *U 552* (Kptlt. Klaus Popp), *U 648* (Oblt.z.S. Peter Stahl), *U 650* (Oblt.z.S. Ernst Witzendorff) and *U 954* (Kptlt. Odo Löwe). After 1 May all of these U-boats, except *U 258*, *U 386*, *U 528* and *U 532*, were supposed to create a new group codenamed 'Fink'. ONS 5 was sailing on a northerly route, closer to Iceland, so it could stay in range of Allied aviation for as long as possible. On 24 April aircraft sank *U 710*, which had the bad luck to pass too close to the convoy whilst returning to Germany. On 28 April the convoy was sighted by *U 650*, whose report summoned more four U-boats, but also betrayed its presence to the escorts who were monitoring wireless traffic with their HF/DF. Now alerted to the ambush forming ahead, the convoy commodore changed course in an attempt to evade it, but that night four U-boats attacked, although only *U 258* was successful, sinking the American

▲ Deformation of a ballast tank on a Type VII caused by the explosion of a depth charge, late spring 1943. (CAW)

▶ Minor damage to the deck abaft the conning-tower aboard a Type VII. (CAW)

destroy the U-boats hunting there. And so it would be. The efforts of March had exhausted the U-bootwaffe. Most of the boats were at the end of their patrols and had to return to base for replenishment and repairs. So in April, with fewer U-boats at sea and stronger escort forces thanks to Churchill's orders, Allied losses halved. But in late April more U-boats went on patrol as new submarines entered service, and by then the number of U-boats operating against convoys in the Atlantic reached its peak. The signals intelligence war intensified also, a conflict the Allies were also beginning to win. They proved much faster at decoding enemy intercepts than the Germans were.

However, on 25 April the Germans changed their codebooks again, taking the Allies by surprise and preventing them from finding out about the 'Star' group concentrating on the route of Convoy ONS 5, comprised of

ship *McKeesport* (6198 GRT) on the 29th. *U 386* (Type VII) as well as *U 532* and *U 528* were heavily damaged by the escorts' determined counter-attack and had to return to base. This was not a favourable beginning for the U-boats. Certainly such an opening was not favourable for the Germans. In response to the commodore's reports that he was under attack, the Admiralty dispatched the 3rd Support Group – four destroyers under Commander MacCoy, a veteran of the Arctic convoys – to assist, as well as detaching the destroyer HMS *Oribi* from Convoy SC 127 to reinforce them.

On the following day, in rapidly deteriorating weather, *U 192* attacked the convoy but without result, and due to the worsening conditions lost contact with the convoy, which was itself beginning to break up in the storm. In the meantime, German signals intelligence had located Convoy SC 128 and the U-boat command decided to concentrate its efforts on that convoy, forming a patrol line across its route with the boats from two groups, 'Specht' and 'Star'. Two more groups were also directed to the area: 'Amsel I' with *U 107*, *U 504* and the Type VIIs *U 402* (KKpt. Siegfried Freiherr von Forstner), *U 575* (Kptlt. Günter Heydemann), *U 621* (Oblt.z.S. Max Kruschka) and *U 638* (Kptlt. Oskar Staudinger), and the all-Type VII 'Amsel II' with *U 266* (Kptlt. Ralf von Jessen), *U 377* (Kptlt. Otto Köhler), *U 383* (Kptlt. Horst Kremser) and *U 634* (Oblt.z.S. Eberhard Dahlhaus). On 1 May 'Specht' and 'Star' combined to form 'Fink', which now consisted of *U 125*, *U 168*, *U 192*, *U 514*, *U 531*, *U 533* and the Type VIIs *U 209* (Kptlt. Heinrich Brodda), *U 226* (Kptlt. Rolf

◄ A Flotilla Commander greets a U-boat crew upon their return from patrol, late summer – early autumn 1941. (CAW)

◄ A Type VIIC U-boat after returning from a patrol, spring 1942. The Flotilla Commander, after receiving the CO's report, speaks to the crew aboard the boat. (CAW)

▲ A Type VIIC after returning from a patrol off the US coast, spring 1942. The Flotilla Commander is listening to the Commanding Officer's report aboard. Note the pennants displaying the tonnage of vessels sunk. (CAW)

Borchers), *U 231* (Kptlt. Wolfgang Wenzel), *U 260* (Kptlt. Hubertus Purkhold), *U 264* (Kptlt. Hartwig Looks), *U 270* (Kptlt. Paul-Friedrich Otto), *U 358* (Kptlt. Rolf Manke), *U 378* (Kptlt. Erich Mäder), *U 381* (Kptlt. Wilhelm-Heinrich Graf von Pückler und Limburg), *U 413* (Kptlt. Gustav Poel), *U 438* (Kptlt. Heinrich Heinsohn), *U 552* (Kptlt. Klaus Popp), *U 584* (Kptlt. Joachim Deecke), *U 614* (Kptlt. Wolfgang Sträter), *U 628* (Kptlt. Heinrich Hasenschar), *U 630* (Oblt.z.S. Werner Winkler), *U 648* (Kptlt. Peter Stahl), *U 650* (Oblt.z.S. Ernst Witzendorff), *U 662* (Kptlt. Heinz-Eberhard Müller), *U 707* (Oblt.z.S. Günter Gretschel), *U 732* (Oblt.z.S. Klaus-Peter Carlsen) and *U 954* (Kptlt. Odo Löwe).

What was thought to be SC 128 was sighted on 1 May, but after *U 209* and *U 438* were damaged and then went

missing, contact was lost. *U 628* reported restoring contact with the convoy, but discovered that it was actually ONS 5, which had previously evaded the U-boats. 'Fink', 'Amsel I' and 'Amsel II' were therefore assigned to deal with this convoy. On 30 April the convoy escorts were reinforced by the destroyer HMS *Oribi*, and the scattered ships were got back into formation.

On 3 May the destroyers of the 3rd SG had to leave the convoy due to lack of fuel, but the two sloops and three frigates of 1st SG were ordered to take their place. On 4 May *U 125* began the next phase of the battle by sinking the British ship *Lorient* (4737 GRT), but during the night the counter-attacking escorts severely damaged *U 270* and *U 732* which headed back to base. The Type IX *U 514* was also damaged but was able to continue its patrol. However, the following day the U-boats were able to breach the escort screen.

U 707 attacked from ahead of the target – it let the convoy pass over it, then surfaced behind the ships and sank the British *North Britain* (4635 GRT). Battle had now definitely been joined. The next to attack was *U 628* which slipped through a gap between the escorts and fired torpedoes at five ships, though only succeeding in damaging one of them, the British *Harbury* (5081 GRT), although *U 628* was later able to finish her off. Roughly at the same time *U 264* sank another British ship, the *Harperley* (4586 GRT), and the American *West Maximus* (5561 GRT). *U 638* destroyed the British *Dolius*, but was itself sunk immediately afterwards by the depth charges of the corvette HMS *Sunflower*. In the evening *U 266* sank three ships, but was itself badly damaged itself by the destroyer HMS *Offa*. *U 358* was damaged by the corvette HMS *Pink* and returned to base, but *U 584* took advantage of the confusion, broke through a gap which appeared in the escort screen and sank the American ship *West Madaket* (5565 GRT). The number of U-boats around the convoy kept increasing. The escorts were doing their best, but even B-24 aircraft appearing overhead were unable to do anything. Dönitz, who was personally directing his boats, hoped to repeat the success of March and was holding nothing back. However, the whole situation changed when the convoy ran into fog. The U-boat commanders, who had hoped to overwhelm the escorts with sheer numbers, were suddenly blinded, while the escorts were equipped with radars operating on frequencies that the German Metox detectors could not pick up. The British ships could easily spot the German boats trying to stalk the convoy on the surfaced and all the attacks attempted during the night were repelled. *U 531* was sunk and *U 707* was forced to flee. Just before dawn a Hedgehog salvo destroyed *U 630*. Aboard *U 192* the terrified men on the bridge suddenly spotted the bow of a corvette coming out of the fog like the sword of destiny. The U-boat's commander immediately launched torpedoes in that direction, but missed. The Allied ship's depth charges did not. Set to explode at a shallow depth, they perfectly bracketed the Type IX U-boat and crushed its hull. After being rammed by HMS *Oribi*, *U 125* was scuttled by its own crew. At dawn *U 233* was damaged,

◄ A U-boat returns to a base on the Atlantic coast. The boat is moored alongside a torpedo boat and welcomed by the Flotilla Commander, September 1943. (CAW)

◄ A Type VIIC U-boat welcomed to a Mediterranean base, spring 1942. (CAW)

▶ Another such situation – this time the Flotilla Commander is met in the middle of the gangway, spring 1941. (CAW)

but the damaged *U 533* remained in action. Before dawn on 5 May the 1st Support Group joined the close escort of ONS 5, helping to drive away U-boats operating all around. The sloop HMS *Pelican* stalked *U 438*, getting to within 300m (328 yards) before she was spotted. The boat crash-dived but was sunk by depth charges again on a shallow setting.

In the morning Dönitz received full reports of the battle and was overwhelmed by the scale of his defeat. He immediately ordered all the remaining boats to disengage. Throughout the battle the escorts, without air support, had been able to beat off the attacks of three powerful wolfpacks. Only half of the impressive number of U-boats assembled had been able to attack. The sudden appearance of the fog, which the Germans tried to blame for their defeat, should not have surprised them as it was not an uncommon occurrence in the area. Thirteen Allied ships were sunk. This was the last time that the U-boats were able to sink this many ships in a single engagement, and it had been at the cost of seven of their own, the Type IXs *U 125*, *U 192* and *U 531*, and the Type VIIs *U 638*, *U 226*, *U 438* and *U 630*. Additionally *U 710* and *U 209* – which tried to join the attacking force – were also lost. Seven U-boats were forced to disengage due to damage.

On 27 May Dönitz cancelled all operations against convoys and – acknowledging defeat – withdrew his surviving U-boats from the Atlantic. From then on his boats would only operate there on individual patrols, while the Type VIIs boats would mainly operate in the Mediterranean and the North Sea.

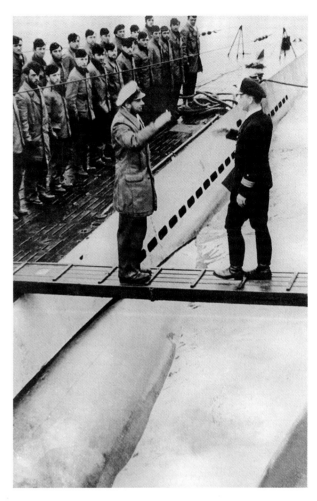

▶ A similar ceremony on the after deck of a U-boat, employed for this purpose because it was wider than the deck forward of the tower. (CAW)

U-Boat Crews

What sort of men made up the crews of the U-boats? The nature of their service required a particular kind of courage, skill and mental and physical toughness. They also had to be technically proficient to operate and maintain advanced equipment far away from the facilities of their bases and dockyards. Their skills and knowledge, coupled with practical experience, made them formidable opponents, and they were idolised in the German media, becoming popular heroes. On the other hand, they were vilified in the Allied press as little better than pirates and murderers, to be destroyed by any means available

Was this a fair assessment? They were loyal servicemen, who fought hard in time of war like every other serviceman. They were excellent seamen and navigators. But it was not the case, as claimed, that they were all volunteers. There were those officers who genuinely chose the submarine service, but many of the crew were posted to it by their superiors.

By the pivotal middle year of the war, 1943, most of those who had served aboard the U-boats from the beginning were either dead or captured, or had been assigned to shore duties as instructors, flotilla commanders or staff officers.

The natural characteristics of the German officer were undoubtedly loyalty and unconditional obedience. They did not pick their postings – their superiors assigned them where they were needed. When the U-bootwaffe was reborn, Dönitz picked his officers personally, Interestingly, he passed over veterans of the First World War, choosing instead younger men who he could train in accordance with his own ideas and tactics. This turned out to be very successful. In any case Kriegsmarine officers were simply assigned to the submarine service and could not do much to influence that posting.

Later in the war, a new type of officer began to serve aboard the U-boats – men who had previously served aboard surface warships or as observers in Luftwaffe maritime patrol aircraft. They began their service in the U-bootwaffe in 1940–1 as watch officers and, after experience of several patrols and completing a special training course, they would be given their own boats. It was often they case that they would go on a patrol 'shadowing' the commanding officer of the boat before they got their own commands. Almost all these officers would have been assigned to their new boat as it was being built, so they could become thoroughly familiar with it well in advance of taking it to sea.

Almost all U-boat officers, with only few exceptions who came from the merchant fleet, were young. U-boat commanders were also quite junior officers. On a battleship, a lieutenant was a minor figure, but in the U-bootwaffe he could be the captain of his own boat and wear the CO's white cap. Interestingly, the smaller and more agile Type VIIs were given to younger, more aggressive commanders, while the larger Type IXs went to older and perhaps steadier men.

The myth of all-volunteer crews arose spontaneously but was assiduously cultivated by the Kriegsmarine, which wanted to be able to claim that, despite all the losses, there were still men willing to serve aboard the U-boats. The officers, capable and professional as they were, were mostly posted to the U-bootwaffe. But the situation was somewhat different for the other ranks. Many were indeed volunteers, attracted to this tough and dangerous service by the significantly higher rates of pay, the ability to use special 'Submariners Only' shops that stocked goods normally unavailable, and certainly by the fame and glamour of the U-boat service. Also, the families of men who volunteered for the U-boats no longer suffered for any offence they may have committed against the Nazi regime.

All candidates for the submarine service had to undergo a tough and exhausting training programme. At first they trained individually on simulators and mock-ups. Then the courses continued aboard older U-boats assigned to training flotillas operating in the Baltic. After graduating from the training programme the men were assigned to existing crews or posted to shipyards where the new boats were being built for them.

Newly-commissioned U-boats joined the 4th Flotilla at Stettin, the 5th at Hel or the 8th at Danzig, where during a six-month programme the crews would get used to working together and train in all kinds of combat missions. In fact, this could be the toughest part of a submariner's career – in many ways tougher than actual combat. Once this was complete, the boat was assigned to operational service as a 'Frontboot' with one of the U-flotillas.

Apart from the training flotillas there were the following operational U-boat flotillas: the 1st and 9th at Brest, the 3rd at La Pallice and 6th and 7th at St.-Nazaire, which were almost exclusively equipped with Type VIIs, the standard boat in the Battle of the Atlantic. The 2nd and 10th Flotillas at Lorient as well as the 12th at Bordeaux were mostly equipped with Type IXs. These units were the mainstay of the German force in the Battle of the Atlantic. There were, however, more combat flotillas: the 5th at Kiel, the 11th at Bergen, the 13th at Trondheim, the 14th at Narvik, the 33rd at Flensburg, the 23rd at Salamis, the 29th at La Spezia and finally the 30th at Constantza. Each flotilla had a well-equipped base, with workshops almost entirely housed in bomb-proof ferroconcrete bunkers, which the Allies struggled to attack effectively.

A patrol would usually take up to two months. After completing a mission crews relaxed in the luxury conditions of former hotels and chateaux, usually in France. Living conditions aboard a U-boat were truly appalling. There was the occasional excitement of an attack on a convoy, but most of the time it was tedious routine in the cramped, dark and poorly-ventilated interior of the boat, followed by a short break in base, a bit of leave, then resupplying and out on patrol again, in the gales and cold of the North Atlantic, without a doctor on board and facing the increasing threat of Allied ASW forces. The crews never really knew the full extent of the losses the U-boats suffered. The figures were classified, and being either at sea themselves or on leave at home, they never really knew which boats failed to come back. But by 1943 they must have known that their losses were mounting. But few would know that by now their life-expectancy was only three or four patrols, and that it would later fall to just one-and-a-half.

The chances of getting out of a sinking U-boat were slim. Of the forty-three boats sunk in March 1943, twenty-nine went down with all hands and less than half of the crew was saved from each of the other fourteen. Statistically, out of a fifty-man crew, just eighteen could expect to survive.

These men had varying feelings about the British, but in most cases the officers admired the traditions of the Royal Navy and almost all of them had read the Hornblower novels! Were these men fanatical Nazis? This is a difficult question to answer. It should be remembered that those of the First World War generation, and the one just after it, lived through a time of crisis in Germany. Hitler, who promised the rebirth of the country, work and food, was admired and even more so when as Chancellor he began to fulfil these promises. Few of these younger officers would have refused to follow him. But there were in fact few Party members in the Kriegsmarine, who were mainly the sons of naval families, raised to obedience and service to the Fatherland from childhood. They fought – as they saw it – for their country. They were avenging the humiliation of the Treaty of Versailles, and later the deaths of the civilians who had died in the Allied bombing raids. The average U-boat man did his duty as he saw it – for his boat and his comrades. The U-boat men saw themselves as a 'navy within the navy', as 'Dönitz's Freikorps'. They were also loyal to their commander, 'Onkel Karl' who welcomed boats back from patrol and spoke to every man aboard.

► After the boat had been welcomed back and the CO had made his report, the mail was distributed. This shows a mail call in late 1941 – early 1942 in the Mediterranean. (CAW)

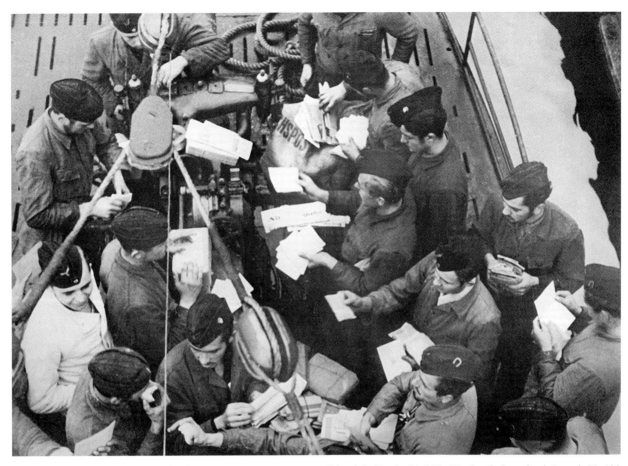

The ships lost by Convoy ONS 5 were:

• On 29 April the American ship *McKeesport* (6198 GRT), sunk by *U 258*.
• On 4 May *Lorient*, sunk by *U 125* (Type IX).
• On 5 May the British *Harpeley* (4586 GRT) and the American *West Maximus* (5561 GRT) sunk by *U 264*, the Norwegian *Bonde* (1570 GRT) and three British ships – *Gharinda* (5306 GRT), *Selvistan* (5136 GRT) and *Bristol City* (2864 GRT) – sunk by *U 266*, the British *Wentworth* (5212 GRT) sunk by *U 358*, the American *West Madaket* (5565 GRT) sunk by *U 584*, the British *Harbury* (5081 GRT) sunk by *U 628*, the British *Dolius* (5507 GRT) sunk by *U 638*, and the British *North Britain* (4635 GRT) sunk by *U 707*.

In September 1943, however, Dönitz once again attempted a large-scale operation in the Atlantic, deploying the 'Leuthen' group to hunt for convoys. It consisted of Type VIIs only, namely *U 305* (Kptlt. Rudolf Bahr), *U 731* (Oblt.z.S. Werner Techand), *U 260* (Kptlt. Hubertus Purkhold), *U 641* (Kptlt. Horst Rendtel), *U 758* (Kptlt. Helmut Manseck), *U 378* (Kptlt. Erich Mäder), *U 229* (Oblt.z.S. Robert Schetelig), *U 386* (Oblt.z.S. Fritz Albrecht), *U 338* (Kptlt. Manfred Kinzel), *U 645* (Oblt.z.S. Otto Ferro), *U 270* (Kptlt. Paul-Friedrich Otto), *U 275* (Oblt.z.S. Helmut Bork), *U 377* (Oblt.z.S. Gerhard Kluth), *U 666* (Kptlt. Herbert Engel), *U 238* (Kptlt. Horst Hepp), *U 422* (Oblt.z.S. Wolfgang Poeschel), *U 341* (Oblt.z.S.

Dietrich Epp), *U 952* (Kptlt. Oskar Curio) and *U 402* (KKpt. Siegfried Freiherr von Forstner). Between 20 and 23 September these boats attacked Convoys ON 202 and ONS 18, but without success, instead losing *U 229*, *U 338* and *U 341*, with *U 386*, *U 270*, *U 377* and *U 422* being damaged and forced to return to base. All of the U-boats had been fiercely attacked by Allied warships. On 23 September the 'Leuthen' boats and the newly-assigned *U 603* (Oblt.z.S. Rudolf Baltz), *U 419* (Oblt.z.S. Dietrich Giersberg), *U 610* (Kptlt. Walter Freiherr von Freiberg-Eisenberg-Allmedingen), *U 539* (Type IX), *U 643* (Kptlt. Hans-Harald Speidel), *U 448* (Oblt.z.S. Helmut Dauter) and *U 631* (Oblt.z.S. Jürgen Krüger) formed the 'Rossbach' group, which now consisted of *U 584*, *U 305*, *U 731*, *U 260*, *U 641*, *U 758* (the only boat not attacked during the previous battle), *U 378*, *U 603*, *U 419*, *U 610*, *U 645*, *U 539*, *U 275*, *U 643*, *U 666*, *U 448*, *U 631*, *U 952*, *U 402*, *U 309*, *U 762* and two Type IXs, *U 91* and *U 336*. This group formed a patrol line and on 8 October found and attacked Convoy SC 143. The attack failed and the Germans lost *U 419*, *U 610*, *U 643* and *U 309*. In anticipation of another convoy, ONS 20, headquarters regrouped the boats and replaced the losses, forming 'Schlieffen'. It consisted of the Type VIIs *U 231* (Kptlt. Wolfgang Wenzel), *U 608* (Kptlt. Rolf Struckmeier), *U 413* (Kptlt. Gustav Poel), *U 281* (Kptlt. Heinrich von Davidson), *U 267* (Oblt.z.S. Ernst von Witzendorff), *U 470* (Oblt.z.S. Günther Grave), *U 448* (Oblt.z.S. Helmut Dauter), *U 631* (Oblt.z.S. Jürgen Krüger), *U 437* (Kptlt. Hermann Lamby), *U 426* (Kptlt. Christian Reich), *U 309* (Oblt.z.S. Hans-Gert

Mahrholz), *U 762* (Kptlt. Wolfgang Hille) and *U 964* (Oblt.z.S. Emmo Hummerjohann), and the Type IXs *U 91*, *U 540*, *U 841*, *U 842* and *U 844*. The operation was a disaster. Three Type VIIs – *U 470*, *U 631* and *U 964* – as well as three Type IXs – *U 540*, *U 841* and *U 844* – were sunk. *U 448* was damaged.

In the meantime *U 279* (Type VII) commanded by Kptlt. Otto Finke was dispatched on 24 September on a secret mission – the boat was to land a German agent on the coast of Iceland. The operation failed, however, as the U-boat was spotted by aircraft and sunk on 7 October.

On 30 October the all-Type VII group 'Schill', comprising *U 333* (Kptlt. Peter-Erich Cremer), *U 211* (Kptlt. Karl Hause), *U 707* (Oblt.z.S. Günter Gretschel), *U 466* (Kptlt. Gerhard Thäter), *U 262* (Kptlt. Heinz Franke) and *U 441* (Kptlt. Klaus Hartmann) and *U 306* (Kptlt. Claus von Trotha), attacked Convoy MKS 28 and the battle which lasted until 2 November lost *U 306* and had *U 441* damaged for no result. The losses were replaced by the Type VIIs *U 228* (Kptlt. Erwin Christophersen) and *U 358* (Kptlt. Rolf Manke). 'Schill' attacked MKS 28 again, but again without success and at the price of *U 707* sunk and *U 466* damaged. Once again the group was reinforced with the Type VII *U 600* (Kptlt. Bernhard Zurmühlen) and the Type IX *U 515* (Type IX) and renamed 'Schill I'. On 18 November it engaged convoys MKS 20 and SL 139, and lost *U 211* sunk and *U 333* damaged.

Several days later, after an attack by enemy surface ships, *U 600* was lost, and *U 515* (Type IX) was detached from the group again and continued its journey towards Freetown.

◀ Letters from home were very important to the sailors, and eagerly anticipated. (CAW)

▼ U-boat men coming ashore with their kit. (CAW)

◀ ▼ After debriefing, the crew finally go ashore, January 1941. (CAW)

▶ After a boat returned from a patrol, the hull was usually inspectd by a diver. (CAW)

▶ Often the 'reception committee' included people from other branches of the services. In this case a delegation from the women's auxiliary service has joined the group. (CAW)

▶ ▶ A Vice Admiral visits a Type VIIC. (CAW)

▲ A U-boat skipper entertains his family aboard, in summer of 1942. A welcoming bunch of flowers has been put into the gun barrel, while the CO's cap hangs on the mount. (CAW)

▲ The tower of *U 564* commanded by Kptlt. Reinhardt 'Teddy' Suhren. A metal silhouette of a cat can be seen in the fork of the stay. The photograph was taken prior to *U 564*'s departure for its fourth patrol from La Pallice on 18 June 1942. Submarine pens can be seen under construction in the background. (CAW)

▼ Summer 1940 – a very precious cargo of beer bottles is lowered into water to cool. (CAW)

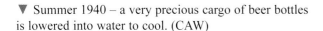

▼ Another view of the same scene – Kptlt. Reinhardt 'Teddy' Suhren in his distinctive black cap with the boat's emblem (cat with arched back) seen on the bridge of *U 564* while talking to officers on the pier. During his six patrols (all aboard this boat) between 3 April 1941 and 1 October 1942 he sank eighteen ships totalling 95,544 GRT, one warship of 900 tonnes and damaged four ships of 28,907 GRT. On 1 August 1942 he was decorated with the Knight's Cross with Oak Leaves and Swords. (CAW)

1944–45

On 29–30 January 1944 the Germans attacked Convoy KMS 39 with the Type VIIs *U 441* (Kptlt. Klaus Hartmann), *U 592* (Oblt.z.S. Heinz Jaschke), *U 650* (Oblt.z.S. Ernst Witzendorff), *U 764* (Oblt.z.S. Hans Kurt von Bremen), *U 281* (Kptlt. Heinrich von Davidson), *U 571* (Oblt.z.S. Gustav Lüssow), *U 212* (Kptlt. Helmut Vogler) and *U 271* (Kptlt. Curt Barleben) in the hastily-formed 'Hinein' wolfpack. Again no successes were scored, and *U 571* and *U 271* were sunk.

On 18 February the 'Hai I' and 'Hai II' groups, composed of the Type VIIs *U 985* (Kptlt. Horst Keßler), *U 386* (Oblt.z.S. Fritz Albrecht), *U 264* (Kptlt. Hartwig Looks), *U 437* (Kptlt. Hermann Lamby), *U 608* (Oblt.z.S. Wolfgang Reisener), *U 709* (Oblt.z.S. Rudolf Ites), *U 989* (Kptlt. Hardo Rodler von Roithberg), *U 406* (Kptlt. Horst Dieterichs), *U 603* (Kptlt. Hans-Joachim Bartelsmann), *U 441* (Kptlt. Klaus Hartmann), *U 963* (Oblt.z.S. Karl Boddenberg), *U 650* (Oblt.z.S. Ernst Witzendorff), *U 764* (Oblt.z.S. Hans-Kurt von Bremen), *U 281* (Kptlt. Heinrich von Davidson), *U 256* (Oblt.z.S. Wilhelm Brauel) and *U 212* (Kptlt. Helmut Vogler) and the Type IXs *U 546* and *U 549* intercepted and engaged an Allied convoy. *U 406*, *U 264* and *U 386* were lost. The last large wolfpack to be formed was 'Preussen', operating in the Northern Atlantic in late February–early March 1944, composed of *U 91* and the Type VIIs *U 985* (Kptlt. Horst Keßler), *U 989* (Kptlt. Hardo Rodler von Roithberg), *U 448* (Oblt.z.S. Helmut

Dauter), *U 437* (Kptlt. Hermann Lamby), *U 608* (Oblt.z.S. Wolfgang Reisener), *U 709* (Oblt.z.S. Rudolf Ites), *U 441* (Kptlt. Klaus Hartmann), *U 262* (Oblt.z.S. Helmut Wieduwilt), *U 603* (Kptlt. Hans-Joachim Bartelsmann), *U 358* (Kptlt. Rolf Manke), *U 963* (Oblt.z.S. Karl Boddenberg), *U 962* (Oblt.z.S. Ernst Liesberg), *U 764* (Oblt.z.S. Hans-Kurt von Bremen), *U 281* (Kptlt. Heinrich von Davidson), *U 256* (Oblt.z.S. Wilhelm Brauel) and *U 212* (Kptlt. Helmut Vogler). By the beginning of March it had lost *U 709*, *U 603* and *U 358* sunk, and *U 441* damaged. These losses were made good by HQ assigning to 'Preussen' the Type IX *U 92* (Type IX) and the Type VIIs *U 267* (Kptlt. Otto Tinschert), *U 986* (Oblt.z.S. Karl-Ernst Keiser), *U 741* (Oblt.z.S. Gerhard Palmgren), *U 672* (Oblt.z.S. Ulf Lawaetz), *U 311* (Kptlt. Joachim Zander), *U 255* (Oblt.z.S. Erich Harms), *U 667* (Kptlt. Heinrich Schroeteler), *U 744* (Oblt.z.S. Heinz Blischke), *U 625* (Oblt.z.S. Siegfried Straub) and *U 653* (Oblt.z.S. Hans Albrecht Kandler). These last three boats were sunk after the first few days of their patrols. On 20 March the group was disbanded and the boats continued their patrols independently.

The Allied invasion of Normandy on 6 June took the Germans by surprise. Willing to respond, Dönitz ordered his U-boats against the invasion force – as they were the only Kriegsmarine vessels able to engage the Allied fleet in the Channel. The boats were *U 767* (Oblt.z.S. Walter Dankleff), *U 1191* (Oblt.z.S. Peter Grau), *U 988* (Oblt.z.S. Erich Dobberstein) and *U 671* (Oblt.z.S. Wolfgang

▶ Two Type VIIs warm up their diesels in port, January 1941. (CAW)

▶▶ Four U-boats moored alongside. The crews are assembling on deck to hear the Flotilla Commander's address, December 1941. (CAW)

▲ A Type VII boat is being prepared for a patrol, Wilhelmshaven, summer 1940. (CAW)

Hegewald). They were sailing from Germany so in order to reduce what would otherwise have been a three or four-week journey they were ordered to sail surfaced at full speed around the British Isles until they reached the southern tip of Ireland. From there they would proceed to south to the western end of the Channel sailing submerged using their snorkels. *U 767*, *U 1191* and *U 988* were sunk in July by aircraft and *U 671* suffered heavy damage after being attacked by surface warships. These four ill-fated boats were expected to cooperate with another group of Type VII boats detached from 'Landwirt', namely *U 275* (Oblt.z.S Helmut Bork), *U 269* (Oblt.z.S. Georg Uhl), *U 984* (Oblt.z.S. Heinz Sieder), *U 621* (Oblt.z.S. Hermann Stuckmann), *U 441* (Kptlt. Klaus Hartmann), *U 764* (Oblt.z.S. Hans-Kurt von Bremen), *U 953* (Oblt.z.S. Karl Heinz Marbach) and *U 212* (Kptlt. Helmut Vogler). All the boats selected for this mission were equipped with snorkels, as to attempt to operate against the invasion beaches without them would have been suicidal. In a month this detachment lost two boats sunk, *U 269* and *U 441*, and two

damaged, *U 764* and *U 212*. U-boats heading towards the landing zones were first attacked from the air, and then by ASW ships patrolling around the invasion force. The orders given to the U-boat commanders were clear: 'Each solider and weapon destroyed prior to landing on the beach decreases enemy's chance for victory. U-boat which will inflict losses on invasion forces will thus fulfil its highest task and justify its existence, even if it is destroyed itself.'

The U-boats tried to get to the invasion force by sailing submerged for over forty hours at a time. Their crews using the oxygen masks of their rescue apparatuses and potassium cartridges to refresh the air. Some boats turned back. All of them were heavily depth-charged – the *average* duration of the enemy attacks was twenty-four hours. *U 275*, *U 953*, *U 984* and *U 269* passed through this hell and survived.

Between D-Day and the end of August more boats were lost in the area, among them *U 390*, *U 672*, *U 212*, *U 415*, *U 740*, *U 821*, *U 373* and *U 970*.

A total of twenty U-boats operated in the invasion area and 45 per cent of them were lost – mostly Type VIIs,

▲ St-Nazaire, a naval base on the Atlantic coast of occupied France. *U 590* (Type VIIC) is preparing to sail on its second combat patrol, spring 1942. During its first four missions the boat was commanded by Heinrich Müller-Edzards, then in the rank of Kptlt. He was not a very successful commander though, sinking only one ship of 5464 GRT. His successor, Oblt.z.S. Werner Krüer, also sank only one ship, *Brazilian*, of 5228 GRT, before – on 9 July 1943 – *U 590* was sunk with all hands in the Amazon delta. (CAW)

▲ A torpedo is loaded aboard a Type VIIC inside a U-boat pen, 1942. (NARA)

which by that time were already effectively obsolete. Seven hundred and sixty-two men were killed and 238 were captured. The losses inflicted by the U-boats were:

- Ships sunk: five escorts, four landing ships and twelve other ships of various types – total 56,845 tonnes.
- Ships damaged: one escort, one landing ship, five others – 36,000 tonnes.

For some considerable time the German high command believed that the Normandy landings were a diversion and the real invasion was still to come. For that reason,

'Landwirt' (mentioned above) was assigned to defend the coast of northern France, still in German hands. As well as the boats already mentioned, it included *U 981*, *U 270*, *U 260*, *U 382*, *U 714*, *U 650*, *U 437*, *U 766*, *U 255*, *U 445*, *U 262*, *U 985*, *U 758*, *U 281*, *U 228*, *U 608*, *U 993*, *U 333* and *U 970*, all of them Type VIIs with snorkels and based at Lorient, St Nazaire and La Pallice. There were also *U 740*, *U 821*, *U 629*, *U 413*, *U 415*, *U 256*, *U 989*, *U 963* and *U 373*, without snorkels and based at Brest.

The Germans also suspected that the Allies might invade Norway. Intelligence reports said that many ships which could be used for such an operation were concentrated in English and Scottish ports. Therefore 'Mitte' was formed to deal with that potential threat, consisting of the Type VIIs *U 1007* (Kptlt. Hans Hornkohl), *U 982* (Oblt.z.S. Ernst Werner Schwirley), *U 276* (Kptlt. Rolf Borchers), *U 397* (Oblt.z.S. Fritz Kallipke), *U 975* (Oblt.z.S. Hubert Jeschke), *U 242* (Oblt.z.S. Wilhelm Pancke), *U 999* (Oblt.z.S. Wilhelm Peters), *U 677* (Oblt.z.S. Paul Weber), *U 1001* (Kptlt. Ernst Ulrich Blaudow), *U 745* (Kptlt. Wilhelm von Trotha) and *U 1165* (Oblt.z.S. Sarto Balert).

On 17 June U-boat HQ reluctantly agreed to use four Type VIIs to transport ammunition to Cherbourg which had been cut off by Allied forces. *U 212* (Kptlt. Helmut Vogler), *U 309* (Oblt.z.S. Hans-Gert Mahrholz), *U 390* (Oblt.z.S. Heinz Geissler) and *U 741* (Oblt.z.S. Gerhard Palmgren) left the bases between 20 and 22 June, each carrying 8000 anti-tank shells and 350,000 rounds of submachine gun ammunition, but on 23 June they were spotted and the entire mission was aborted.

► Two Type VIIC U-boats at La Spezia, end of June 1942. The boat in the foreground is *U 205* commanded by Kptlt. Franz-Georg Reschke. On 16 June 1942 he sank the 5500-ton British light cruiser HMS *Hermione*. She was his second and last kill. (CAW)

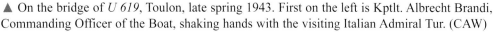

▲ On the bridge of *U 619*, Toulon, late spring 1943. First on the left is Kptlt. Albrecht Brandi, Commanding Officer of the Boat, shaking hands with the visiting Italian Admiral Tur. (CAW)

On 7–8 July 1944 the Type VII boat *U 763* (Kptlt. Ernst Cordes) on 7–8 July 1944 had an adventure unique in the history of the U-bootwaffe. Whilst submerged, a U-boat's only means of navigation was dead reckoning based on time of travel, speed and course. But the unknown factor of underwater currents made this more guesswork than science, and fixes on radio beacons were of little use if only one was available. *U 763* was depth-charged for thirty hours and lost all track of its position. The one radio beacon in Brest was no real help. The commander's surprise can only be imagined when he later found himself not somewhere north of Cherbourg but rather circling among dozens of British ships at Spithead! However, despite this amazing opportunity, he was unable to attack

▲ Kptlt. Albrecht Brandi was one of two Kriegsmarine officers decorated with the Knight's Cross with Oak Leaves, Swords and Diamonds (the other was Wolfgang Lüth, commander of a Type IX U-boat). Brandi sank eight merchant ships with a total tonnage of 25,869 GRT, one auxiliary Royal Navy vessel of 810 GRT, and three warships with a total displacement of 5000 tons, among them the fast minelayer HMS *Welshman*, urgently needed for supply deliveries to Malta. At the very beginning of the war Brandi served as a watch officer aboard *M–1*, flagship of the 1. Minensuchflotille, which assisted the training battle-ship *Schleswig-Holstein* when she bombarded the Polish Military Transit Depot at the Westerplatte in Danzig (now Gdańsk).

◀ Type VIIs being refuelled prior to going out on patrol. (ADM)

► Type VII boats in a base, northern Norway, 1942. (CAW)

► A polar bear bagged by a U-boat crew, on the after deck. (CAW)

◀ ◀ A U-boat leaves its base on patrol. The censor has deleted the coastline forward of the hull to make identification of the base impossible. (CAW)

◀ A Type VIIC U-boat leaves a base in the Mediter-ranean, late spring 1942. (CAW)

▼ A Type VII boat cruising at dusk, late summer 1942. (CAW)

as the boat was armed with the new top-secret 'Lut' torpedoes, which might fail to explode in shallow waters and be recovered by the British. Therefore all *U 763* could do was slip away and head for home.

As the U-boat bases on the French coast were being cut off by the Allied advance, it was decided to redeploy the boats to Germany, where suitable shelters had already been under construction for some time. The last boat to leave was the Type VII *U 267* (Oblt.z.S. Bernhard Knieper).

The Type VII *U 480* (Oblt.z.S. Hans-Joachim Förster) was one of the last six U-boats operating in the English Channel, and one of two among them equipped with 'Alberich' – a special synthetic rubber coating over the entire hull which was supposed to attenuate sound waves and make the submarine 'invisible' to ASDIC. On 19 August *U 480* sank *St. Enogat* and on 22 August the minesweeper HMS *Loyalty*. Then the boat dived to let Convoy FTM 74 to pass overhead on 25 August and then sank the ship *Orminster*. Altogether it sank ships with a total tonnage of 14,000 GRT, managing to survive only thanks to the 'Alberich'.

In October, after receiving optimistic reports on the situation in the Atlantic and English Channel the Germans decided to send six U-boats from the 'Mitte' group – which was kept in readiness in Norway to defend it from any possible invasion – to the English Channel and possibly also further into the Atlantic. Three Type VII boats were sent to patrol the Channel, of which *U 1006* (Oblt.z.S. Horst Voigt) was sunk before reaching the open ocean by an enemy anti-submarine force and *U 246* (Kptlt. Ernst Raabe) was damaged by depth charges and turned back, only *U 978* (Oblt.z.S. Günter Pulst) successfully reaching its patrol area and operating in the Channel for three weeks, sinking one ship (7170 GRT) and damaging another (7176 GRT).

Later those boats were followed by *U 1200* (Oblt.z.S. Heinrich Mangels) and *U 991* (Kptlt. Diethelm Balke). The former was sunk by enemy surface forces on 11 November

▲ The tower of *U 96* (Type VIIC) taken from its after deck by the war correspondent (Kriegsberichter) Lothar-Günther Buchheim. Buchheim later used his experience to write the famous novel *Das Boot* ('*The Boat*'). The photograph was taken at the end of the eighth and last patrol of *U 96* under command of Kptlt. Heinrich Lehmann-Willenbrock, most probably in March 1942. (CAW)

▲ ▶ A Type VII boat follows in the wake of a Sperrbrecher. (CAW)

south of Ireland. Usually three or four U-boats operated in that area and they started to achieve successes. On 6 January 1945 off Cherbourg, *U 486* sank two merchant ships, the frigate HMS *Capel* and probably also the LSI *Empire Javelin*[1] and damaged the frigate HMS *Affleck* so seriously that despite managing to get back to port, she was declared a constructive total loss.

The patrols of *U 680* (Oblt.z.S. Max Ulber), *U 485* (Kptlt. Friedrich Lutz) and *U 325* (Oblt.z.S. Erwin Dohm)

proved fruitless, while *U 772* (Kptlt. Ewald Rademacher) sank four ships (21,053 GRT) and damaged another (7176 GRT) so seriously that she would not return to service, but the U-boat was then itself sunk by an aerial depth charge.[2]

In late November–early December 1944 *U 1202* (Kptlt. Rolf Thomsen) operated in the Irish Sea and sank a ship there, so immediately further U-boats were deployed there: *U 285* (Kptlt. Konrad Bomhaupt), *U 1055* (Oblt.z.S.

▶ An early Type VII boat departing on a combat patrol. (CAW)

[1] It is not quite certain what was the cause of this ship's loss. Other 'suspects' are *U 322* and mines.

[2] According to later publications by Axel Niestlé of the US Naval Institute *U 772* was sunk on 17 December 1944 by depth charges from the frigate HMS *Nyasaland*. Before the same author had claimed that the 'killer' was a Wellington from No 407 Squadron RAF.

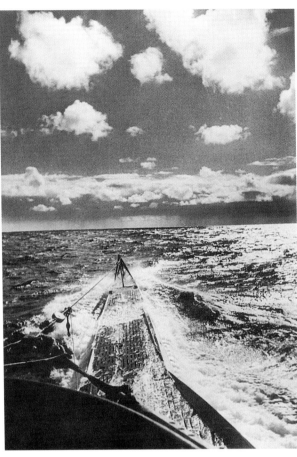

◀ ◀ A Type VII boat in calm seas. Even in good weather waves broke over the deck. (CAW)

◀ In rougher seas the waves swamped the entire deck and every now and then the bow disappeared completely. (CAW)

◀ Rendezvous of two Type VIICs. (CAW)

▶ A Type VIIC heads for its designated patrol area. (CAW)

▶ When a boat was surfaced, its deck was often swamped by waves, making working the gun difficult at best. Therefore sometimes even the removal of this weapon was called for, especially since in convoy battles it was useless anyway. Even engaging lone ships on the surface became increasingly dangerous, as an enemy aircraft could catch the attacker by surprise. The deck guns were no longer installed on Type VIIC/41 model, which only mounted anti-aircraft weapons. (CAW)

Rudolf Meyer) and *U 1172* (Oblt.z.S. Jürgen Kuhlmann). In December and January six ships totalling 27,820 GRT were sunk in that area.

The Marinegruppenkommando West (Command Naval Group West) as well as Heeresgruppe Nord (Army Group North) often requested the U-bootwaffe to detail U-boats to transport military material to the ports besieged by the Allies, but it considered that U-boats were entirely unsuited to such work and furthermore did not want to divert boats from its own operations and usually refused. However, in November and December 1944 the Type VIIs *U 773* (Oblt.z.S. Hugo Baldus) and *U 722* (Oblt.z.S. Hans Reimers) transported a cargo of 30–40 tonnes of anti-tank ammunition to St Nazaire and returned to Norway with a load of anti-magnetic iron ore.

Fearing that Allied aircraft carriers might be used to launch attacks on Norway, a blockade of Scapa Flow was ordered by the high command. This extremely dangerous mission was assigned in December to the Type VII boats *U 297* (Oblt.z.S Wolfgang Aldegarmann) and *U 1020* (Oblt.z.S. Otto Eberlein). A month later further Type VIIs were deployed to that area. Of these, *U 1020* and *U 274* (Oblt.z.S. Günther Jordan) failed to return. On 14 January 1945 the operation was terminated.

In February 1945 *U 245* (KKpt. Friedrich Schumann-Hindenberg) carried out Operation 'Brutus'. Its objective was to attack convoys running between the Thames and the Scheldt. After sinking the ship *Henry B. Plant* (7240 GRT) and a small Dutch tanker, *U 245* safely returned to base at Heligoland.

▲ Another photograph showing conditions on the fore deck when cruising. It shows a Type VIIB U-boat. (CAW)

► One more set of photographs showing bow and stern of a Type VII boat. These were taken from the bridge of *U 96* (Type VIIC) by Lothar-Günther Buchheim. The upper photo was taken on 18 February 1942, the lower on 3 March – both during the eighth and last patrol of *U 96* under Kptlt. Heinrich Lehmann-Willenbrock. (CAW)

▲ ▲ The situation on the after deck was no better – it was also frequently awash. (CAW)

► A Type VII boat heads for its designated patrol area. (CAW)

◄ ► When combat operations were terminated, the U-boats surrendered to the Allies. Soon afterwards, in 1946, the scuttling of the U-boats commenced – it was codenamed 'Deadlight'. It involved some Polish warships, and these photos were taken from them. (All photographs Museum of the Polish Navy)

On 18 April Type VII *U 255* (Oblt.z.S. Helmut Heinrich) was one of two to conduct a minelaying operation in the area of Les Sables, laying eight TMC mines. Further planned minelaying operations off Dundee, Cherbourg, Hartlepool and Portland Bill were all cancelled, however.

On 3 May peace negotiations between Generaladmiral von Friedeburg and Field Marshal Montgomery began. Earlier – on 30 April – Kriegsmarine vessels were ordered to be prepared for scuttling upon receipt of the codeword 'Regenbogen'. During the negotiations, however, the Allies demanded that the fleet be surrendered, so execution of that order was reluctantly called off by Dönitz. From 4 May on, the U-boats were ordered to terminate all combat operations, hoist black flags and proceed on the surface to designated ports. Nevertheless the act of mass suicide had already started. Between 2 and 5 May 1945 the following Type VIIs were scuttled by their own crews: *U 71, U 72, U 236, U 267, U 290, U 316, U 339, U 349, U 351, U 370, U 382, U 397, U 428, U 446, U 475, U 552, U 554, U 560, U 612, U 704, U 708, U 717, U 721, U 733, U 746, U 748, U 750, U 822, U 903, U 904, U 922, U 924, U 958, U 979, U 1056, U 1101, U 1132, U 1161, U 1162, U 1192, U 1193, U 1196, U 1201, U 1204, U 1205* and *U 1207*. Also scuttled were a number of Type VIIC/41s: *U 323, U 827, U 828, U 929, U 999, U 1007, U 1008, U 1016, U 1025, U 1166, U 1168, U 1170, U 1275, U 1303, U 1304, U 1306, U 1308* and *U 1277*. The last of these was scuttled off the Portuguese coast on 6 June 1945. *U 963* also sank near the coast of Portugal. This was only stopped by Dönitz himself who asked his commanders to understand the situation and obey orders. He pointed out that failure to surrender the fleet to the victors might result in reprisals against German civilians. Therefore the remaining U-boats sailed to be taken over by the Allies. Only two failed to obey and fled to Argentina: the Type IX *U 530* and the Type VII *U 977*. The commanding officer of *U 977*, Oblt.z.S. Heinz Schäffer left part of his crew, mainly married petty officers who wanted to stay with their families, in Norway and departed for a long journey. The boat stayed submerged for sixty days, a record, and after evading Allied patrols in the Atlantic arrived in Argentina in August. The local authorities interned the boat and treated the crew very courteously, but upon American demands they handed both the boat and its crew over to them. After two years in the USA, where the German crew was interrogated endlessly, the officers and sailors were sent to Great Britain where the entire process was repeated. Eventually the Germans were released and repatriated. Their legendary action aroused plenty of interest in the world and resulted with many legends about the escape of some high-ranking Nazis, maybe even Hitler himself, from the Reich.

The Allied Operation 'Deadlight' put a definitive end to the German submarine service. Between November 1945 and February 1946 British warships towed U-boats out to sea and sank them. This was the fate of 115 U-boats, among them the following Type VIIs: *U 218* (VII D), *U 244* (VII C), a stubborn boat, which broke its tow line

and had to be sank by gunfire from the Polish destroyer ORP *Piorun*, *U 245*, *U 249*, *U 255*, *U 278*, *U 281*, *U 291*, *U 312* (all Type VIICs), *U 293*, *U 294*, *U 295*, *U 298*, *U 299*, *U 318*, *U 328* (all Type VIIC/41s), *U 313*, *U 363*, *U 368*, *U 369*, *U 427*, *U 481*, *U 483*, *U 485*, *U 637*, *U 668*, *U 680*, *U 716*, *U 720*, *U 739*, *U 760*, *U 764*, *U 773*, *U 775*, *U 776*, *U 778*, *U 779*, *U 825*, *U 826*, *U 901*, *U 907*, *U 928*, *U 956*, *U 968* (all Type VIICs), *U 930* (Type VIIC/41), *U 975*, *U 978*, *U 991*, *U 992*, *U 994* (all Type VIICs), *U 977* (returned by Argentina), *U 1002*, *U 1004*, *U 1005*, *U 1009*, *U 1010*, *U 1019*, *U 1022*, *U 1023* (all Type VIIC/41s), *U 1061* (Type VII F), *U 1052*, *U 1102* (Type VIICs), *U 1103*, *U 1104*, *U 1109*, *U 1110*, *U 1163*, *U 1165* (all of them Type VIIC/41s), *U 1194*, *U 1198*, *U 1203* (Type VIIC), *U 1271*, *U 1272*, *U 1301*, and *U 1307* (Type VIIC/41).

Operations in the Mediterranean

In 1941 Hitler ordered U-boats to commence operations in the Mediterranean. Only Type VII boats were deployed in this theatre. Taking these boats from the Atlantic was a great loss to German operations and significantly weakened the groups operating against the convoys – not that strong at this time anyway. The following boats operated in the Mediterranean: *U 73*, *U 74*, *U 75*, *U 77*, *U 79*, *U 81*, *U 83*, *U 95*, *U 97*, *U 133*, *U 205*, *U 223*, *U 224*, *U 230*, *U 259*, *U 301*, *U 303*, *U 331*, *U 343*, *U 371*, *U 372*, *U 374*, *U 375*, *U 380*, *U 407*, *U 409*, *U 410*, *U 414*, *U 421*, *U 431*, *U 433*, *U 443*, *U 450*, *U 453*, *U 455*, *U 458*, *U 466*, *U 471*, *U 557*, *U 559*, 561, *U 562*, *U 565*, *U 568*, *U 573*, *U 577*, *U 586*, *U 593*, *U 595*, *U 596*, *U 602*, *U 605*, *U 616*, *U 617*, *U 642*,

U 652, *U 660*, *U 755*, *U 952*, *U 960*, *U 967* and *U 969*. They were all Type VIICs, except for *U 73*, which was a Type VIIB. *U 573* was interned in Spain.

The following boats were damaged or sunk in the Straits of Gibraltar while trying to enter the Mediterranean. In 1941 *U 96*, *U 558*, *U 432* and *U 202* were damaged and turned back, while *U 208* and *U 451* were sunk. *U 371*, *U 97*, *U 559*, *U 331*, *U 75*, *U 79*, *U 205*, *U 81*, *U 433*,

▲ A U-boat is towed towards its designated scuttling place.

◄ Explosives are planted.

U 565, U 431, U 95, U 557, U 562, U 652, U 372, U 375, U 453, U 568, U 374, U 74, U 77, U 83, U 573, U 133 and *U 577* all made the passage successfully. In 1942 *U 572* and *U 25* turned back, while *U 73, U 561, U 458, U 605, U 660, U 593, U 595, U 617, U 755, U 596, U 259, U 407, U 380, U 443, U 602* and *U 301* got through. *U 133, U 259, U 301, U 371, U 372, U 374, U 559, U 568, U 573, U 595, U 605, U 652* and *U 660* were lost in the Mediterranean that year. In 1943 *U 732* and *U 340* were sunk and the damaged *U 667* had to turn back, while *U 224, U 414, U 303, U 616, U 410, U 409, U 960, U 223, U 450, U 642* and *U 230* made it, and in 1944 *U 761, U 392* and *U 731* were sunk and *U 343, U 952, U 455, U 969, U 586, U 967, U 421, U 466* and *U 471* made it.

Operations off the United States' Coast

Type VII U-boats which participated in Operation 'Paukenschlag' in 1941– operations against Allied navigation off American coast: *U 701* (Degen), *U 201* (Schnee) and *U 552*. Lost: *U 701, U 576* and *U 352*.

Type VIIs which carried out the most successful combat patrols:

- *U 99* (Kptlt. Otto Kretschmer) – February–March 1941, sank seven ships (61,711 GRT).
- *U 47* (Kptlt. Günther Prien) – June–July 1940, sank eight ships (51,483 GRT).
- *U 100* (Kptlt. Joachim Schepke) sank seven ships (50,340 GRT) in three hours during a patrol in September 1940.

The following Type VII boats have their places among the twenty U-boats with the highest tonnage sunk:

- *U 48* (Type VIIB) – 12 patrols – 51 ships sunk (306,875 GRT), 3 ships damaged (20,480 GRT).
- *U 99* (Type VIIB) – 8 patrols – 35 ships sunk
- *U 96* (Type VIIC) – 11 patrols – 27 ships sunk (181,206 GRT), 5 ships damaged (41,931 GRT).
- *U 552* (Type VIIC) – 15 patrols – 29 ships sunk (163,529 GRT), 3 ships damaged (26,910 GRT).
- *U 47* (Type VIIB) – 10 patrols – 30 ships sunk (16,2769 GRT).
- *U 94* (Type VIIC) – 10 patrols – 26 ships sunk (141,852 GRT), 1 ship damaged (8022 GRT).

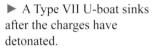

► A Type VII U-boat sinks after the charges have detonated.

TYPE VII U-BOAT LOSSES

Number	Area	Cause
1939		
U 45	Atlantic	Surface warships
U 27, U 35	North Sea	Surface warships
U 36		Sub
1940		
U 31, U 32	Atlantic	Surface warships
U 51	Atlantic	Sub
U 33, U 49, U 50, U 53, U 55	North Sea	Surface warships
U 54		Mines
U 102		Accident
1941		
U 41, U 47, U 76, U 99, U 100, U 207, U 208, U 401, U 434, U 551, U 556, U 567, U 574, U 651	Atlantic	Surface warships
U 206		Aircraft
U 570		Aircraft + Surface warships, Captured by the Allies
U 452	North Sea	Aircraft + Surface warships
U 75, U 79, U 204		Surface warships
U 433	Med.	Surface warships
U 95		Sub.
U 451		Aircraft
U 557		Collision
U 580, U 583	Baltic	Collision
1942		
U 82, U 85, U 90, U 93, U 94, U 136, U 210, U 213, U 215, U 252, U 352, U 353, U 356, U 357, U 379, U 581, U 587, U 588, U 619, U 626	Atlantic	Surface warships
U 98, U 132, U 216, U 253, U 254, U 408, U 578, U 582, U 597, U 599, U 611, U 627, U 654, U 658, U 661, U 701, U 705, U 751, U 754, U 756		Aircraft
U 261, U 412	North Sea	Aircraft
U 88		Surface warships
U 335		Sub
U 702	Med.	Mines
U 74, U 372, U 411, U 331, U 559, U 568, U 605		Surface warships
U 652, U 259, U 577		Aircraft
U 670, U 222, U 272	Baltic	Collision
U 133	Med.	Mines
U 374		Sub.
U 573		Handed over to Spain
U 457, U 585, U 589, U 655	Arctic Ocean	Surface warships
1943		
U 69, U 87, U 135, U 201, U 202, U 209, U 225, U 226, U 229, U 274, U 282, U 306, U 334, U 340, U 381, U 405, U 432, U 436, U 438, U 444, U 449, U 576, U 600, U 606, U 607, U 609, U 613, U 631, U 634, U 635, U 638, U 640, U 645, U 648, U 710, U 732 U 84, U 86, U 89, U 134, U 211, U 217, U 221, U 232, U 258, U 265, U 266, U 268, U 273, U 279, U 280, U 284, U 304, U 332, U 336, U 337, U 338, U 341, U 359, U 376, U 383, U 384, U 388, U 391, U 402, U 403, U 404, U 417, U 418, U 419, U 420, U 422, U 435, U 440, U 442, U 447, U 454, U 456, U 465, U 467, U 468, U 469, U 470, U 558, U 563, U 564, U 566, U 569, U 572, U 584, U 590, U 591, U 594, U 598, U 604, U 610, U 614, U 615, U 620, U 623, U 624, U 628, U 630, U 632, U 633, U 643, U 646, U 657, U 662, U 663, U 664, U 665, U 669, U 706, U 707, U 752, U 759, U 951, U 954, U 964	Atlantic	Surface warships

Number	Area	Cause
U 966		Aircraft
U 553, U 753, U 439, U 659		Accident, collision
U 227, U 389	North Sea	Aircraft
U 308, U 644		Submarine
U 769, U 770		Aircraft in harbour
U 647		Mines
U 73, U 83, U 205, U 297, U 224, U 375, U 409, U 414, U 443, U 458, U 561, U 562, U 593, U 617	Med.	Surface warships
U 77, U 755		Aircraft
U 301, U 303, U 431		Sub.
U 602		Accident
U 37, U 346, U 649, U 670, U 718, U 768, U 983	Baltic	Collision
U 346		Accident
U 395		Aircraft in Kiel
U 345		Mines
U 639		Sub.
U 101		Scuttled

1944

Number	Area	Cause
U 91, U 238, U 257, U 264, U 302, U 305, U 322, U 333, U 358, U 378, U 386, U 392, U 400, U 406, U 424, U 445, U 448, U 473, U 575, U 592, U 603, U 608, U 618, U 621, U 641, U 653, U 666, U 709, U 719, U 731, U 734, U 736, U 741, U 743, U 744, U 757, U 761, U 762, U 765, U 962, U 970, U 984, U 986, U 1200	Atlantic	Surface warships
U 231, U 243, U 270, U 271, U 283, U 311, U 342, U 364, U 373, U 426, U 441, U 625, U 629, U 821, U 955, U 976		Aircraft
U 385		Aircraft + surface warships
U 981		Aircraft + Mines
U 415, U 667, U 703		Mines
U 263		Mines?
U 377, U 925, U 972		Missing
U 212, U 214, U 247, U 269, U 297, U 390, U 394, U 413, U 671, U 672, U 674, U 678, U 713, U 767, U 959, U 961, U 971, U 973, U 988, U 1006	North Sea	Surface warships
U 240, U 241, U 292, U 317, U 319, U 423, U 476, U 477, U 478, U 484, U 675, U 715, U 735, U 740, U 742, U 772, U 777, U 906, U 908, U 980, U 982, U 990, U 993, U 996		Aircraft
U 484		Surface warships + Aircraft
U 771, U 974, U 987		Submarine
U 673, U 737, U 1209		Collision
U 92		Withdrawn from service
U 228, U 437, U 998		Damaged and withdrawn from service
U 223, U 343, U 371, U 407, U 450, U 453, U 616, U 960	Med.	Surface warships
U 81, U 596, U 380, U 410, U 642, U 952, U 969		Aircraft
U 230, U 466, U 471, U 565, U 967		Scuttled
U 486		Sub
U 455		Mines
U 421		Withdrawn from service
U 277, U 288, U 289, U 314, U 344, U 347, U 354, U 355, U 360, U 362, U 365, U 366, U 387, U 472, U 601, U 921	Arctic Ocean	Surface warships
U 347, U 361	West of Narvik	Allied Aircraft
U 28, U 80, U 738, U 416, U 1013, U 1015	Baltic	Accident, Collision
U 239, U 474		Damaged and withdrawn from service
U 250		Aircraft + surface warships
U 479		Mines

1945

Number	Area	Cause
U 248, U 285, U 286, U 300, U 307, U 309, U 399, U 425, U 486, U 636, U 676, U 714,		Surface warships

Number	Area	Cause
U 722, U 774, U 905, U 965, U 989, U 1001, U 1014, U 1018, U 1024, U 1051, U 1063, U 1169, U 1172, U 1195, U 1199, U 1208, U 1274, U 1276, U 1278, U 1279		
U251, U 320, U 321, U 326, U 382, U 393, U 396, U 579, U 622, U 681, U 927, U 1017, U 1055, U 1065, U 1106, U 1107		Aircraft
U242, U 260, U 275, U 296, U 325, U 367, U 480, U 676, U 677, U 745, U 923, U 1021, U 1169, U 1273, U 1302,		Mines
U 246, U 396, U 398, U 650, U 683, U 1055		Missing
U 963		Ran aground
U 1053, U 1206		Accident
U 96, U 237, U 276, U 348, U 350, U 682, U 711, U 747, U 749, U 982, U 1167, U 1210		Sunk in harbour in Allied air raids
U 977		Fled to Argentina

1945 – ...

Number	Area	Cause
U 218, U 244, U 245, U 249, U 255, U 278, U 281, U 291, U 293, U 294, U 295, U 298, U 299, U 312, U 313, U 318, U 328, U 363, U 368, U 369, U 427, U 481, U 483, U 485, U 637, U 668, U 680, U 716, U 720, U 739, U 760, U 764, U 773, U 775, U 776, U 778, U 779, U 825, U 826, U 901, U 907, U 928, U 930, U 956, U 968, U 975, U 978, U 991, U 992, U 994, U 997, U 1002, U 1004, U 1005, U 1009, U 1010, U 1019, U 1022, U 1023, U 1052, U 1061, U 1102, U 1103, U 1104, U 1109, U 1110, U 1163, U 1165, U 1194, U 1198, U 1203, U 1271, U 1272, U 1301, U 1307	North Sea	Sunk in Operation 'Deadlight'
U 286, U 307, U 425, U 679	Arctic Sea	Surface warships
U 78	Baltic	Coastal artillery
U 262, U 310, U 315, U 324, U 712, U 758, U 1197		Stricken
U 256, U 953, U 957, U 1057, U 1058, U 1064, U 1105, U 1108, U 1171, U 1202, U 1305		Surrendered or taken over by the British
U 1201, U 1275		Scuttled
U 995		Damaged by an air raid, handed over to Norway, then taken over by the British and again handed over to Norway. Currently a museum ship in Laboe.

Index

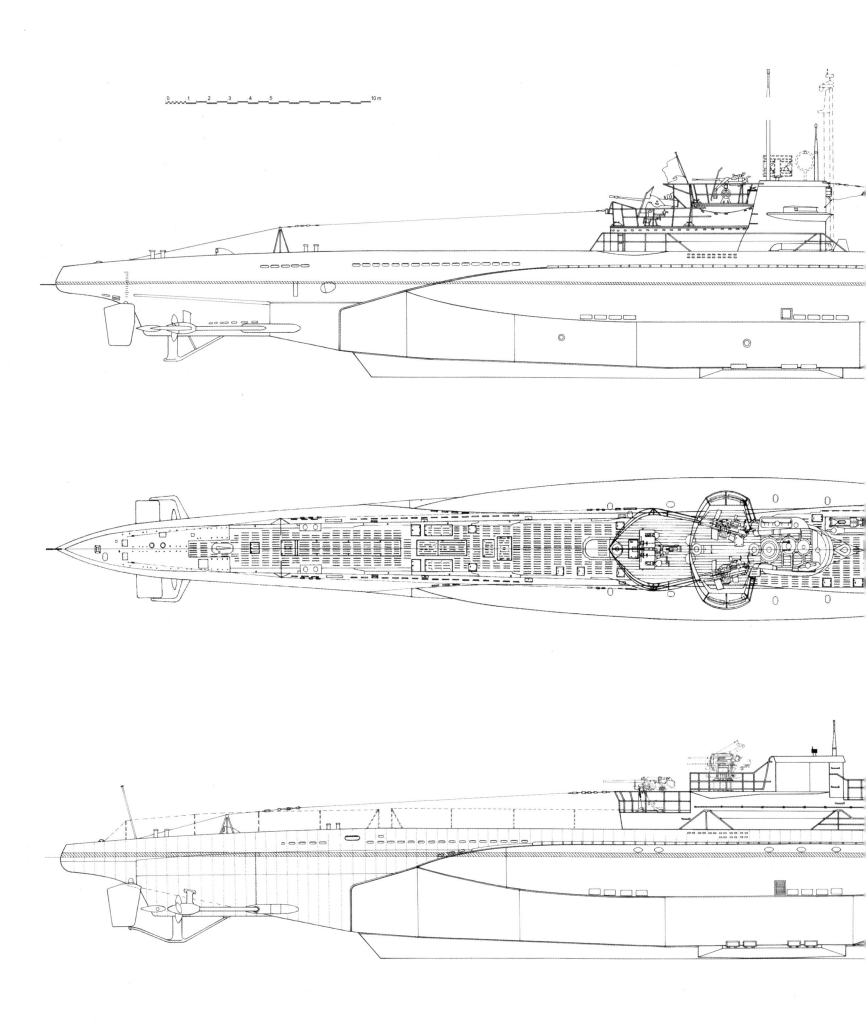